Birds with Human Souls

Birds

with Human Souls

A Guide to Bird Symbolism ∫ *Beryl Rowland*

THE UNIVERSITY OF TENNESSEE PRESS

Copyright © 1978 by The University of Tennessee Press/Knoxville.
All rights reserved. Manufactured in the United States of America.
First edition.

Library of Congress Cataloging in Publication Data

Rowland, Beryl.
  Birds with human souls.
  Bibliography: p.
  Includes index.
  1. Folk-lore of birds. I. Title.
GR735.R68   398'.369'82   77-4230
ISBN 0-87049-215-2

Books by Beryl Rowland
  Companion to Chaucer Studies (editor), 1968
  Blind Beasts: Chaucer's Animal World, 1971
  Animals with Human Faces, 1973
  *Chaucer and Middle English Studies in Honor of Rossell
    Hope Robbins* (editor), 1974
  Birds with Human Souls, 1978

Frontispiece:
  Birds descend on fallen Babylon. Add. MS 17333, f.36

To Margaret

Preface

That strange and remarkable poet Emily Dickinson was able to confront a bobolink or robin at eye level as it hopped along the path in her Amherst garden, and appreciate both symbol and fact simultaneously. Today such birds are vanishing, and we rarely meet them face to face. In Europe 150 million small birds are slaughtered annually, with the great winter migration ending not in the African sun but on the dinner tables of France, Belgium, Italy, Cyprus, Syria, Lebanon, Turkey, or in the pickle jars. In North America if one cannot purchase oven-ready redwings, curlews, lap-wings, robins skewered en brochette or served as tasty canapés, the reason is probably practical rather than humanitarian: the preparation is too much trouble. Pâté de foie gras is still imported and eaten even though this delicacy is the result of the inhuman practice of ramming unwanted food down the throats of geese while they scream at the pain. If birds are viewed at close quarters, it is because someone has caged them, an act which, as in the case of Blake's robin, must surely put all heaven in a rage. In western Flanders there are regular Sunday morning birdsong competitions involving heavy betting. Finches are shut up in glass-fronted boxes and judged on the number of times each bird utters the distinctive note which marks the end of its song. The winner is the one that sings the note most often in an hour, and everything is done, including the use of drugs, to make the birds sing only the ending.

What man does not directly destroy, his environment will. The spring can indeed be silent. Some of us urban dwellers have already experienced the ultimate desolation of not seeing a bird fly nor hearing it sing. The warm west wind, instead of being full of birds' cries, throbs with the rasp of power mowers, electric saws, cars, motorbikes, and airplanes.

For our delight in birds we rely more and more on memories and traditions derived not from life but from

In earlier times birds were hunted for sport, especially in May.

books. In doing so, we discover that the history of the bird in human thought is a fascinating and inexhaustible subject. This book is the result of my happy exploration of bird symbolism through the centuries. Occasionally birds themselves cannot be identified with certainty, especially in an age of different avian terminology and definition. But I think that the phantom scientific ornithologist peering critically over my shoulder disappeared when he realized that my concern is not, of course, with birds as they are in nature but as they exist in the mind.

In my work I have had the invaluable assistance of many libraries including the Renaissance Library at Victoria College, University of Toronto, the British Museum, the Bodleian, and the Huntington. My gratitude is due to all these, and especially to the Scott Library at my own university, where the staff have been indefatigable in procuring innumerable rare books for me. I am also grateful for the unfailing moral support of McLaughlin College under Dr. George Tatham, assisted by M. Klein, and for the secretarial aid of R. Dallison and P. Truman. Finally, I wish to thank the generous, unknown scholar who read this work when it was in manuscript and reported to the publisher: "This work was fun to read and must have been fun to write." If I can share the enjoyment I experienced in considering this subject, I am grateful.

February 11, 1977

Beryl Rowland
MCLAUGHLIN COLLEGE
YORK UNIVERSITY
TORONTO, ONTARIO

Acknowledgments

The author wishes to thank:

THE BRITISH LIBRARY for permission to reproduce photographs of birds descending on fallen Babylon (Add. MS 17333, f.36), Cock (Orien. MS 481, f.104v), Coots (MS Harl. 4751, f.38), Dove & Venus (MS Harl. 4425, f.138v), Goose (Add. 42120, f.169v), Goshawk (Add. 42120, f.163), Griffin (Harl. MS 3244, f.38v), Hen & chickens (Add. 42120, f.166v), Lark (Harl. MS 4431, f.125v), Nightingale (Roy 10 E IV, f.177), Phoenix (Harl. 4751, f.45), Vulture (Harl. MS 3244, f.51), Wren (Roy 19 B XV, f.37v).

THE BODLEIAN LIBRARY for permission to use photographs of birds singing to the Holy Family (MS Canon Misc. 476, f.37v.ii), Blackbird (Bodl. MS Douce 308, f.92v), Caladrius (Bodl. MS 764, f.63v), Cockfight (Bodl. MS 264, f.50), Crane (Bodl. MS Ashm. 1511, f.57), Dove and Noah (Bodl. MS Douce 311, f.13), Ducks (Bodl. MS 764, f.86v), Eagle (Bodl. MS Ashm. 1511, f.74), Falcon and lure (Bodl. MS Douce 219, f.55v), Finch (Bodl. MS 264, f.112), Geese (Bodl. MS 764, f.83v), Hawking in May (Bodl. MS Douce 144, f.10), Hen (Bodl. MS Ashm. 1462, f.16), Heron (Bodl. MS Ashm. 1511, f.65), Ibis (Bodl. MS Ashm. 1511, f.59), Jay (Bodl. MS 764, f.68), Kestrel (Bodl. MS New Coll. 65, f.73), Kingfisher (Bodl. MS Ashm. 1511, f.67), Kite (Bodl. MS Ashm. 1511, f.58), Magpie (Bodl. MS Ashm. 1511, f.48v), Ostrich (Bodl. MS Ashm. 1511, f.52), Owl (Bodl. MS 764, f.73), Parrots (Bodl. MS 764, f.63), Partridge (Bodl. MS 764, f.75v), Pelican (Bodl. MS Ashm. 1511, f.46v), Pheasant (Bodl. MS Douce 219, f.60), Quails (Bodl. MS 764, f.82v), Robin (Bodl. MS 264, f.75), Stork (Bodl. MS 764, f.64), Swallows (Bodl. MS 764, f.81v), Swans (Bodl. MS Douce 308, f.88v), Woodpecker (Bodl. MS Douce 308, f.97v), Boys shooting at popinjay (Bodl. MS Douce 276, f.4).

THE WESTMINSTER CHAPTER HOUSE LIBRARY for permission to use photographs of Griffin and Man (MS 22, f.19v), Peacock (Westminster MS 22, f.41v).

THE PIERPONT MORGAN LIBRARY for permission to use photographs of Bats (MS M81, f.54v), Coot (MS M81, f.65), Crow (MS M81, f.55), Hoopoe (MS M81, f.63v), Nightingale on her eggs (MS M81, f.54), Parrot (MS M81, f.50v), Quail (MS M81, f.56v), Raven (MS M81, f.55), Siren (MS M81, f.17), Swallow (MS M81, f.56), Turtledove (MS M81, f.66).

UNIVERSITÄTSBIBLIOTHEK, HEIDELBERG, Gerfalcon (Cod. Pal. Germ. 848, f.7), Swan Poet (Cod. Pal. Germ. 848, f.146), Falcon (Cod. Pal. Germ. 848, f.184v), the last photograph being kindly supplied by the Institut für Film und Bild in Wissenschaft und Unterricht, München.

PHAIDON ART BOOKS for permission to use the photograph of the Harpy from Heinz Mode, *Fabulous Beasts & Demons* (1975).

Contents

Introduction

Even birds looking for food may illustrate the workings of Divine Providence.

In one of the great moments of dramatic literature, Mephistophilis conjures up Helen whose beauty destroyed the ancient city of Troy. The scholar Faustus, who has sacrificed his soul for experiences such as this, exclaims:

> Was this the face that launch'd a thousand ships,
> And burnt the topless towers of Ilium?
> Sweet Helen, make me immortal with a kiss!
> Her lips suck forth my soul: see where it flies!

No words can be more tragically ironic. Faustus is doomed. He imagines his soul soaring in ecstasy; instead, he will be dragged down, screaming with terror, into the infernal abyss. Traditionally, only the soul of the dead escaped from the mouth when kissed.

The idea of the soul as a winged creature or bird is not new here. It is a widespread and extremely ancient belief that the soul assumes the form of a bird or, put more extremely, that all birds are human souls. The Egyptians depicted an androcephalic bird as their sign for the soul. In the fourth century B.C., Plato gave an extraordinary detailed picture of the soul growing wings and feathers, saying that "when it is perfect and fully winged it soars on high and regulates the entire world." In the Roman catacombs the upward flight of the bird was used to represent the aspiration of the soaring soul, released at last from the body. Birds pecking at grapes signified the souls of the redeemed taking the Eucharist. In fourteenth-century paintings of the Madonna and Child the bird in the plump hand of the Infant was the symbol of the soul which He had come to save. The bird escaping from the mouth of the martyr St. Quintinus as his torturers cut off his head has the same meaning; in the story of the two dead prophets who were revived after three and a half days when "a breath of life from God entered them," a French apocalyptic manuscript of the fourteenth century shows two birds flying into their mouths.

The idea that the bird represented the soul as opposed to the body, the spiritual in contrast to the earthly, seems to have been universal. The medicine man or shaman owed his power to the popular belief that he was able to leave his body and fly about the universe like a bird. "In this case," writes Henderson, "the bird is a most fitting symbol of transcendence. It represents the peculiar nature of intuition working through a 'medium,' that is, an individual who is capable of obtaining knowledge of distant events—or facts of which he consciously knows nothing—by going into a trance-like state." As Joseph Campbell has pointed out, in the cave paintings at Lascaux a shaman, lying in a trance, wears a bird mask; the shamans of Siberia wear birds' costumes and are believed to have descended from a bird. Primitive tribes still see the human soul as a bird. The Bororos of Brazil think that the soul-bird passes out of the body in dreams; the Bella Coola Indians conceive of the soul as a bird enclosed in an egg at the nape of the neck; if the shell breaks the soul will fly away and the man will die.

The bird has always been a favorite baby-bringing symbol, for if it is the soul, it is also the divine breath of life. As a generative symbol, it has both male and female attributes. As the procreator, it is the male organ. Roman phallic amulets are winged; in Italian, bird (*l'ucello*) means "penis"; in German, the popular term for the sexual act is *vögeln*, "to bird." The bird is also the maternal breast, the life-giving milk: whereas the ancient gods take the form of a bird to seduce mortals, the mother deities, such as Ishtar, Aphrodite, and Diana, display prominent breasts and have a bird as their totem. In the Hebraic account of the creation, the Spirit of God broods like a bird upon the waters and fertilizes with its Divine Breath; in other accounts of the creation, the bird is the Mother of the Gods who flutters over the abyss and brings forth life. Sometimes in medieval paintings of the Madonna and Child the artist substitutes a bowl or domed scepter for the bird or, in the case of the *Madonna Lactans*, he omits the bird altogether. Clearly, the bird clasped by the Holy Child symbolizes the maternal breast as well as the soul and is the same bird which serves as food or as the bringer of food in innumerable legends. Quails, sent by Jehovah, feed the Israelites; crows, ravens, and a robin feed the saints in the desert. Verbally, such food is inspiration or a divine message: in the Old Testament, a winged seraph comes to Isaiah and gives him prophetic power by placing a glowing coal on his lips; in the New Testament, according to many medieval representations of the Annunciation, the dove impregnates Mary by the ear, causing the *logos* of God to be made flesh.

Birds give their wings to angels, and they sing like angels. Their harmony reflects the harmony of heaven itself. Especially on St. Valentine's Day do they sing "with voys of aungel" in their harmony. Just as St. Valentine followed God's command to procreate and multiply when he strove to increase the number of the faithful, so the birds implement God's decree by mating on the saint's day. Birds are never far from Paradise. When they are not singing services at its very gates, they are caroling blithely in Nature's honor in an earthly garden of delight or luring mortals into fairyland by their magic notes.

It is a rare bird that is found in Hell. Specific birds may be bad and they may haunt the living as revenants or represent the Seven Deadly Sins. But they are not like animals whose sensual natures illustrate the baser traits of humanity. Taken collectively, they most commonly represent the spirit with its capacity for joy, and they sing of the day of Grace.

Poets have always envied the divine power of the bird, and some, such as the Romantics, believed they could acquire it for themselves. Today, Shelley's ecstatic carolings are less meaningful than the modest, poignant questions of Thomas Hardy in "The Blinded Bird":

Who hath charity? This bird.
Who suffereth long and is kind,
Is not provoked, though blind
and alive ensepulchred?
Who hopeth, endureth all things?
Who thinketh no evil, but sings?
Who is divine? This bird.

Aptowitzer, pp. 150–68; "Armonye of Byrdes," *passim*; Bunker, p. 420; Chaucer, *PF*, 386–89; "Devotions of the Fowles," pp. 6–7; Eliade, p. 105; Henderson, p. 151; Jones, pp. 326–27; Marlowe, *Doctor Faustus* xiii,91–93; "La Messe des Oisiaus," pp. 4–7; Neilson, pp. 216–27; Plato, *Phaedrus*, 246c; Schnier, p. 99; Wormhoudt, pp. 179–80.

BIBLIOGRAPHICAL NOTE

One of the pleasures in this kind of study lies in the discovery of specialized works of which one previously knew little or nothing. The most memorable of these demonstrate how closely, even for the most dedicated scientific ornithologist, the study of birds is a study in human culture. These works are of many kinds, ranging from the encyclopedic *A Dictionary of Birds* by Alfred Newton, D'Arcy Wentworth Thompson's *A Glossary of Greek Birds*, the monumental work on folklore by Edward Armstrong, to Harting's dated but fascinating

Birds of Shakespeare, with its excellent modern introduction by Grundy Steiner, and an unforgettable work on the English robin by David Lack. One of the most delightful recent publications is Topsell's *The Fowles of Heauen or History of Birds*, edited by Thomas P. Harrison and F. David Hoeniger from a manuscript in the Huntington Library and presumably intended as a counterpart to Topsell's *The Historie of Foure-Footed Beasts and Serpents*. Although he never finished his translation of Aldrovandi, Topsell's descriptions and anecdotes are always entertaining, and the work is particularly valuable for the careful annotations of the editors and for the numerous illustrations of birds, so exquisitely tinted as to have the appearance of original watercolors.

While I refer to these and other works, my purpose has been, of course, to use the material to show birds in new perspectives or to give different emphases. I have taken my evidence from a variety of key works: the Bidpai and the Aesopic fables; Greek and Roman natural histories such as Aristotle's *Historia animalium*, Pliny's *Historia naturalis*, Aelian's *De natura animalium*, and Oppian's *Cynegetica*; the *Physiologus*, which moralized traditional zoological beliefs early in the Christian era and proliferated into innumerable illustrated bestiaries in the Middle Ages; accounts of ritual and myth recorded by Herodotus, Ovid, and Plutarch; the Septuagint version of the Hebrew Bible; the Vulgate text of the Bible; the exegetical writings of Tertullian, Ambrose, and others; Isidore of Seville's *Etymologiarum sive originum*, an important source book for medieval scholars, which repeated much of the earlier lore in order to support erroneous etymologies.

Also examined are various medieval encyclopedic works such as Alexander Neckam's *De naturis rerum*, Bartholomaeus Anglicus' *De proprietatibus rerum*, which was translated into English by Trevisa in 1397; (Pseudo) Vincent de Beauvais' *Speculum*, (Pseudo) Rabanus Maurus' *Allegoriae in universom sacram scripturam*, the sermons of Honorius of Autun, Odo of Ceriton, and John of Sheppey and others; the medieval Latin and French bestiaries; the *Gesta Romanorum*, a collection of allegorized tales, and *The Golden Legend*, a compilation of saints' lives.

In addition, numerous works of the Renaissance period are taken into account: the popular emblem books which contained short verses, illustrated by engravings, to express a conceit of a moral or philosophical kind; Horapollo's *Hieroglyphics* (1505), a work on Egyptian symbolism, originating in the fourth or fifth century and relying on folklore and the Greek and Roman histories rather than on a sound knowledge of hieroglyphics; the works of the Italian naturalist Aldrovandi (1522–1605) and others. By using such works I have been able to turn to the finest imaginative literature of many periods and try to show the complex and magnificent role of the bird in it.

Where standard classical texts are cited, editions are not described in the bibliography. Similarly, when Church Fathers are quoted, reference is made to the volumes of *Patrologia Latina* (*PL*) and *Patrologia Graeca* (*PG*), edited by J.-P. Migne, without additional bibliographical note. I refer to the *Allegoria in sacram scripturam* as belonging to Rabanus Maurus, although Migne's attribution is in fact incorrect. After each section in the text, the most important sources only are given, including secondary sources, for which full details are supplied in the Selected Bibliography. Spellings, especially with regard to *v* and *u* in some titles and quotations, have been normalized.

Birds with Human Souls

Birds sing to the holy family.

Albatross

The albatross has usually been regarded as a good omen. The editors of Oliver Goldsmith's work on birds explain why:

In the West Indies these birds are said to foretell the arrival of ships; which is frequently true, and may arise from a very natural cause. They always fish in fine weather; so that, when the wind is rough at sea, they retire into the harbors, where they are protected by the land; and the same wind that blows them in, brings likewise whatever vessels may be exposed to its fury, to seek a retreat from it. They devour fish with great gluttony and are often so gorged as to be unable to fly. Their cry resembles the braying of an ass.

Good omen or not, the albatross was also a victim of maltreatment by egg-snatchers. Its tasty eggs, weighing a pound each, were much in demand. According to J.E. Davis, captain of the *Challenger*:

a push with a stick on the breast of the poised bird, as she sits on the side of the nest, is sufficient to send it sprawling on its back, and before it can regain its upright position, the prize egg is gone, and the wail of the despoiled mother, as she perches again on her rifled nest, tells the tale of her woe. The action of these birds is sometimes most ludicrous.

Coleridge's guilt-ridden mariner abused the albatross. He and his fellow sailors were stuck in the ice when the great white seabird soared above the ship:

> At length did cross an Albatross,
> Through the fog it came;
> As if it had been a Christian soul,
> We hailed it in God's name.

Miraculously, with the bird's appearance, the ship moved forward and a south wind sprang up. Then the Mariner killed the bird, thereby committing an act which was wanton and ominous, as the sailors immediately realized:

> And I had done a hellish thing,
> And it would work 'em woe:
> For all averred, I had killed the bird
> That made the breeze to blow.
> Ah wretch! said they, the bird to slay,
> That made the breeze to blow!

Terrible things began to happen. The ship suddenly stopped. There was no drinking water:

> Ah! well-a-day! what evil looks
> Had I from old and young!
> Instead of the cross, the Albatross
> About my neck was hung.

Had the Ancient Mariner been a pipe-smoker the explanation for his action would have been obvious: sailors used to kill these birds to manufacture pipe stems from the long wing bones and make tobacco pouches from the webbing of the feet. As it stands, the question is one for the psychoanalysts, and, most conveniently, poor Coleridge's life is a fully documented case book. He was a brilliant scholar and conversationalist. In his personal affairs he was undisciplined and unreliable, eccentric, and firmly addicted to opium. A voluminous writer, he produced three "golden poems" which in themselves assure his permanent recognition as a great poet, yet his life was unhappy and he was haunted by a sense of remorse and paranoia:

> Like one, that on a lonesome road
> Doth walk in fear and dread,
> And having once turned round walks on,
> And turns no more his head;
> Because he knows, a frightful fiend
> Doth close behind him tread.

As noted later with regard to the vulture, the great white bird was a mother or breast symbol. Coleridge's choice of symbol must have been determined by a deep conflict associated with his mother, possibly by incestuous feelings which he experienced as a fatherless child boarding in the highly disciplined Bluecoat School in London. Like the Ancient Mariner, Coleridge never freed himself from a sense of guilt. And he seems to have realized that the only possible relief was to be found in open acknowledgment:

> Since then, at an uncertain hour,
> That agony returns:
> And till my ghastly tale is told,
> This heart within me burns.

> I pass, like night, from land to land;
> I have strange power of speech;
> That moment that his face I see,
> I know the man that must hear me:
> To him my tale I teach.

Coleridge was not likely to have seen an albatross. According to Witherby, the only one ever found in England was an exhausted bird picked up near Linton in Cambridgeshire toward the end of the nineteenth century. But his Mariner was not the first nor the last to shoot one in the South Seas. Wordsworth claimed that he gave the idea to Coleridge after reading Shelvocke's *Voyage Round the World*. Captain Shelvocke in 1719 had a strange experience when his ship the *Speedwell* passed through the Straits of LeMair en route to the island of Chiloe on the coast of Chile. He had already seen some albatrosses near the River Plate and had observed that their wing span was twelve or thirteen feet. On Thursday, October 1,

1719, one sailor cried out "that his hands and fingers were so benumb'd that he could not hold himself, but before those that were next to him could come to his assistance, he fell down and was drown'd." Despite the summer season they had continual squalls, sleet, snow, and rain. They saw neither fish nor seabird "except a disconsolate black Albitross who accompanied us for several days, hovering about us as if he had lost himself." Then Hatley, whom Shelvocke calls his second captain, noticing "in one of his melancholy fits, that this bird was always hovering near us, imagin'd, from his colour, that it might be some ill omen. . . . He, after some fruitless attempts, at length, shot the Albitross, not doubting (perhaps) that we should have a fair wind after it." Three weeks later the fore-topmast was carried away, and the ship continued to battle with contrary winds until it came within sight of the coast of Chile on November 14. "I must own, that this navigation is truly melancholy," observed Shelvocke. He saw himself and his crew as "separated from the rest of mankind to struggle with the dangers of a stormy climate." In 1841 Charles Baudelaire, sailing around the Cape to Bourbon Island, found sailors still wantonly destroying albatrosses. As he watched *ces rois de l'azur* (kings of the blue) flop piteously on deck—each bird recently so beautiful and now *comique et laid* (comical and ugly)—he regarded the albatross as a symbol of the poet: grounded amid derisive shouts, like the bird, the prince of the skies, his massive wings prevented his escape.

Coleridge's poem is, I believe, wholly responsible for the symbolism of the albatross still in use. Toward the end of 1975 when a prominent British speculator suddenly crashed financially and badly shook the world stock markets, London newspapers several times referred to one of his subsidiary companies as being an albatross around his neck. The figurative meaning was too obvious to require explanation.

Baudelaire, p. 13; Beres, p. 111; Davis, see Goldsmith, ii, 204n; *EB.*, i, 491; Goldsmith, ii, 204–206; Jameson, p. 58; Schnier, p. 102; Shelvocke, p. 73; Witherby, iv, 81–83.

Alerion

The alerion is known in heraldry as a kind of eagle, and Boutell notes that some early heralds represented it without feet and beak. The Dukes of Lorraine were said to have borne the device to commemorate an exploit of their crusading ancestor Godfrey de Bologne. Apparently three alerions perched on Godfrey's arrow when he was shooting against David's Tower in Jerusalem. According to Paradin, these birds foreshadowed Godfrey's future greatness and power. Even if the alerions were eaglets, as some have supposed, the story seems improbable. Some inventive genealogist may have noticed that alerion is an anagram of Lor[r]aine.

In medieval times the bird is described in Prester John's account of the marvels of the East. Here and in some of the bestiaries its characteristics seem to derive partly from the eagle and partly from the phoenix:

> The Physiologus says that the alerions have lordship over all other birds in the world and their colours are like fire. And their wings are as sharp as a razor; and the alerion is larger than an eagle and there is only one pair in the world. . . .

The alerion was the symbol of a very distinguished rich man who continued to make money, however dishonestly. At his death, said the moralist, the Devil would take his soul and worms would eat his corpse. The sharp wings of the alerion were the deeds of the wicked man, and his soul was damned because of his greed.

Boutell, p. 97; Cahier & Martin, II, 162–63; Godefroy, I, 218; McCulloch, pp. 197–98; Paradin, pp. 39–40; Prester John, *Rutebeuf*, II, 456.

Bats are not birds, but they look like them.

Bat

When Robert Browning referred to bats in *Pippa Passes*, apparently his main intention was to provide a rhyme for his next line. Instead, he produced a shocking literary gaffe:

6

> Then, owls and bats
> Cowls and twats.   (iv.ii.96)

Twat was not a part of a nun's garb, as he supposed, but of her anatomy. He had mistaken the meaning of this four-letter word which he had found in a satire "Vanity of Vanities" (1660), written in an age less decorous than his own:

> They talked of his having a cardinal's hat
> They'd send him as soon an old nun's twat.

Browning's lines do not even rhyme, for in his day *twat* rhymed with *what*, not *bat*. But at least his pairing of owls and bats is sound. These two creatures of ill omen are frequently mentioned together. Appearing mainly at night, they are commonly thought to be predatory and sinister, emblems of spiritual darkness.

Among the ancients the bat was a varied symbol, so varied, in fact, as to demonstrate for the Reverend Topsell, a clergyman translating Aldrovandi's work on birds early in the seventeenth century, "the inconstancie of the heathenishe learning." A bat sitting on the spear of a Sicilian tyrant was a favorable augury; on the other hand, to the Egyptians, as Horapollo observed, the bat not only symbolized the good mother—for the bat is the only winged creature which has teeth and breasts—but the man "who was weak yet audacious" because the bat "flies though destitute of feathers."

Medieval preachers almost unanimously condemned the bat. They pointed out that in the Bible bats were regarded as unclean and that Isaiah foresaw sinners on Judgment Day abandoning their idols of gold and silver to bats and moles (ii.20–21). These moralists made much of the curious belief that the strength which should have given sight to the bat passed into the creature's leather-like wings. Such blindness became the symbol of moral blindness. The envious who could not see good in others were like bats. Men who flew about in search of honors instead of looking at God were like bats. They had lost their sight and their strength had passed into the "wynges of pryde and of ambicion." Equally persistent was the bat's reputation for duplicity. According to Étienne de Bourbon's story—which, in itself, is an Æsopian fable found in many collections of stories, in the sermons of Jacques de Vitry and others—when in the company of birds the bat tried to hide its four feet and stretch its wings; when in the company of animals it did the opposite. Similarly hypocrites pretended to be pious when among the virtuous but assumed a very different character when in the company of those who lived dissolute lives.

During the Renaissance the reputation of the bat varied. It continued to be a symbol of maternal fecundity as it had been to the Egyptians; when it flew into the holes of rocks it became a type of piety, seeking Christ, the true rock. On the other hand the bat also retained less praise-worthy attributes as Topsell observed:

> Others compare Batts and their qualities to the diversities of sinners. ffirst they say leacherous persons are like Batts bycause the eyes of the Adulterer wayte for the twylight; so doe Batts. Againe they live by eatinge dust of walls and in narrowe chinkes: so doe the Covetous, for they care for nothinge but this worlde: like the enemyes of our Lord, they licke up the dust . . . . Moreover this bird will eate the oyle out of the Churche Lampes: so the envious rob good people of the grace and praise which belongeth unto them; they are glad of another mans harme but sory for another mans good . . . . They sticke to the walls and live in secreate holes betwixt the tiles of houses or ruynes of Chimneyes. Even so doe proud persons ad-vaunce themselves above their neighbours by the goods, lands, and favours of other men.

"Bat-fowling" was a term used in Shakespeare's day for catching various birds by night. It was also a slang term for robbing a store at dusk. According to Harting:

> the rogue pretended to have dropped a ring or a jewel at the door of some well-furnished shop, and, going in, asked the apprentice of the house to light his candle to look for it. After some peering about, the bat-fowler would drop the candle, as if by accident.
>
> "Now, I pray you, good young man," he would say, "do so much as light the candle again." While the boy was away the rogue plundered the shop, and having stolen everything he could find, stole away himself.

The folklore which accrued to the bat enhanced its sinister reputation. The bat was the companion of witches, and its wings were given to devils or it was itself the Devil incarnate. If, like birds, the bat was a soul creature, it belongs to the lost and the damned. As Kittredge observed in 1929, in Nigeria a belief persisted that a bat could be taken from the mouth of a possessed person. Some centuries earlier a physician in Provence made use of a similar belief to cure a patient who claimed to be possessed by the Devil.

> The shrewd doctor, falling in with the man's humour, visited him one day with a priest and a surgeon, and took along a bat in a bag. He explained that he would relieve him if he would consent to a slight operation. Prayer was offered, and the surgeon made a small incision in the man's side.

At the same time the physician let the bat out of the bag. "Behold, the devil is gone," he exclaimed. The patient believed him and was cured.

At the end of the Victorian era, to those curious lexicographers Farmer and Henley the bat was accepted as a term for a woman of the town, plying her trade by night. They observed that "the equivalent French term, *hirondelle de nuit*, i.e., 'a night swallow,' is more poetic."

8

In ancient China the bat was a symbol of happiness. Five bats were often used in Chinese decorations to symbolize the Five Blessings, those of old age, wealth, health, love of virtue, and a natural death.

Étienne de Bourbon, p. 250; Harting, pp. 159–60; Horapollo, p. 118; Kittredge, p. 135; *M.E. Sermons*, pp. 231–32; Pyles, p. 1; Rabanus Maurus, *PL*, 112, col. 1077; Topsell, pp. 59, 61, 62; Williams, p. 25.

Bittern

Along with cranes, swans, herons, and woodcocks, roasted bittern was once such a popular dish that only the occasional straggler is seen in Britain now. In 1802 the bird fetched half-a-guinea (fifty-three new pence) in the poultry market, more than the average weekly wage of an agricultural laborer. Because of its rarity few people today have seen this solitary bird which crouches almost motionless in the marshes by day and seeks its food in the twilight; nor have they heard the bird's eerie mating call from which its generic name, *Botaurus*, is said to derive. Yet these distinctive characteristics of the bittern gave it a positive symbolism in early times and made it an objective of superstitious dread for centuries.

As a symbol of desolation it appears in some Biblical versions which foretell the destruction of Babylon and Nineveh. According to Isaiah and Zephaniah, these once bustling cities were to become a wasteland, the ruins of their palaces echoing with the bittern's cry. This cry in itself was a symbol of impending calamity. To cause the booming sound the bird was thought to insert its beak into some mud or a hollow reed. The "bitoure bombleth in the myre" in Chaucer's *Wife of Bath's Tale*, and if the traditional lore was implicitly denied by Drayton, it still persisted in his contemporary Topsell:

> The voice of this fowle is most admirable, ffor fasteninge his beake in the waters or in the earth he roareth like a Bull, which is usual with him in the Springe when he is stirred with lust for procreation.

Goldsmith denied this belief of "the common people," but like Willughby, Bishop Hall, and others, he testified to the dread which the bittern's boom aroused in the hearts of most villagers:

> It is impossible for words to give those who have not heard this evening call an adequate idea of its solemnity. It is like the interrupted bellowing of a bull, but hollower, and louder, and is heard at a mile's distance, as if issuing from some formidable being that resided at the bottom of the waters. . . . I remember, in the place where I was a boy, with what terror this bird's note affected the

whole village; they considered it as the presage of some sad event; and generally found or made one to succeed it.

Goldsmith spoke feelingly of the "detestation" with which the bittern was held "by the vulgar," and perhaps the popular attitude may have been responsible for the pejorative symbolism of the bird even earlier. In medieval times the bird was the symbol of greed. The moralist disapproved of the bird whether it was making "a huge sound" or sitting noiselessly with its bill in the air, and even credited it with possessing two stomachs. "Lyk a botore, I have also Two wombys" (like a bittern, I have also two stomachs), says Gluttony in Lydgate's *Pilgrimage of the Life of Man*. In the Renaissance the bittern was accused of sloth by emblem writers, although Topsell maintained that it was a "subtile and industrious birde." Peacham gave an individual pejorative symbolism to the bittern in his *Minerva Britanna* in 1612:

> The Fenny Bitter [bittern], that delights to breed
> In thickest sedge, by moore, and riverside,
> By thrusting low his bill into a reede,
> All summer long, at morne and eventide:
> Though neere, yet makes farre seeming such a sound
> That oft it doth, the Passenger astound.
>
> This Figure fits, two sorts of people base,
> The Coward one, that will with wordes affright
> When dares not looke, true valor in the face:

The other is, the proud vaine-glorious wight [man],
Who where he comes, will make a goodly show
Of wit, or wealth, when it is nothing so.

A similar idea occurs in the sixteenth-century proverb, "A bittern will never make a good hawk," which regards the two birds as symbols of baseness and nobility respectively and implies that the bittern despite his pretentions cannot elevate himself.

Chaucer, *WBT*, 972; Drayton, *The Owle*, 921; *Polyolbion*, xxv.103; Goldsmith, II, 185; Harrison, pp. 44, 120; Henkel and Schöne, cols. 862–63; Lydgate, *Pilgr.*, 13031; Owst, p. 202; Peacham, p. 63; Rogers, p. 510; Swann, p. 18; Topsell, p. 92; Witherby, III, 156–57.

Blackbird

Wallace Stevens discovered thirteen ways of looking at a blackbird. Why a blackbird? Black represents death, evil, and the descent to the grave, while a bird, in terms of general symbolism, stands for everlasting life and the ascent to heaven. To Stevens, therefore, the bird symbolized the tension between soul and body, between the spiritual and the material.

The idea of the blackbird as a multivalent symbol is

not new. Theocritus called the bird holy because of its sweet song, and other writers saw the bird as a symbol of solitariness as well as of song because they believed that the Latin word for blackbird, *merula*, derived from *mera volans* (flying alone). Albertus Magnus, the great medieval scientist, knew of a blackbird that had learned nine different musical strains, and its heart put under the head of a sleeping man could make him reveal all his secrets "with an high voice." The Mondovi Bestiary said that the blackbird sang only twice a year and therefore symbolized "all of us who should confess our sins at least twice a year." In Richard de Fournival's *Bestiary of Love*, a man and woman look at a single blackbird in a cage. "This bird," wrote the poet, "sings only for two months in a year, and it is that much more precious for the rarity and beauty of its melody." The bird was a symbol both of poet and lover. The bird's blackness, on the other hand, made it the symbol of death, and occasionally the bird appeared as a foreshadowing of Christ's crucifixion in paintings of the Virgin and Child. The bird might also be the form of a fiend; when a blackbird flew before the face of St. Benedict, the saint suffered agonies of sexual temptation. According to St. Gregory, he was only able to resist by tearing off his clothes and casting himself naked upon the nettles and briars growing around his cell.

The blackbird is similarly identified with sensual passion in a debate between the blackbird and the nightin-

*The blackbird singing sweetly in a cage
is like the captive lover.*

gale by the Scottish poet Dunbar. The blackbird boasts of the "lusty life" in the service of love; the nightingale, usually identified with romantic love, piously declares that "all luve is lost bot upon God allone."

The blackbirds in the nursery rhyme are not easy to interpret:

> Sing a song of sixpence,
>   A Pocket full of rye:
> Four and twenty blackbirds,
>   Baked in a pie.

When the pie was opened,
  The birds began to sing
Was not that a dainty dish,
  To set before the king?

The king was in his counting-house,
  Counting out his money;
The queen was in the parlour,
  Eating bread and honey.

The maid was in the garden,
  Hanging out the clothes,
There came a little blackbird,
  And snapped off her nose.

The meaning of the four and twenty blackbirds baked in a pie has been vigorously argued. Some have taken the nursery rhyme literally. An Italian cookery book of 1549 translated into English in 1598 as *Epulario* or *The Italian Banquet* gave instructions to make pies "so that birds may be alive in them and flie out when it is cut up." The recipe is as follows:

> Make the coffin of a great Pie or pasty in the bottome whereof make a hole as big as your fist, or bigger if you will, let the sides of the coffin bee somewhat higher than ordinary pies, which done, put it full of Flower [flour] and bake it, and being baked, open the hole at the bottome, and take out the Flower.

A small pie, well-filled with goodies, is baked and put inside the large pie, and in the space between the two the cook places many small live birds. When the pie is set before the guest and opened, "all the birds will flie out, which is a delight and pleasure shew to the company. And because they shall not bee altogether mocked, you shall cut open the small pie. . . ." John Nott, cook to the Duke of Bolton in 1723, described a further elaboration in his *Cook's and Confectioner's Dictionary or the Accomplish'd Housewife's Companion*. According to his account, one pie filled with birds and another with frogs are brought to the table. When the lid of one pie is lifted out jump the frogs:

> This makes the Ladies skip and scamper, and lifting the Lid of the other, out fly the Birds which will naturally flie at the light, and so put out the Candles, and so with the leaping of the Frogs below, and flying of the Birds above, it will cause a surprising and diverting Hurley-burley amongst the Guests in the Dark.

The only other literal reading involves a poet laureate called Henry James Pye who wrote some poor verses for the king's birthday in 1790, but the nursery rhyme is earlier than this date.

Allegorical interpretations are more numerous. Some scholars have suggested that the birds represent the hours of the day, with the king as the sun and the queen as the moon; or choirs of monasteries about to be dissolved by King Henry VIII; or manorial title deeds presented to the same king; or the letters of the alphabet for the printing of the English Bible. The queen has been identified with Catharine of Aragon and the maid with Anne Boleyn, and moralists have identified the same maid as a sinner and the blackbird as the Devil, snapping off her nose.

In 1919 the Duke of Windsor heard a parody of the nursery rhyme in a Canadian border town and repeated it to his father, George V. Apparently the parody pleased the king more than any other information which the duke brought back from his tour:

> Four and twenty Yankees,
> Feeling very dry,
> Went across the border,
> To get a drink of Rye.

> When the Rye was opened,
> The Yanks began to sing
> "God Bless America,
> But God Save the King."

While the blackbirds in the royal pie seem light-hearted enough, at the time when the Italian cookery book was published the blackbird was not always highly esteemed as an item of diet. Edward Topsell observed that according to some physicians the taste of the flesh, being sharp, increased melancholy. The blackbird loves solitude, he said.

> Whereupon the Auncients paynted a blackbird to figure a melancholy man who delighteth not so much in any thinge as in woodes and waters.

Applied externally, however, the blackbird might be beneficial either physically or psychologically.

> A dissolved blackbirde in olde oyle easeth the cricke in the necke; and the ache in the hippes. And the olde Magi made an amulett of the feete of a hare and the head of a blackbirde bound to the left arme make men bold and fitt to enterprise greate and waightie matters.

In the nineteenth century, "blackbird" was a common term to denote an African slave, and even early in the twentieth century it was applied to a Polynesian indentured laborer who, while not called a slave, was often one in fact. Another symbolic use of the bird occurs in a popular song of the 1920s in which the blackbird represents all that "care and woe" which the singer is packing up and leaving behind him.

Albertus Magnus, *Secrets*, p. 60; *Animal.* XXIII.27; Aldrovandi, II, 610; Dunbar, "Merle and the Nychtingall," ll. 24, 64; *Epulario*, biiii; de Fournival, p. 33; Friedmann, p. 10;

Holbrook, p. 301; Klingender, pp. 76–77; *Mondovi libellus*, biiv; Nott, pref., n.p.; Opie, pp. 394–95; Gregory, *PL*, 66, col. 132; Theocritus, *Ep.* 4, 9–10; Topsell, pp. 102–104; Witherby, ii, 136.

Bunting

To people living in the Far North the most welcome of all buntings is the snow bunting or snowflake. Its cheerful twitter as it feeds on the windswept fields in biting sub-zero weather is one of the most frequent and happiest of all winter bird sounds. Like Hardy's thrush, the bird is a symbol of hope and promise.

Halliwell in his *Dictionary of Archaic and Provincial Words* gave a number of interesting meanings for bunting: sifting flour, mean and shabby, a large piece of timber, a boy's game played with sticks, a shrimp, a term of endearment, the woodlark. Bunting is also a loosely-woven cloth for making flags. The derivation of the word is uncertain: *bonten* / bunten means to sift or bolt meal, and it seems possible that the corn bunting may derive from this word. This derivation seems more likely than the Scottish *bunt*, meaning gay, lively, brisk, especially when one thinks of a young woman called Bessie Bunting in medieval times. Bessie was the miller's girl "withe lippes so red as cherry." Certainly she was all that the Scottish adjective implied but in particular she was interested in what the poet euphemistically called "daliance." Since all activities having to do with the milling of flour—grinding, sifting, kneading and baking—have sexual connotations and appear in many early bawdy jokes, Bessie's surname probably owes its derivation to the Middle English *bunt*: to sift, as well as to the small bird, *emberiza calandra*, which is somewhat careless about the way it builds its nest and falls an easy prey to the predator.

Sexual implications also seem to be hinted at in the nursery rhyme:

> Baby, baby bunting,
> Daddy's gone a-hunting,
> Gone to get a rabbit's skin
> To wrap the baby bunting in.

The yellow bunting, if it is to be identified with the yellowhammer in England and the yellow yeldring or yorling in Scotland, has an explicit association with the pudendum in Robert Burns' "The Yellow Yellow Yorlin'." Here the bluntness seems especially amusing in a poem which still adheres to the ancient framework of the traditional pastourelle:

14

It fell on a day, in the flow'ry month o' May,
All on a merry merry mornin',
I met a pretty maid, an' unto her I said,
I wad fain fin' your yellow yellow yorlin'.

O no, young man, says she, you're a stranger to me,
An' I am anither man's darlin,
Wha has baith sheep an' cows, that's feedin' in the hows,
An' a cock for my yellow yellow yorlin'.

But, if I lay you down upon the dewy ground,
You wad nae be the waur ae farthing;
An' that happy, happy man, he never cou'd ken
That I play'd wi' your yellow yellow yorlin'.

In Shakespeare's day, in proverbial expression, the bunting was a poor creature. In *All's Well That Ends Well* when young Bertram praised his follower Parolles, who was in fact an unpleasant, scheming fellow, the old Lord Lafew expressed surprise and observed: "I took the lark for a bunting." Another proverb stated that "a goshawk begets not a bunting." On the other hand, Topsell, writing in the same period, used a bit of pseudo-natural history to liken the behavior of buntings to that of reasonable men. Buntings live in summer in couples and in winter in flocks "so as they resemble the fashions of reasonable men whom the Sommer of prosperitie part asunder and desire a solitary life, more for desire of wealth then [than] content of nature, but in the Winter of adversitie they cleave together." Apparently unaware that birds fluff up their feathers in cold weather and look larger, Topsell found that God ordained that in the winter while the birds found less food they should grow fatter. "So is it," said this Elizabethan clergyman, "with poore men, whose bodies are in farre better estate then [than] the richer mens, and many tymes the adversities of this life make mens soules in better likinge then [than] their welfare and prosperitie." Topsell added that the bird was delicious to eat even if only the rich could afford it, and it must therefore be regarded as a sign of God's mercy. According to one of the editors of Goldsmith's work on birds, the bird was similarly valued in the last century. The ortolan bunting is apparently very thin when it arrives in France, but "human ingenuity" soon makes it fit to eat. Trapped and kept in a room totally dark save for one light surrounded by oats and millet, the buntings confine their whole attention to the food, "and it is said that they will thus die of suffocation from their own fat, if left entirely to themselves."

EB., IV, 802; Goldsmith, II, 151–52; Rowland, "The Mill," pp. 69–79; Shakespeare, *All's Well That Ends Well* II.v.6; Swann, p. 60; Topsell, pp. 71–72.

15

Buzzard

One of the earliest English dictionaries of slang defined the buzzard as a "foolish soft fellow, easily drawn in and gulled or trickt." The popular proverb "You cannot make a sparrowhawk out of a buzzard"—that is, you cannot make a noble or skillful bird out of one that is ignoble or clumsy—is even earlier. The pejorative meaning continued up to the beginning of this century when Farmer and Henley in their dictionary of slang defined the buzzard as a stupid fellow. Oliver Goldsmith traced this value to the appearance of the bird:

> He is a sluggish, inactive bird, and often remains perched whole days together upon the same bough. He is rather an assassin than a pursuer; and lives more upon frogs, mice, and insects which he can easily seize, than upon birds, which he is obliged to follow. . . . His figure implies the stupidity of his disposition; and so little is he capable of instruction from man, that it is common to a proverb, to call one who cannot be taught or continues obstinately ignorant, a *buzzard*.

Edward Topsell observed that the buzzard is not a good flier and quoted a German proverbial expression addressed to a lazy person: *du sitzest wie ein Busshart* (you sit like a buzzard). In Italy, a timorous person was called a buzzard because the bird never dared to approach cities or crowded places. Nevertheless, despite its "slouthfull pusillanimitie," the bird was believed to be extremely lascivious and to possess three testicles.

In general the buzzard served as an image of base and witless people, particularly among the Elizabethan satirists. "As blind as a buzzard" was a common proverb. Roger Ascham blamed some of the evils in his day on "those blind buzzards, who in late years, of wilfull maliciousness, would neither learn themselves, nor teach others anything at all." That quarrelsome pedant, Gabriel Harvey (1545–1630) found "none so hawty [haughty] as the basest Bussard," and his old enemy Thomas Nashe (1567–1601), whose powers of invective and unsparing wit were far superior, castigated certain pamphleteers as "brainless Bussards."

Ascham (ed. Giles), III, 201; Goldsmith, II, 49; Harvey (ed. Grosart), II, 277; Nashe (ed. McKerrow), I, 9; Robertson, "Buzones," pp. 741–44; Rolland, II, 15; Topsell, p. 85.

Caladrius

Some people say that this bird actually exists. Réau states that it is a kind of white plover which has been transformed into a fabulous bird. No plover, as far as I know, will sit on your bed when you are ill and tell you by its glance whether you are to live or die. Moreover, this bird was very class-conscious and discriminatory about its patients: you would not have been able to get a caladrius under the health insurance plan or with the Blue Cross. It only visited royalty, and for this reason in illustrations of the bird making its famous ocular diagnosis the patient often has a splendid crown on his head, however uncomfortable it might have been to wear in bed. According to most accounts, if the bird looked away from the patient, he would die; if it looked at him, he would recover; in some cases the bird effected a rapid cure by popping its beak in the sick man's mouth, transferring the disease to itself, and flying away with it to the sun; in other cases hypnosis seems to have been used. Sometimes the disease was specified. Jaundice used to be called "the royal disease" perhaps because the patient turned the color of gold or got the disease as a result of rich living, or because the sufferer was the more easily cured by good wine and the food of kings, as Isidore said. Naturally, this disease merited the attention of the caladrius. The bird was also believed to cure blindness either with its dung or with the marrow in its thigh bone.

In antiquity, as T.H. White observes, the bird was assumed "to be everything from a white parrot to a woodpecker or a seagull, but there was a general agreement

The caladrius looks at a king.

that it was a bird of the rivers." White himself thought that the caladrius was a white wagtail. Identification must have been made more difficult by the fact that, as Suidas explained at the end of the tenth century, "Bird sellers were reluctant to display a caladrius except for immediate cash, lest the bird's glance might heal the intended purchaser free of charge." The bird's name is said to derive from *charadra* (mountain streams). In the list of unclean

Alexander the Great meets the caladrius.

birds in Leviticus and Deuteronomy the Hebrew *anaphah* became *charadrios* in the Septuagint, and *caladrie* in Middle English. Aristotle speaks of the caladrius in connection with ravines and cliffs; Aelian, in the third century A.D., mentions the bird specifically in connection with jaundice. By medieval times there was a tradition that the bird was one of the eastern marvels which interested Alexander the Great, and illustrations show Alexander conducting medical tests in opulent bedrooms with the bird nearby. In many of these illustrations the bird is yellow or has some yellowish coloring, and the great naturalist Conrad Gesner (1516–65) found yellow to be the essential color of any bird reputed to be able to cure jaundice.

The emphasis on the *white* bird is in the bestiaries where the fullest descriptions are found. The reason for its whiteness becomes clear when we look at the symbolism:

> The caladrius is a type of our Saviour. For he is all white, because he has committed no sin, neither is there any guile found in his mouth. But Christ coming down from heaven turned His face away from the Jews, because of their unbelief, and turned to us Gentiles, bearing our infirmities. . . . but the caladrius in Leviticus is one of the unclean birds which must not be eaten or imitated. . . . because it has a long neck and seeks food for itself out of the very bowels of the earth. Here it typifies the contemplative man who keeps up an appearance of religion and reads about heavenly things but lives in a wordly fashion and must not be copied. . . .

Verses in the Psalms in which God either turns His face away or is exhorted to turn His face toward man support the symbolism. In consequence, as Hippeau observes, the caladrius was frequently employed as a symbol of justice

18

or of divine clemency. In a fourteenth-century *Bestiaire d'Amour* by Richard de Fournival the love-sick writer thinks of his lady as the caladrius. If she turns away from him he will die. The lady replies that she wishes she were the bird because then she could avoid getting pregnant: "If I were as wise as the caladrius which you tell me about, I should not have to beware of bringing forth that which is so pleasant to conceive. Ha! True God! Guard me from conceiving anything which would be dangerous to bring forth!"

Since that time the bird has received little attention except from the ornithologists. T.H. White has suggested that it may be the sinister bird mentioned in Shakespeare's "The Phoenix and Turtle." The poem begins by summoning birds to the funeral rites of the turtledove and phoenix, symbols, so Richard Wilbur suggests, of constancy and love. A bird "on the sole Arabian tree" is to serve as the herald, the swan is to be "the priest in surplice white," and the crow is to go among the mourners. The second stanza is addressed to a bird which is unwelcome:

> But thou shrieking harbinger,
> Foul precurrer of the fiend,
> Augur of the fever's end,
> To this troop come thou not near.

It has been suggested to me by Norman Sanders, however, that this shrieking harbinger is the screech owl, which is alluded to in the same way in both *Hamlet* and *A Midsummer Night's Dream.*

Aelian, XVII.13; Aldrovandi, III, 536–37; Aristotle, *H.A.* VIII.3; IX.11; *Athiopische Phys.*, pp. 14–15; *Best. Divin*, p. 92; Brown, pp. 302–303; Cahier & Martin, II, 129; *De Bestiis, PL*, 177, cols. 48, 77; Druce, "Caladrius," pp. 381–416; Evans, pp. 145–47; de Fournival, pp. 28, 116; Friedmann, pp. 10–16; Gesner, II.iii.256–57; Ham (ed.), p. 233; Honorius, *PL*, 172, col. 958; Isidore, iv.8.13; McCulloch, pp. 99–101; Meyer (ed.), p. 437; *Physiologus*, pp. 98–101; Réau, 1.87; Suidas, *Lexicon*, s.v. χαραδριος; Thompson, pp. 311–14; T.H. White, pp. 115, 128; Wilbur, p. 1404; Woodruff, p. 247.

Chough

Larger than the jackdaw and almost the size of a crow, the chough (pronounced chuf) is as noisy and gregarious as these birds. Like the crow also, it was the bird which decked itself out in fine feathers but deceived no one; and it was the tell-tale bird which informed the husband of his wife's infidelity.

The fable of the tell-tale bird probably accounts for the chough's persistent association with the detection of guilt.

Chaucer's Wife of Bath makes an elliptical allusion to it, as though it were very familiar to the audience, and Macbeth, horrified at the appearance of the ghost of his victim, declares:

> It will have blood, they say; blood will have blood.
> Augures and understood relations have
> Stones have been known to move and trees to speak;
> By maggot-pies and choughs and rooks brought forth
> The secret'st man of blood.

Various medieval writers associated the bird especially with thievery, although, as Topsell subsequently pointed out, the ancients also praised the chough for its life-long affection to its mate. When tamed, Topsell added, the chough could be taught to speak, but its voice was never pleasing. Given wine to drink, the bird was "lascivious above measure." The chough's inadequacies gave rise to several proverbs: *gracculus inter musas* (a chough among the muses) signified "an unlearned man in the schooles." Another proverb stating that choughs held their peace when swans sang meant that "when fooles are silent, then wise men may teach profitable things." Their physical appearance, added Topsell, was often a bad portent, foretelling cold and rain or famine and sterility. Devils were known to have transformed themselves into choughs.

Aldrovandi, I, 762; Chaucer, *PF*, 345; *WB Prol*, 232; Gold-smith, II, 93; Shakespeare, *Macbeth* III.iv.122–25; Topsell, pp. 131–39.

Cock

Most people who have heard of Socrates know that he was a Greek philosopher sentenced to death in 399 B.C. on the grounds that his ideas were corrupting Athenian youth. His final words, uttered as the poisonous draft of hemlock froze his lower limbs, have proved to be a teaser. "I owe a cock to Aesculapius," he remarked to his disciples, "pay it and do not neglect it." Some have suggested that his request was the last example of the famous Socratic irony. The cock was a sacred bird, and Socrates was displaying his scepticism. The explanations given by the early Christian Fathers were harsh. Origen, Chrysostom, and Theodoret considered that Socrates, for all his wisdom, was being idolatrous or petty: he was concentrating on the trivial or, even worse in Lactantius' view, he was running scared of the hereafter. The Renaissance philosophers refuted such accusations. Socrates' cock was man's soul. His soul had the same value as that of philosopher and mathematician Pythagoras who, when he said "feed the cock," meant "feed the soul." Socrates was saying that he owed his soul to the great Doctor of Souls. Later scholars have suggested that Socrates was indicating his acceptance of exclusive Greek religious rituals known only to the few. The cock was the last offering made by those who had been inducted into the Greater Mysteries, and the dying philosopher was indicating his awareness that he also was to undergo the last test or discipline and was about to witness the revelation.

As far as Aesculapius, the legendary Greek god of medicine, is concerned, the cock was sacred to him and was sacrificed by those whom he cured. In ancient Greece the cock was also the symbol of the sun and was sacred to Apollo, Athena, Demeter, Latona, Hermes, and Hercules. In ancient China, the cock was the chief embodiment of *Yang*, representing the warmth and light of the universe.

In the Christian era the cock's early associations with light, healing, and regeneration made it the symbol of resurrection or of eternal life; on early funereal monuments and in epitaphic verse, it was the guide of the souls of the dead, or the triumphant soul itself. In medieval times the cock was the good Christian, saint or priest. The uncanny intelligence, for which Pliny himself had praised the cock, was reinforced by Job xxxviii.36: "Who hath put wisdom in the innermost parts of man? Or who hath given understanding to the cock?" Gregory, Rabanus Maurus, Eucherius, Neckam, and others saw the cock as a teacher of the church "because God is wisdom conferred upon teachers." Ambrose, in his famous hymn, "*Aeterne Rerum Conditor*" introduced the cock into the liturgy:

> Gallo canente, spes redit,
> Aegris salus refunditur,
> Mucro latronis conditur,
> Lapsis fides revertitur.

> (With the singing of the cock
> hope returns, health is restored
> to the sick, the sword of the robber
> is put away and faith returns to
> the fallen.)

Prudentius composed a hymn to the song of the cock in which the bird not only heralded God's light, but was the Judge himself.

The iron cock perched on the top of the church represented more than an obvious symbol of day and of light. According to Durandus, Bishop of Mende, who explained the symbols of Christian ritual in the *Rationale divinorum officiorum*, a liturgical treatise written in Italy about 1286, this cock was the preacher, "who preacheth boldly and exciteth the sleepers to cast away the works of darkness, exclaiming 'Woe to them that sleep!' " The iron rod on which the cock sat symbolized the preacher's "discourse

St. Peter's cock symbolized the call to repentance.

...that he speaketh not of man but of God."

The cock which perched for centuries on crucifixes at crossroads in many European countries was thought by Victor Hugo to be a reminder of treachery. He was alluding, of course, to the cock of St. Peter, the cock which, as Christ had prophesied, crew when the disciple lied three times out of fear. St. Peter's denial is one of the most poignant incidents in the New Testament (Luke xxii.54–62):

> Then took they him, and led him, and brought him into the high priest's house. And Peter followed afar off. And when they had kindled a fire in the midst of the hall, and were set down together, Peter sat down among them. But a certain maid beheld him as he sat by the fire, and earnestly looked upon him, and said, "This man was also with him." And he denied him, saying, "Woman, I know him not." And after a little while another saw him, and said, "Thou art also of them." And Peter said, "Man, I am not." And about the space of one hour after another confidently affirmed, saying, "Of a truth this fellow also was with him: for he is a Galilean." And Peter said, "Man, I know not what thou sayest." And immediately, while he yet spake, the cock crew. And the Lord turned, and looked upon Peter. And Peter remembered the word of the Lord, how He had said unto him, "Before the cock crow, thou shalt deny me thrice." And Peter went out, and wept bitterly.

Rather than representing treachery, however, this cock of St. Peter's was the symbol of the call to repentance. As the bestiaries remarked:

> At the crowing of this bird hope returns to all men, the

troubles of the sick are relieved, the pain of wounds is lessened, fevers die down, faith comes back to the fallen. Jesus looks back upon the waverers and sets the wanderers straight.

An even longer exegesis was popular:

In the middle of the night Peter denies; with the approach of day at cock crow he repents. Whereas he wandered in the midst of the darkness of his error he now wept at the remembrance of the much to be desired light. And that true light changed completely and set everything right. As the first servant girl denotes wavering, the second girl consent and the third, a man, the deed done, so we deny God thrice when we delight in evil, when we consent to evil, and when we do evil deeds. So must the cock crow to us, the preacher must teach us the way of truth, and the Holy Spirit visit and inspire our hearts.

The cock's divine properties became magical in folklore. In early religious beliefs, such as those recorded in the *Zend-Avesta*, the crowing of the cock put demons to flight. In *Hamlet*, the cock "that is the trumpet to the morn" dispelled ghosts; in folk tales and ballads the cock-crow caused fairies and ghosts to lose their power over mortals and to vanish. Sometimes God assisted. According to an attractive Danish youth who was set upon by elf queens,

If God had not help'd me in time of need
With crowing of cock so shrill,
I surely had stay'd with these elfin queens
In cavern beneath the hill.

On the other hand the magical crowing brought disaster to two friends dining on a cock in Bologna. When the steaming bird was placed before them, they observed merrily, "This fowl is so well cut up that neither St. Peter nor Christ Himself could put it together again." According to Aldrovandi:

At these words the rooster suddenly sprang up, alive and covered with feathers, clapped his wings and crowed, scattering the sauce upon the men who were dining together. Straightway there followed a punishment worthy of their sacrilege and rash blasphemy; for as they were sprinkled with pepper they were stricken with leprosy.

The color of the cock was important. Red cocks, black cocks, and cocks of unspecified color were all sacrificed in ancient, medieval, and modern sorcery; and in one of the earliest witchcraft trials, in 1324, Dame Alice Kyteler was accused of sacrificing a variety of cocks to a demon at the crossroads, tearing them limb from limb, and using their entrails for magical powders and potions. The solar cock was yellow, the Christian cock white. In China the cock's white color was emblematical of purity of heart, and at wedding ceremonies white sugar cocks were eaten by the bride and bridegroom. Also white was the cock which, according to Pliny, terrified the lion but which Sir Thomas Browne thought to be "a very unsafe defensative . . . against the fury of this animal"; the red cock was sacrificed in Egypt to Osiris, a sun god, and in China it was pasted on a house as a protection against fire. The black cock, offered by the Druids to the evil spirits and used by the French in order to raise them, was valuable therapeutically. Three drinks of water from its skull restored speech to a mortal maiden struck dumb by the fairies; buried with clippings of the patient's hair and nails, a black cock cured an epileptic. Epilepsy was transferred to it if the patient threw money into St. Tecla's well in Denbighshire and slept on the church altar table with a cock in his arms, and as late as 1850 a witness reported seeing a cock staggering about with the "fits," as a result of the ritual. Even St. Peter's cock becomes black in D.H. Lawrence's *The Virgin and the Gypsy*: Yvette, denying her sexual interest in the gypsy, thinks of herself as Peter, "and it was a strange, lustrous black cock which crew in mockery of her."

The ancestor of St. Peter's cock was, of course, the prophetic cock which the Greeks and Romans closely inspected for auguries. To the ancients, while the cock displaying homosexual tendencies threatened terrible disasters and had to be instantly seized and burned alive, the way in which a cock approached its food might be a favorable sign from the gods. Medieval writers continued to examine the cock's eating habits. They found them praiseworthy but no longer regarded them as divine portents: "The cock," said Bartholomew, "sechith his mete with his bile [bill] and with feet, and scharpith and over torneth st[r]awe and poudir: and whan he fyndith a grayne he clepith and crieth to him his hennes." This bit of natural history enhanced the cock's reputation and made him generous as well as vigilant. In a manuscript at Cluny the virtue Liberality is portrayed as a woman riding a cock and scattering coins from a vase. The cock on a tower represents "vigilance and guardianship" to the Renaissance writer Alciatus; with a horn at its feet, the cock is "vigilant for peace and arms," according to Paradin; with a laurel branch in its beak and the caption "By vigilance," Aldrovandi saw it as a man "who spends his life in watchfulness but not in sleep and leisure, so that by good works he may attain eternal glory." The cock, standing on a skull and holding an hourglass with the motto *Vigilate quia nescitis diem neque horem* (watch because you know neither the day nor the hour), was the device of the Antwerp printer, Guislain Janssens. The cock also symbolized the sense of sight in a mural depicting the wheel of the Five Senses in the tower of Longthorpe near Peterborough.

The fighting cock celebrated in Greece and Rome gave

rise to an obvious symbolism. Often repeated was the story of the hero Themistocles who came across two fighting cocks as he led his troops against the Persians, and who declared the birds to be a pattern for the warrior. On Christian tombs a carving of two fighting cocks represented the courage of Christians in their persecution. Preachers such as Berchorius made analogies which were repeated for many centuries: the spurs of the cock were its martial weapon, its comb a helmet, its tail a banner, and the actual fighting was a pitched battle. A somewhat curious use of the cock's knightly qualities can be found in a medieval bestiary of love where the cock became the courtly lover:

> The cock crows at dawn and dusk, which are like both day and night together; this is like love which is neither all hope or all despair; and midnight signifies utter despair. When I have no hope of your love . . . it is like midnight . . . .

In heraldry, according to John Guillim, the cock was the Knight amongst Birds—"a compleat Souldier armed *a Cape a pee*."

In the early seventeenth century Topsell still repeated the idea of the cock being an armed soldier "having his Combe for a helmett, his spurres for a sword, his beake for a speare, his taile for a standard, and after combate his owne voice to proclaime his victorie and singe his tri-

Cockfighting was popular in the Middle Ages.

umph." The same writer also domesticated the cock's vigilance and generosity. The cock became the pattern of the good and watchful father who hatched the eggs of his offspring if his wife died; when the cock gave food to his hens the bird was like the loving husband or the liberal man. On the same theme, Aldrovandi wrote that "the ardent love of the rooster towards his family also teaches us to love our wives and to reject all prostitutes, who are nothing more than a pestilence and destruction to husbands. Therefore the ancients were accustomed to carve the image of a rooster and hen kissing each other upon the tombs of prominent persons to indicate by their conjunction a lawful marriage."

Yet this uxoriousness which made the cock a symbol

of conjugality also had far-reaching pejorative implications. Aristotle had said that the barnyard cock was peculiarly salacious, and Pliny described how it fought for its wives and then dominated them with inordinate vanity and aggressiveness. Perhaps as a result of the reputation given it by the early natural historians, the cock appeared on the fist of Lady Wrath (Dame Ire) as she proudly rode a boar in the procession of Gower's Seven Deadly Sins, but usually the associations were sexual. The most common symbolism is conveyed by delicate innuendo in an early lyric:

> I have a gentil cok,
> Croweth me day;
> He doth me risen erly
> My matins for to say.

> I have a gentil cok,
> Comen he is of gret (great family),
> His comb is of red corel,
> His tail is of jet . . . .

Only the unusual roosting place of the cock reveals the bird's symbolism:

> . . . every night he percheth him
> In myn ladyes chaumber.

The same symbolism, punningly used by Shakespeare and others, appears in Cock Walk of the London stews, cock-bawd, cock-alley (meaning the pudendum), and cock-ale, an aphrodisiac or strong ale.

It is the phallic cock which D.H. Lawrence identified with the resurrected Christ in "The Man Who Died," a short story originally published in Paris as "The Escaped Cock," and presumably intended to be very daring. In this story Christ releases a tethered cock, and its newfound freedom is the symbol of His own sensuality which has been almost extinguished by His devotion to humanity.

As a verb, according to Farmer and Henley, *cock* is usually applied to women in the passive voice, i.e., "to want cocking" or "to get cocked." Writing at the end of the Victorian era, these two strange compilers of the most famous dictionary of slang produce a number of associated terms. Cocktail might be in America "a drink composed of spirits—bitters, crushed ice, sugar, etc., the whole whisked briskly until foaming, and then drunk hot," but in England it was commonly a "prostitute; a wanton." In contemporary American slang, a "cock-teaser" is a taboo term said to be "universally known to male students," meaning "a girl or young woman who displays affection but . . . ."

While the cock's salaciousness caused its parts to be served in all kinds of medicine as a cure for impotency, it also made the bird a symbol of impiety. Aldrovandi observed that the bird:

leaps upon his mother in copulation, as the hippopotamus does, and he likewise cruelly treads upon his father. For this reason the most wise legislators of the ancients thought he should be included with a viper, a monkey, and a dog in the parricide's sack, so that those who are guilty of the same crime might be afflicted with the same punishment and pay the penalty equally. It is well known that in Aristophanes, *Clouds*, Pheidippides, who had beaten his father, looks upon his deed as done by example of the rooster, for the latter also treats his father roughly.

A converse meaning of the cock was given by Isidore. He derived its name from *castratio*. The bestiaries repeated Isidore's derivation and stated that the cock was the only member of the bird family to have his testicles removed. For the same reason the priests of Cybele were called *galli* (cocks). In 1612 Henry Peacham depicted Ganymede, Jove's favorite, riding on a cock, on the grounds that he was a "foule Sodomitan." The meaning survives in the American underworld where cock is a term for a catamite, especially for one used as a decoy by extortionists to blackmail susceptible men. On the other hand, a "queer rooster" had a different meaning for Grose in 1775: he was "an informer that pretends to be sleeping, and thereby overheard the conversation of thieves in night cellars."

The most famous literary cock is Chanticleer of Chaucer's *Nun's Priest's Tale*. In this amusing beast epic

Chaucer shows how well he knew the traditions. Chanticleer is splendidly regal, a courtly lover to his favorite hen, and generous to all his wives:

And with a chuk he gan hem for to calle.
For he hadde founde a corn lay in the yerd. . . .
He chukketh whan he hath a corn yfounde,
And to him rennen thanne his wyves alle. (4364–73)

He has, as Pliny had said in the second century, an instinctive knowledge of astronomy and an ability to foretell events. His proverbial vigilance enables him to detect the fox lurking among the cabbages; his knightly arrogance and pride in his voice make him almost fatally susceptible to flattery. If the Church Fathers saw the cock as the *doctor Ecclesiae*, fighting the temptations of the world, the flesh, and the devil, Chanticleer is the priest who succumbs to all three. Only his proverbial intelligence enables him to save his life and—since a fable should have a moral—to realize the consequences of vanity:

Lo, swich it is for to be recchelees
And necligent, and truste on flaterye. (2626–27)

(See, that's what comes of being careless and negligent and trusting in flattery.)

Aelian, ii.28; Albertus Magnus, *Secrets*, pp. 80, 92; Alciatus, pp. 76–79, xv; Aldrovandi, ii, 183–354; see also Lind, pp.

178–243; Ambrose, *PL*, 16, col. 1473; *American Slang*, s.v. cock-teaser; Barke, pp. 27–28; Bartholomew, XII.17; Berchorius, pp. 208–209; Browne, *Pseudodoxia*, III.xxvii; Cahier & Martin, II, 31; Chew, pp. 138, 193, 356n.38; Chrysostom, *PG*, 60, col. 414; Dahlberg, p. 282; Durandus, I, 22; Eucherius, *PL*, 50, col. 750; Evans, pp. 162–63; de Fournival, p. 9; Garner, *PL*, 193, col. 73; Gower, *Mirour*, I.ll. 877–80; Gregory, *PL*, 76, cols. 527–28; Guillim, p. 164; Isidore, xii.7.50; Jean de Condé (ed. Novati), pp. 486–87; Kittredge, p. 94; Knight, p. 4n; Lactantius, *PL*. 6, col. 417; Neckam, p. 121; Origen, *PG*, 11, col. 1294; Paradin, p. 225; Peacham, p. 48; Plato, *Phaedo*, 118A; Pliny, x.xxiv; Prudentius, pp. 4–9; Rabanus Maurus, *PL*, 112, col. 939; Réau, I.102; Shakespeare, *Hamlet* I.i.147–64; Steadman, "Chauntecleer," pp. 236–44; Theodoret, *PG*, 83, col. 1006; Topsell, p. 26; Thompson, pp. 33–44; Twining, pl. LXXVIII, pp. 177–78; Typotius, p. 7.x; Varty, pp. 31–42; Williams, pp. 163–64; Wimberly, pp. 190, 240; *Zend-Avesta, Vendidad*, 34, 38.

Except for its baldness the coot was once greatly admired.

Coot

The popular expressions "silly old coot" and "as bald as a coot" have associations so far removed from Tennyson's babbling brook flowing "from haunts of coot and fern" that few writers are likely to use this bird as a praiseworthy symbol. Yet earlier natural historians and theologians thought highly of the coot, and the symbolism given in *De Bestiis* was often repeated by the bestiary writers:

The coot is very intelligent and the most prudent of all birds. It neither eats cadavers, nor gads about from one place to another, but remains in one place, staying there until the end and finding there its food and rest. Thus, the faithful man lives and is preserved by the will of God. He does not fly hither and thither like a heretic. Nor does he enjoy worldly desires or carnal lusts, but, just like this bird [the coot], he does not eat flesh and remains and finds his peace always in one place, that is to say the catholic and apostolic Church.

These writers usually give a little natural history:

The coot is a pond-dweller, building its nest in the middle of the water or on a stone surrounded by it, and always it finds delight in the deep water; and when it foresees a storm, it flees to play in its nest.

One bestiarist, Philippe de Thaon, regarded this coot as the symbol of a hermit and the nest as a hermitage.

The poet Skelton (1460–1529) did not share the medieval view of the coot. Among those who are to mourn the death of Philip Sparrow is

> . . . the mad coot,
> with bald fact to toot.

Topsell, translating Aldrovandi nearly a century later, saw the coot as a "weaker creature," epitomizing inferiority when compared to other birds. Despite the bird's bad

Coots are sensible birds.

reputation, however, the heart of a "rawe coote" was good for epilepsy, and several families used the coot as their heraldic crest. Both he and Aldrovandi gave a proverbial expression which has not survived: to compare a swan to a coot was to "expresse a great dissimilitude," to denote two things which were poles apart. On the other hand, an expression already in use in medieval times, "as bald as a coot," may still be heard.

The bird has attracted little attention since. Farmer and Henley in their dictionary of slang gave coot as a synonym for "buffle-head," or "cabbage head." The explanation was that the *fulica atra*, the bald or common coot, like the ostrich, was said to bury its head when pursued, thinking that none could see it.

Aldrovandi, III, 97; *Best. Divin.*, pp. 254–56; *De Bestiis, PL*, 177, col. 56; McCulloch, pp. 104–105; *MED.*, s.v. *cote*; Philippe de Thaon, ll. 2749–64; Topsell, pp. 216–17; T.H. White, pp. 107–108.

Cormorant

Siwash Rock on the shores of English Bay, Vancouver, is a favorite spot for cormorants. Usually three sit there on a small twisted tree stump, black against the blue water. They are sinister, predatory creatures, very watchful, and capable of remaining still for long periods without losing their alert, confident air. The ornithologist Newton thought that Milton's well-known comparison of Satan to a cormorant might have arisen because Milton knew that "when gorged, or when the state of the tide precludes fishing, they are fond of sitting on an elevated perch, often with extended wings, and in this attitude they will remain motionless for a considerable time, as though hanging themselves out to dry." Milton, however, may have been thinking of the cormorant's traditional characteristics. Satan, alighting on a tree to plot the downfall of Adam and Eve, is a voracious creature:

Thence up he flew, and on the Tree of Life,
The middle tree and highest there that grew,
Sat like a cormorant . . . .

In Milton's day the cormorant was trained to fish. A strap around its neck prevented the bird from devouring its take. Usually the bird seizes its prey within a few seconds of seeing it and rises to the surface with the captive in its bill. While the usual diet is fish, the cormorant has been known to eat a conger eel measuring two-and-a-half feet and a kitten eleven inches long. King James I who kept cormorants at Westminster created a new office, "Master of the Royal Cormorants." After this office lapsed as a result of the Civil War, James' former keeper, at the age of ninety-five, petitioned Charles II to restore the rank to him. Milton would probably have known of the sport of fishing with a cormorant since it was described by George Sandys whose work Milton knew. The image in *Paradise Lost* is appropriate: like the trained cormorant, Satan will capture his prey but eventually will have to surrender it to his master, God.

Not surprisingly, the cormorant was predominantly a symbol of a voracious appetite; "The hote [hot] cormeraunt of glotenye," Chaucer called the waterfowl. But although its greed soon became proverbial, comparatively little was made of the cormorant in medieval times, except as a symbol of Christ rising from Hell or as a symbol of the Devil seeking to capture mankind like fish.

The Elizabethans applied the cormorant as a term of abuse to all kinds of people—bailiff, debt collectors, farmers, money lenders, in fact any "wretch that lives on the spoile of the needy." Shakespeare made use of the name as an adjective to express insatiability. He speaks of "the cormorant belly," "this cormorant war," and "cormorant devouring time." In Michael Drayton's poem which attacks political and social evils, *The Owle* (1603), while the kestrel represents a gouging landlord, and the sparrow a lecherous courtier, the cormorant is a monopolist. Thomas Nashe, writing in an age when there were no government handouts for the Arts, abuses his patrons with the image: "This is the lamentable condition of our time, that men of Arte must seek almes of Cormorants, and those that deserve best be kept under by Dunces."

Chaucer, *PF*, 362; Greene (ed. Grosart), xi, 253, 283, 285; Harrison, *They Tell of Birds*, p. 112; Harting, pp. 259–65; Lodge (ed. Hunterian Club), iv, i, 73; Mills, pp. 414–15; Milton, *Paradise Lost* v. l. 196; Nashe (ed. McKerrow), i, 36, 159–60, 164–65, 204; ii, 106; iii, 178; Newton, *EB.*, vii, 162; Sandys, p. 219; Shakespeare, *Love's Labour's Lost* i.i.4; *Troilus and Cressida* ii.ii.6; *Coriolanus* i.i.116; Swainson, p. 143; Tillyard, pp. 71–75; Turner, p. 111.

Crane

Cranes dance; not hesitantly, as you might expect, but with all the aplomb of Scottish country dancers tackling "Marie's Wedding." Marjorie Kinnan Rawlings in her novel *The Yearling* thought that they danced a cotillion:

> The cranes were dancing a cotillion as surely as it was danced at Volusia. . . . In the heart of the circle several moved counterclockwise. . . . The outer circle shuffled around and around. The group in the center attained a slow frenzy.

The circular movement was important: to the ancients the ring dance associated the cranes with the sun. The cranes brought the spring and were surrogates of the resurgent sun god. Their dance epitomized both fertility and death rituals. When Theseus returned from Crete after slaying the Minotaur, he and his young friends, according to Plutarch, landed on Delos and danced the *geranos* or the crane dance: they went through the motions of "threading" the Cretan labyrinth whereby the hero had been able to slay the monster in the center and find his way out afterwards. This spiral dance, in Robert Graves' view, "imitated the fluttering love dance of courting cranes." The tradition was that each movement consisted of nine steps and a leap. As Polwart says in his *Flyting with Montgomery* (1605):

> The crane must aye
> Take nine steps ere shee flie.

This dance was common to rituals enacted in funerary labyrinth and tumuli in many parts of the world. As late as the eighteenth century the Ostiks of Siberia dressed their dancers in the skins of cranes. China also had her ritual crane dancers:

> Ho-lu, king of Wu, offered his daughter a fish of which he had already eaten a portion, thereby apparently breaking a food-communion taboo. She committed suicide and in order to propitiate her spirit and avert evil consequences the king sacrificed dancers by burying them alive. He constructed a magnificent tomb for her remains, furnished with objects of great value. An underground passage, the prerogative of royalty, led to the sepulchral chamber. The dance of the white cranes was enacted in the market-place of the capital. The crowd was ordered to go and see the spectacle and to follow the cortège. It was so arranged that boys and girls entered the subterranean passage with the crane dancers. Then a machine . . . was set in motion to close the passage and bury the dancers and their followers alive.

Next to the phoenix, the crane was the most celebrated in Chinese legend. The black crane was said to reach a fabulous age; human beings assumed its shape, and the bird showed a peculiar interest in mortal affairs. The crane was one of the commonest emblems of longevity and was usually shown under a pine tree—also a symbol of age. The soul of the dead was represented as riding on the crane's back to the "Western Heaven." Armstrong remarked thirty years ago that the figure of the crane was still prominent in Chinese funeral ceremonies:

> A picture of one is placed on top of the catafalque when coffins are carried to the grave, and the wheeled sedan chair in the funeral cortège containing an image of the departed is sometimes drawn by a paper crane. In South China I have seen a white paper model of a crane suspended from the window of a house in which someone had died.

Yeats' bird must be a crane:

> Two Chinamen, behind them a third,
> Are carved in lapis lazuli,
> Over them flies a long-legged bird,
> A symbol of longevity.

In Japan also the crane was the symbol of longevity and happiness, and was believed to carry to heaven those who had attained immortality.

Equally ancient was the bird's reputation for vigilance.

The crane holding a pebble in its foot is an illustration of proverbial watchfulness and prudence. Flying in formation in a strong wind, the crane was said to pick up a stone. The bird used the stone as ballast or dropped it to find out by the noise it made whether the crossing was over sea or land. According to Aristotle and Pliny, when the crane acted as night sentinel during migration, it stood on one foot and held a pebble in the other. If the watcher fell asleep the noise of the falling pebble woke it; if danger threatened, the bird dropped the pebble to warn the rest of the flock. To Horapollo, the crane on guard duty symbolized the man who protected himself from the plots of his enemies. The bird was also a symbol of a watchful man skilled in celestial matters. Cranes always flew very high, said Horapollo, to inspect the clouds for rain.

To the medieval bestiarists the crane was a symbol of the Christian's foresight and wisdom; in such a way should man guard against the machinations of the devil:

Et garde de dormir, c'est à dire que tu ne l'oblies par péchié que tu fais; et que tu soies adès veillant en bien fais.

(And take care of sleeping; that is to say, do not forget through sin what you are doing and be watchful in well-doing.)

Gerald of Wales saw the crane as the symbol of the watchful prelate, and Wither gave the same significance

The crane holds a stone to keep itself awake.

in the Elizabethan period when he placed the crane on top of the crozier of the bishop, the overseer of the church. To other emblem writers such as Valeriano, Reusner, and Alciatus, the crane was the symbol of prudence or of vigilance, often associated with justice, and as such it appeared in a portrait of Queen Elizabeth. Valeriano also regarded the bird as a symbol of perseverance, as a man who persisted in his way of life unchanged, as democracy, and as *observator ordinis* (the keeper of rank). Thynne, in his emblem, saw the crane as a symbol of discretion. He depicted the Strymonian cranes carrying stones in their bills to keep themselves from uttering a cry when crossing the dangerous Taurus hill, for fear of arousing their foe. He concluded:

> Soe men, whome art and nature doth adorne,
> Should silent be, for feare of followinge hate.

He entitled his emblem "Our Betters or Enemies Not To Be Provoked With Wordes." In Topsell's view the crane traditionally signified "a wise man that warily avoided the treacheries of his adversaries." Its flight symbolized astrology or "any loftie and sublime studie." In his opinion the organization of the cranes was a symbol of true democracy. He, too, laboriously explored the habits of the crane to find an extended allegory of the good Christian. Just as the eagle was the enemy of the crane "so is the divell to every good Christian man or woman." Ripa regarded the crane in flight as the emblem of an inquisitive man investigating sublime things at a distance. His contemporary, Spenser, on the other hand, seems to have thought little of the crane: in the *Faerie Queene*, Disdain walks like a crane, and Gluttony has the neck of a crane. The last allusion may be to the bird fattened for the table. Topsell referred to the ancient practice of sewing up the eyes of "Cranes and Swannes, and so feede them in darkenes whereby they grewe very fatt in a short space."

The cranes' flight was said to have inspired the invention of letters. The birds fly in v-formation and the characters of all early alphabets nicked with a knife on bark or on clay tables were naturally angular. Lucan said that at the beginning of their flight "the cranes described various chance-taught figures: but later when a loftier wind beats on their outspread wings, they combine at random and form disordered packs, until the letter is broken and it disappears as the birds are scattered." Isidore repeated the statement, and the *Aviarium*, the medieval collection of pseudo-natural history of birds, observed that the cranes follow one another in letter order (*ordine litterato*). According to the fables of Hyginus, the curator of the Palatine library under Augustus, Mercury invented certain letters of the alphabet after watching the flight of cranes "which make letters as they fly." Mercury's counterpart in Egypt was Thoth, the god whose symbol was the crane-like white ibis, and he too was credited with inventing hieroglyphs.

Aelian, III.13; Alciatus, p. 87, xvii; Aldrovandi, III, 334–35, 353; Aristotle, *H.A.* IX.10; Armstrong, "Crane Dance," pp. 71–76; Cahier & Martin, II, 142; Chew, p. 138; de Fournival, p. 47; Gerald of Wales, *Top. Hib.*, v, 46–47;

Graves, pp. 227, 233; Ham (ed.), p. 234; Horapollo, pp. 143, 145; Isidore, xii.7.14; Lucan, *Pharsalia* v.716; Matthews, p. 159; McCulloch, pp. 105–106; Morgan, p. 128; Picinelli, iv.xxxxi; Pierre de Beauvais, ii.142; Pliny, x.xxx; Plutarch, *Theseus*, xxi; Reusner, ii.xxxiv.95; Ripa, ii.iii.173 (*Vigilanza*); ii.ii.349 (*Investigatione*); Spence, p. 100; Svendsen, pp. 66–67; Swan, p. 413; Thynne, no. 50; Topsell, pp. 201–209; Valeriano, ff.128v–129; Williams, p. 84; Wither, iii, no. 15; Yeats, *Lapis Lazuli*, ll. 37–40.

Crow

The long-lived crow was supposed to be able to foretell the future.

As W.J. Brown remarks, crows "seem to have been all that the raven was, only, as befitted their size, in a less degree." The French peasants, for instance, used to say that whereas bad priests become ravens, bad nuns become crows. Virgil declared that the *cornix* (crow) was an ominous bird, calling down rain; Ovid and others said that it was unpleasantly garrulous. Cicero quoted as a proverbial expression *cornicum oculos configere* (to delude the most wary), an allusion to the crow's habit of attacking the eyes first. The bird's divine powers were usually regarded as sinister. The Greek proverb "go to the crows" used in Aristophanes' *Clouds* meant "drop dead!" Reverence and fear toward the bird persisted in modified forms over the centuries.

Drawing from the Roman writers and from early collections of bird and animal tales, medieval authors found the crow a suitable figure for a variety of sins. They made

35

use of two fables in particular: the fable of the white crow which Apollo turned black as a punishment for tattling about his unfaithful wife; the fable of the crow which decked itself in peacock feathers and disdained its companions, only to be despised by the peacocks which were not deceived by the fine plumes. In the heyday of anti-feminism, both fables served to illustrate what was wrong with women. The Church Fathers pointed to the bird in order to rebuke women for using cosmetics and false hair. Boccaccio, writing of a man reduced to despair by a widow's vanity, garrulity, and disloyalty, named his work *Corbaccio*, a title which, while it has caused some argument among critics, seems to symbolize the black widow herself. The monk Matheolus, in a typically medieval anti-feminist diatribe, used the crow to denounce the inability of women to keep silent—*cornix mutatur quia garrula* (the crow is changed because she is garrulous). Later Ripa put the crow, *cornacchia* (meaning "a loose woman" in modern Italian), in the hand of a woman personifying loquacity. He placed *two* crows in the hands of Irresolution because the bird's supposed cry "*cras! cras!*" (to-morrow! tomorrow!) had won for it a reputation as a procrastinator.

The crow in borrowed feathers was a useful figure in other ways. In a sonnet by Chiaro Davanzati in the thirteenth century this crow was the poet's rival. Similarly, several centuries later, in a letter in *A Groatsworth of Wit*

(1592) by Robert Greene, the crow was also the writer's rival—this time no less than William Shakespeare himself:

> For there is an upstart crow, beautified with our feathers, that with his tiger's heart wrapped in a Player's hide, supposes he is as well able to bombast out a blank verse as the best of you . . . .

To the emblem writer Camerarius the crow in fine feathers was the symbol of all those who were ambitious and arrogant.

Some of Greene's contemporaries discovered in the classics a more favorable symbolism for the crow. Clergyman Topsell, translating Aldrovandi, justified the crow as a good symbol on etymological grounds: "in Greek Corona the Crowne which signifieth the toppe of happines, derived from Korone, a Crowe." Juvenal, he noted, made the crow a symbol of a long and happy life:

> The patterne of his happie life
> ffrom Crowes he tooke whose yeres are rife.

Among the Egyptians, Topsell stated, the crow symbolized "undivided amitye and love betwixt man and wife," and in his own day the emblem writers made the crow the symbol of concord. Furthermore, he declared, the crow was a divine bird because it predicted rain.

In the same period one interpretation arose which strikingly reversed another aspect of the crow's traditional

36

symbolism. In Suetonius' *Life of Domitian* are two lines *nuper Tarpeio quae sedit culmine cornix* / *"Est bene" non potuit dicere, dixit: "Erit"* (recently the crow which sat on the top of the Capitoline Hill not being able to say "It is well," said "It will be"). According to Tibullus, another Latin writer, the crow was hope that nourished life, and tomorrow (*cras*) would always be better. These two passages together inspired the idea that the crow's well-known cry "*cras! cras!*" was a symbol of Hope. "Which bird is accompanying you?" Hope is asked in Alciatus' emblem, "the crow, most faithful of augurs; / When he cannot say, 'All is well,' he says, 'All will be well.'" Probably because of the popularity of Alciatus' *Emblemata* the crow became widely accepted as the symbol of Hope, appearing on columns in engravings and sculpture, particularly in the Netherlands. It also became the attribute of Pandora. Pandora was the inquisitive girl who opened the forbidden box or jar and let all the evils loose in the world. According to Hesiod: "only Hope remained there . . . under the rim of the great jar, and did not fly out at the door." Beginning with Rosso Fiorentino, artists introduced the crow hanging to the rim of Pandora's box, a small but perky figure dwarfed by the grotesque personifications of evil which had already issued forth—such as Avarice grasping her purse, Despair tearing her hair, and Wrath with a dagger attacking a youth. Emblem writers also had a good word to say for the crow which plucked out the eyes of its victim. The crow or raven on the head of an armed man recalled the story given by Livy and Pliny of the bird which helped Valerius to victory by blinding his adversary. This bird, said Geoffrey Whitney, signified the Lord's providence. On the other hand, under the title *Luxuriosorum Opes* (the wealth of profligates) Whitney makes the crow a symbol of the spendthrift. He uses Ovid's account of the crow sent by Phoebe to find water. In this story the crow arrives at a fountain, sees some figs and neglects its errand until the figs ripen. Whitney adds:

> So fooles, theire goods unto no goodnes use
> But flatterers feede, or waste them on the stewes.

Of more recent times, the crow's image has shockingly deteriorated, and now it has neither dignity nor respect. The crow's association with its more sociable close relative, the rook, seems to have compounded the degradation. Very early the verb *to rook* meant "to cheat"; by Smollett's time a *rookery* had become a gambling den, then it was a brothel, slum or barracks, and today in America it is a place frequented by hoboes. A crow in the late nineteenth century, according to Farmer and Henley, was "a confederate on watch whilst another steals. Generally a man, but occasionally a woman acts as a crow." Proverbial expressions still current, such as "to have a crow to pluck" and "to eat crow," are a reminder of the bird's unpleasant connotations. Crow's feet, a figurative term which Chaucer used, are still something that no one wants around the eyes. No one likes to be called an old crow, either, although crows have been known to reach the age of seventy or eighty without losing the sprightliness of their movements or the sparkle of their eyes. Whether anyone now bears toward the crow the deadly hatred with which the Somali Arabs are said to have pursued and killed the bird, is doubtful. Their detestation was apparently inspired by the Muslem version of the tell-tale bird. When Mohammed was hiding in a cave from his enemies, the crow, at that time a light-plumaged bird, spotted him and screamed "*ghar! ghar!*" (cave! cave!) to indicate the place of concealment. Mohammed's enemies, however, did not understand the bird, and passed on. When the Prophet came out of the cave, he turned the crow's feathers completely black and ordered it to cry "*ghar*" as long as crows should live.

Alciatus, pp. 178–82,xliii; Aldrovandi, I, 744; Barclay, p. 162; Bartholomew, XII, 10; Brown, p. 274; Camerarius, III.lxxxi; Cassell, pp. 83–91; Chaucer, *Tr*, ii.403; Cicero, *Mur.* ii.25; Garver, p. 308; Ham (ed.), p. 237; Hesiod, *Works and Days*, ll. 96–98; Horapollo, pp. 18–19; Jacques de Vitry, p. 105; Matheolus, 1.52; McKenzie, p. 423; Morgan, pp. 127–28; Ovid, *Met.* II.548; Panofsky, *Pandora*, pp. 28–37; Pliny, x.xiv; Ripa, II.ii.450; II.ii.363; Suetonius, xxiii.2; Tibullus, *Carmina* II.vi.20; Topsell, pp. 226–31; Valeriano, xx, f.49; Virgil, *Georg.* 1.388; Whitney, p. 113.

Cuckoo

Chaucer called the cuckoo "unkynde"; Shakespeare said it mocked married men—"Cuckoo, Cuckoo, O word of fear, / Unpleasing to a married ear." This cuckoo is a far cry from the bird synonymous with spring in one of the oldest English songs: "Summer is icumen in / Llude sing cuccu." Chaucer's and Shakespeare's bird is the one whose habits gave rise to the unpleasant word *cuckold*. The bird's own name came from its mating call. Its habit of depositing its eggs in another bird's nest made it the symbol of unfaithfulness. In ancient Rome the word became a term of reproach for foolish men. In Plautus' *Asinaria* the wife Artemona says to her husband whom she has caught *flagrante delicto*: "What? Is the cuckoo [*cuculus*] lying there still? Get up my gallant, and go home." In France, according to Littré, *cocault* applied to both men and women. In England the word became *cuckwold/cuckold* and was applied to the male only, who, it was assumed, fostered another man's brood. Writing at the beginning of the seventeenth century, Topsell thought the term appropriate in spirit but not in letter:

> Daily experience teacheth the contrary. For not Cuckoes but other birds doe hatche Cuckoes and straingers to their kinde. Yet forasmuch as a Cuckoe is a foolishe birde, and respecteth not so much her breede as her egge, it may well resemble a Cockolde, that watcheth not his wifes dishonestie but for his oune lusts sake (which shee serveth) reteyneth both a whoore and a bastard alsoe.

When Chaucer described the cuckoo as "unkynde," he meant that the bird was unnatural, acting against normal feelings. In addition to being a synonym for conjugal infidelity, the bird represented ingratitude because it was supposed to eat its parents. Such ingratitude was proverbial in France and Germany, and the passage in Shakespeare's *Lear* so often quoted by philologists to demonstrate the absence of the genitive case in Elizabethan English, makes the point clear:

> The hedge-sparrow fed the cuckoo so long
> That it had it head bit off by it young.

A similar idea was expressed earlier in Chaucer's *Parliament of Fowles* where the merlin contemptuously addresses the cuckoo as

> "Thow mortherere of the heysoge on the braunche
> That brought the forth . . . ."

("You murderer of the hedge-sparrow on the branch,
Who brought you forth . . . .")

Other qualities attributed to the bird are avarice, jealousy, misfortune, cowardice, and stupidity. According to Neckam, "the cuckoo, a tedious trifler with its useless repetition of its frequent note, constitutes a type of avarice, proclaiming and announcing 'Give, give.'" In the temple of Venus, Chaucer's personification of Jealousy had a cuckoo sitting on her hand. In a poem by Chaucer's contemporary, John Clanvowe, the cuckoo which debates with the nightingale represents jealousy, ill-luck in love, and the betrayed husband, regarding all love as evil. To Milton the cuckoo was a similar symbol, "the rude bird of Hate," indicative of his own failure in love. At this time the feminine form of *cuckold* was *cuckquean*. Some writers have linked the word with the cucking stool to which women were fastened and then ducked in a pond as a punishment for various offenses. The derivation of cucking stool, however, is not from *cuckquean* but from *cuk* to defecate, and the cucking stool was the *cathedra stercoris*. Other unfavorable characteristics of the bird were summed up by Topsell:

> These Cuckoes are a base and fearefull Creature, beinge afraide of every small birde. Wherefore the Authours of Hieroglophickes doe picture a Cuckoe to signifie a Coward and fearefull man.

39

In crying out only their name, cuckoos were like Braggadocians or boasters:

> So they love to talke of nothinge but themselves and
> their oune acts, envynge the just prayses and merits
> of other men, and extollinge the dunghill of their oune
> fame.

In ancient times the cuckoo, while possessing a phallic significance, was hardly a common adulterer. Zeus changed himself into a cuckoo to seduce Hera in her youth; in a bas-relief representing their marriage, a cuckoo sits upon the god's scepter. The god Indra in India also assumed the shape of a cuckoo for purpose of seduction. According to Gubernatis, the kokilas or Indian cuckoo was for the Hindu poets what the nightingale has been for English poets, and the term most frequently applied to the bird was that of "ravisher of the heart." Even Topsell who called the cuckoo base and vulgar admitted that it had been termed a bird of good luck (*boni ominis avem*) and said that the Germans used to choose their wives according to the prognostications in the cuckoo's voice. In Scandinavia vestiges of the bird's association with Freya, goddess of love, remain in Danish wedding customs where the image of the cuckoo represents longevity and fruitfulness. Chaucer called the cuckoo a fool and the meaning is still used. According to the *Dictionary of American Slang*, the implications can range from stupidity and unconventionality to insanity. The meaning of "cuckoo's nest," however, is more restrictive and has been the slang for *pudendum muliebre* both in the last century and this. *Gowk*, the name of the cuckoo in Scotland, has apparently had wider application, particularly to victims of April Fool's jokes. The word itself is from the Old Norse. *Gok* was current in Middle English to denote the European cuckoo but was borrowed early in the Cornish dialect to make the noun an adjective *goki*, meaning fool, foolish.

Alciatus had an emblem entitled *Cuculus* which Topsell translated:

> Why doe so many call the race of Countrey Clownes
> Cuckoes, what is their cause assignd?
> In Springe the Cuckoe sends her twise doubled sounds
> and blames the hand that hath not prunde his vyne.
> Shee leaves her younge in neasts of forreyne breede
> like a false spouse defilde with strangers seede.

As Topsell explained, in ancient Rome the man who did not cut his vines until he heard the cuckoo was called a cuckoo because he was regarded as negligent. The arrival of the cuckoo meant that spring had come.

It was as a symbol of spring that the cuckoo gave rise to the strangest of myths. Countrypeople thought that if they could keep the cuckoo with them the spring would last forever. Hence the idea of "penning" the cuckoo in an enclosure, usually made of a clump of trees on a mound or hill. The idea was originally attributed to the foolish men of Gotham, but penning the cuckoo was once a widespread ritual. J.E. Field, writing in 1913, described as many as fifteen sites with the name of "Cuckoo Pens" in Oxfordshire, Berkshire, Buckinghamshire, Gloucestershire, and elsewhere.

The cuckoo was by almost universal consent the sign of spring, *annunciatrix optatae laetitiae* (the announcer of the greatest happiness). Picinelli, however, saw the cuckoo as a symbol of the Virgin Mary *parturiente*, on the grounds that she gave birth in Bethlehem rather than in her native town.

Alciatus, pp. 218–219, lx; Aristotle, *Generation*, 750a; Chaucer, *KnT*, 1810, 1930; *PF*, 358; Clanvowe, pp. 347–58; Field, *passim*; Hardy, *passim*; Lampe, "Tradition," p. 51; Plautus, *Asinaria* v.ii.925; Picinelli, IV.xxv; Pliny, x.xi; Shakespeare, *Lear* I.iv.235–36; Swainson, p. 121; Swan, p. 405; Swann, p. 68; Topsell, pp. 243–44; Vincent of Beauvais, *Spec. Nat.* XVI.lxvii.

Dove

If you want to exchange glances with a pigeon, the best thing to do is to run up to the attic of one of those old Victorian houses in London and put your chin on the windowsill. Even if none of the pigeons outside deign to look at you directly, you will be the nearest that you can be to an eye-level confrontation. And you will be surprised at what you see: hard, mean-looking eyes. Here is a larger version of the dove of peace, and its expression is as cold, shrewd, and secretive as that of a CIA agent. If you have wondered why Chaucer, Lydgate, and others speak of the dove "with her meek eyes," the explanation is that these poets were not looking at nature; they were thinking of the bird's symbolism. Pigeons or doves, according to *Birds of America,* "are by no means the peaceful birds they are popularly supposed to be—fierce, bloody, and stubborn conflicts often occur during the breeding season." As a symbol, however, the dove is predominantly the bird of love. The traditional symbolism, as Katherine Holloway, an amateur birdwatcher, points out, only becomes appropriate when one considers the soft, black-pearl eyes of the mourning dove.

The symbolism is complex: in ancient civilizations the dove was the symbol of fertility and of the soul; in the Vedas the dove was Yama's messenger of death, or the forerunner of some tragic event; in China it was symbolic of longevity, faithfulness, and filial piety; among the ancient Hebrews the dove was the symbol of purity, of persecuted Israel, and the image of the spirit of God; in the Christian world the white dove was the symbol of the

The dove was Venus' bird.

Holy Ghost, of Christ, of the Church, of the Virgin, of the souls of the redeemed, of spiritual love, of innocence, of defenselessness, of charity, of martyrdom, of sorrow, and of the Ascension. No other bird had such importance in the Christian faith. According to Martigny and Pugin, the most ancient eucharistic vessels were gold or silver representations of the dove, which were suspended near the altar. The same dove, of painted wood, enclosed in a glass ball, eventually degenerated into *Suppenbringer* (soup maker) in Austrian and Bavarian farmhouses. It was originally suspended over the bed in order to promote conception, but after the fourposter went out of style the dove was transferred to the living room to hang over the dining table. When a soup tureen was placed under the ball, the rising steam condensed on the cold glass and dripped into the soup.

The bird was sacred among the Assyrians, Egyptians, and Hebrews, and in semitic languages the word for dove is associated with fertility. All the great female goddesses had their doves, representing both sacred and profane love. The most famous of the dove goddesses was Venus whose chariot was drawn by doves; on her sacred island doves were sacrificed in honor of Adonis, a rite deriving, so Frazer thought, from an older form of worship in which a holy man personifying the goddess's lover was the victim. Virgins consecrated to the Ishtar cult were called doves (*hu*), a euphemistic expression for prostitutes. The

42

dove-like spirit which fluttered over the abyss and brought forth life in Genesis i.2, was originally feminine, possibly deriving from earlier Babylonian myth. Jehovah, according to Graves, is another name for *Ia-Hu*, an ancient god name of wide distribution, and *Ia-Hu* is a combination of "the Exalted One" and "Dove." In some Christian heresies the dove goddess survived as the third member of the Holy Trinity until removed by the decree of the Nicene Council.

We find examples of the phallic symbolism of the dove in all ages. A Bohemian love charm instructs a young girl to go into the woods on St. George's Eve, catch a male dove, and the following morning carry it to the hearth. There she is to press it to her bare breast, mutter an incantation, and let it fly up the chimney (a widely recognized vaginal symbol). Ernest Jones, in an interesting analysis of the psychological implications of the sacred dove stated:

> The most unequivocal indication of the symbolic signification of the dove is to be found in the extra-Canonical legend which states that a dove escaped from Joseph's genital organ and alighted on his head (an unconscious symbol of the erect phallus) to designate him as the future husband of the Virgin Mary; the story is weakened in the writings of the later Christian Fathers, who say that the dove escaped from Joseph's rod [!].

The symbolism is even more apparent in medieval representations of the Annunciation in which the bird hovers either near the ear or the lap of the Virgin. The basic situation has a certain parallel to the pagan myth in which Zeus seduced the mortal maid Phtheia in the form of a dove; in the Christian myth the holy dove fertilizes the Virgin. The Word is made Flesh. The Immaculate Conception is through the ear as in the hymn:

> *Gaude, Virgo, Mater Christi*
> *Quae per aurem concepisti.*
>
> (Rejoice, Virgin, Mother of Christ
> You who have conceived through the ear.)

Sometimes a well-developed infant follows the bird, being propelled down golden beams by a wind blown directly from the rounded cheeks of God above. The implications are made specific in an illustration in a manuscript of the *Bible Moralisée*. In one circle a bun is being put in the oven; in the circle below, the Virgin holds the Infant in her arms and a dove hovers about her left ear.

The dove's kiss was the natural equivalent of the miraculous fertilizing breath which inflated the Virgin. Tenderness, billing and cooing, and passion are all associated with the dove. Traditionally doves are *maxime in coitu fervidae*, and the dove (Latin: *columba*) gave a special name to the soul kiss, "the columbine kiss." Both in classical Latin poetry and in a genre known as the *basium*, developed in the Renaissance by neo-Latin poets, the kiss was accompanied by the lover's dying in a sexual sense. The ecstasies of Petronius provided a model:

Qualis nox fuit illa, di deaeque,
Quam mollis torus. Haesimus calentes
Et transfudimus hinc et hinc labellis
Errantes animas. Valete, curae
Mortales. ego sic perire coepi.

(What a night was that, ye gods and goddesses! How soft the couch! We clung, passionate together and transfused our straying souls back and forth through our lips. Farewell, mortal cares! Thus I began to die.)

The Shulamite in the *Song of Songs* was the dove desiring to be kissed by its mate: *Osculetur me osculo oris sui* (i.l). The generative significance of the act was reinforced by a folk belief concerning the peculiar mating of doves. Even in the early seventeenth century the Reverend Topsell referred to the belief as being still current that crows and doves conceived at the mouth, "although Aristotle denyeth the latter." The symbolism of the dove's kiss was subsequently given a more general application by the Church Fathers. The divine breath, as represented by the dove, was love itself, and the kissing dove was the image of unity and peace which the faithful should have in their contact with each other. According to St. Augustine, *simplicem se esse debere sicut columbam, habere cum fratribus veram pacem quam significant oscula columbarum* (one should behave simply like the dove, have with one's brothers the true peace which the dove's kisses signify).

As symbol of rebirth, the dove's important role in the myths of the creation of the world, Noah, Jonah (whose name means dove), the baptism of Jesus, when John the Baptist testified that he saw "the spirit descend as a dove from heaven" (John i.32), is not surprising. As the traditional symbol of fire from early times, its appearance to the three young believers in the fiery furnace (Daniel iii.13–26) is also appropriate. Especially is the dove represented in illuminated manuscripts in scenes of the Day of Pentecost, when the Spirit, as Tongues of Fire, descended on the Apostles. The same association explains why the Holy Dove appears in rays of light or in flames.

Although the dove appears most frequently in representations of the creation of the world, the Annunciation and the Baptism of Christ, the application in terms of Christian symbolism was much wider. The dove's simplest significance, as seen on early Christian tombs or in illustrations where the bird emerges from the mouths of the dying, was as the soul of the faithful. Sometimes the bird carried an olive branch, in itself an emblem of peace and deliverance since the time that the dove brought a branch back to the Ark as a sign that the waters had receded.

44

Among the Christian Fathers, explanations for the symbolism of the dove range from explicit statements to elaborations on symbolic meanings of the colors and parts of the bird or of their significance in numerical groups. To Rabanus Maurus the dove was the Holy Spirit, Christ, the Church, the Preachers and their eloquence, the foolish man of Hosea vii.2, the man who despised the world, the active life, the gift of the Holy Spirit, the cries of the penitents. To Garner, the dove symbolized God's Grace, Christ, the Holy Spirit, and the Church. In *De Bestiis*, the writer considered in detail the dove of Psalm lxvii.14, whose wings glistened with silver and its feathers with yellow gold—"*Alae columbae nitebant argento, / et pennae ejus in pallore auri.*" This dove stood for many things: the Church, the faithful, the prelacy. The red feet of the dove were the feet of martyrs; the silver feathers the preachers of the Church. The dove's yellow eyes signified maturity. All the dove's properties had a moral significance: in building in holes of rocks, the dove was the man who placed his hopes on the Passion of Christ; in resting on streams in order to see the shadow of the hawk, it was the man who read the Scriptures in order to avoid the wiles of the Devil; it had twin children, signifying love of God and love of neighbors. Whoever possessed the properties of the dove, concluded the moralist, "takes to himself the wings of contemplation whereby he flies to heaven." The bestiaries also included the

Noah's dove is a symbol of peace.

45

preaching in hair shirt and ashes; gold, the three youths thrown by Nebuchadnezzar into the furnace for refusing to worship the golden image; white, John the Baptist and the whiteness of baptism; stephanite, Stephen, the first martyr.

The turtledove received special treatment. Whereas the dove traditionally had an ambivalent symbolism, the turtledove always symbolized faithfulness and innocence. The qualities of the turtledove described in the bestiaries remained with it, and the dove was a popular symbol of faithfulness in love, especially faithfulness to a dead mate, in both the Middle Ages and the Renaissance. According to the bestiaries:

> The turtledove loves its mate very much and lives chastely with him and keeps to him alone. If it happens that her mate is taken by a vulture or falcon she will not take another mate but all the time she longs for him that she has lost . . . .

This bird was like the mother church which remained faithful to Christ after His death. It was also like the souls of the faithful and served as a model for widowhood. Aldrovandi in 1599 summed up the tradition when he observed that the turtledove was "Salvatoris typus" (a type of savior), a symbol of the wisdom of the Father, of the preacher, and of men leading chaste and solitary lives. The *voice* of the turtle which was "heard in our land" in

Turtledoves are faithful in love.

meaning of the colors of the dove: red was the predominant color because Christ redeemed man with his blood; black symbolized obscure sermons; speckled, the diversity of the twelve prophets; "the color of air," Elisha, who was snatched up through the air; cinder-colored, Jonah

46

the *Song of Songs* (ii.12) was that of the Virgin when she said, *"Ecce ancilla Domini!"* (Behold the handmaid of the Lord!). The turtledove was also the symbol of Mary Magdalene, and of Christ and the holy preachers.

The bestiaries attributed their observations to the *Physiologus*, but the *Physiologus* itself discusses not the turtledove but the *columba*, and then only in connection with Christ's advice, "Be ye as wise as serpents and as innocent as doves" (Matthew x.16). This dove, according to the *Physiologus*, also signified Christ, the Holy Spirit, the Church, the Virgin Mother, Grace, Charity, Sacred Teaching and Scripture, Spiritual Nature, the Teachers of the Church, simple and upright men.

All these values are used by medieval homilists and biblical commentators. In lyrics Christ was *columba potens* (the powerful dove), the Virgin Mary the *colvere of Noe* (the dove of Noah). Two doves were usually the turtledoves, the sacrifice that a mother made after the birth of her child when "the priest shall make atonement for her and she shall become clean" (Leviticus xii.28). The seven doves or the dove with the seven rays proceeding from it usually meant the seven gifts of the Holy Spirit, such as wisdom, piety, strength, counsel, understanding, knowledge, and fear. The twelve doves could represent the Apostles or the faithful and could have these meanings in representations of the crucifixion. As a general symbol of inspiration, the dove also hovered about St. Thomas Aquinas, while the saint, dressed in the Dominican habit, sat writing at a table.

Other values given to the dove are very different. Among the Egyptians, according to Horapollo, a man enthusiastic about the flute and dancing was portrayed by the turtledove; the ordinary dove signified a man who was ungrateful to his benefactors. Aldrovandi claimed that the turtledove was an Egyptian heroglyphic for "mulier lactans," the nursing mother. In medieval representations of the Seven Deadly Sins, Lust, in the guise of a seductive young woman, rode a goat and carried a dove on her wrist. On false etymological grounds the turtledove was associated with the Sin of Sloth because Latin, *turtur* (turtledove) was connected with the Latin *tardus* (late). Both the dove and the turtledove appeared in various medieval recipes:

If any man would take of the milk of a woman, giving suck to her own daughter of two year old, and let it be put in a glassen vessel, or hanged up in a Dove or Culver house where they go in and forth, Doves will abide and be multiplied there, until they be innumerable.

If the heart of this fowl [turtledove] be borne in a Wolf's skin, he that beareth it shall never have an appetite to commit lechery from thenceforth. If the heart of it be burned, and be put above the eggs of any fowl, there can never young birds be engendered of them from thenceforth. And if the feet of this fowl be hanged to a tree, it shall not bear fruit from thenceforth. And if an hairy place, and an Horse, be anointed with the blood of it, and with water wherein that a Mole was sodden, the black hairs will fall off.

By Elizabethan times the two turtledoves had lost any significance as a religious offering and become any placating gift: "I have here a dish of doves, that I would bestow on your worship," says Gobbo trying to curry favor with Bassanio in the *Merchant of Venice*.

Swainson said that the dove in some country areas even in the last century was a bird of ill-omen, but an anecdote in B.R. Haydon's autobiography suggests that the dove represented a different value. The poet Wordsworth told him that his wife and a friend were walking in a wood where a stock dove was cooing. "A farmer's wife coming by said 'Oh, I do like stock doves.' Mrs. Wordsworth, in all her enthusiasm for Wordsworth's poetry, took the old woman to her heart. 'But,' continued the old woman, 'some like them in a pie; for my part, there's nothing like 'em stewed in onions.'"

In the language of the streets pigeon and dove had various meanings. According to Captain Francis Grose, "to fly a blue pigeon" meant to steal lead from a church, and pigeons were rogues engaged in a particular kind of lottery fraud. "Soiled doves," stated Brewer in 1900, were "women of the demi-monde." A carrier pigeon, according to Farmer, was a girl "who travels up and down the railways seeking clients." A columbine (Latin *columba*, dove), had a similar meaning. It is hard to say whether there is any symbolic significance in the proverbial saying:

> Who would hold his house very clean,
> Ought lodge no priest nor pigeon therein.

Albertus Magnus, *Secrets*, pp. 58, 84–85; Aldrovandi, II, 517, 518, 523, 525; Augustine, *PL*, 35, col. 1427; *De Bestiis, PL*, 177, cols. 15–20; *Birds of America*, II, 37; *Bible Moral.*, MS. Bodl. 2706.f.59; Cahier & Martin, III, 262–64; 275–83; Camerarius, III.lix; Chaucer, *PF*, 341; Evans, p. 98; Frazer, *Adonis, Attis and Osiris*, pp. 114–15; Garner, *PL*, 193, col. 71; Graves, p. 337; Greene (ed. Grosart), II, 35, 90–91, 119, 188, 257; III, 11; IV, 109; V, 61–62, 72, 86; VIII, 65; IX, 79–80, 130, 256; Haydon, p. 555; Horapollo, pp. 78; 107; Jones, pp. 268–341; Lodge (ed. Hunterian Club), I.iii.49; I.v.95; III.iv.27–28; Lydgate, *Pilgrimage*, p. 22, l.810; Martigny, I, 162–65; McCulloch, pp. 111–12, 178; Meyer (ed.), p. 440; Morgan, p. 128; Neumann, p. 141n; Petronius, *Satyricon*, 79, 8; Perella, pp. 189–91, 253–59; Pliny, x.lii; Pugin, p. 37n; Rabanus Maurus, *PL*, 112, cols. 898–99; Réau, II, 12; Shakespeare, *Merchant of Venice* II.ii.124–25; Spence, p. 58; Swainson, p. 168; Topsell, p. 176; Twining, p. 60; Utley, p. 471; Wenzel, p. 107.

Duck

For centuries the duck has been an emblem of happiness in China. The mandarin duck was the most highly prized. The Chinese regarded it as an emblem of faithful married love because this breed had a reputation for constancy exceeding even that of the turtledove. Mandarin ducks were said to pair for life and if separated were believed to pine away and die.

In the West in medieval times the duck had little life as a symbol. Although Isidore noted that the Latin name for duck *anas* derived from *assiduitas*, "constancy" in swimming, he drew no symbolic implications from his erroneous etymology. Vincent of Beauvais said that drakes sometimes kill the female in the enthusiasm of their mating, and presumably Chaucer was alluding to this trait when in the *Parliament of Fowls* he described the drake as "stroyere of his owene kynde." Whether Chaucer was also using natural history in *The Miller's Tale* when he pictured the old husband merrily pursuing his young wife like a white duck swimming after her drake is hard to determine. The sexual differentiation is curious, but the allusion may have an ironic appropriateness. According to ornithologists, "the female is not purely passive but will follow the male about, assuming coition posture, calling and pushing against him . . . ."

Ducks are always swimming.

Aldrovandi, the great natural historian, has not much to say about the duck. The bird was thought to be sacred to Neptune, he observed, and he quoted the ancient natural historians' opinion that the duck foretold violent winds when it plunged frequently into the water and

49

flapped its wings. Like the *mergus*, the diver, a bird which is said to be over fond of going under water and to symbolize those who were preoccupied with sex, the duck usually had a bad reputation. The emblem writers regarded the bird both as a symbol of treachery and of the common people. In *dolus in suos* (treachery to one's own), Whitney shows four ducks flying into a net which has been put out by two hunters who are hiding behind a tree. A tame duck is just outside the net. His verses tell of the tame duck which acted as a decoy, flying aloft with the wild ducks and then bringing them down.

> By this is mente, all suche as doe betraie,
> Theire kindred neare, that doe on them depende,
> And oft doe make, the innocent a praie,
> By subtill fleighte, to them that seeke theire ende.
> Yea unto those, they Should moste frendship showe,
> They lie in waite, to worke theire overthrowe.

Under the emblem *imparilitas* (inequality) Whitney shows ducks and geese feeding on the ground while a falcon flies above. The picture is symbolic of the difference in men's estate. The first are lowly creatures; the falcon is princely.

In more recent literature, according to T.H. White, there have been "half-a-hundred wild ducks." One of the most famous of literary ducks is the wounded bird kept in the attic in Ibsen's play *The Wild Duck*. As Tindall observes, this bird "embodies the meaning of the play and, by the aid of action, speech, and immediate context, presents it." The play tells what happens when Gregers Werle insists on stripping life bare of all illusions for his friend Hjalmar. Because of Gregers' obsession with the truth, Hjalmar learns that his wife was formerly the mistress of Gregers' rich father, that he may not be the father of fourteen-year-old Hedvig, and that the invention by which he hopes to grow rich is useless. The wild duck is Hedvig's most precious possession, symbolizing her aspirations. To others she is the wild duck, a tragic creature, destined in time to become totally blind. "O, you can imagine we haven't the heart to tell her of it," Hjalmar says. "She dreams of no danger. Gay and careless and chirping like a little bird, she flutters onward into a life of endless night." The illusions of Hedvig are the substance of her existence. Her death is the symbolic destruction of the wild duck and of a naïve faith in life.

In *Dr. Zhivago*, the wild duck is also a symbol of illusions. A wild drake, wrapped up in a torn piece of some printed broadside, is given to Dr. Zhivago by a chance acquaintance, a deaf mute who, like Gregers Werle, is bent on changing the world even if he must destroy it first. While Dr. Zhivago accepts the gift reluctantly, his wife is delighted because of the food shortage. The bird appears at her dinner party, the occasion on which Dr. Zhivago in an impromptu address shows a realization that his hopes are misplaced and that he and his milieu are doomed.

Aelian, vii.7; Aldrovandi, iii, 182, 245; Chaucer, *PF*, 360; *MllT*, 3575–76; Isidore, xii.7.51; Jackson, pp. 39–45; Tindall, p. 123; Vincent of Beauvais, *Spec. Nat.* xvi.xxvii; T.H. White, p. 243; Whitney, pp. 27, 407; Williams, p. 120; Witherby, iii, 336.

Eagle

The way of the eagle was one of those things which baffled a writer of the Biblical proverbs:

"Three things are too wonderful for me; four I do not understand: the way of an eagle in the sky, the way of a serpent on a rock, the way of a ship on the high seas, and the way of a man with a maiden."

A knowledge of ancient civilization or even of the writings of his colleagues might have solved the mystery for him. The Bible itself has many references to the bird's distinctive characteristics—its high, swift flight, its training of its young, its nesting in inaccessible places, its longevity and strength. Early civilizations were almost unanimous in regarding the eagle as a symbol of the divine. In some Eastern countries it was a god itself; among the Greeks it was Zeus's bird, bearer of the thunderbolt and lightning and was even identified with the supreme deity; among the Romans the eagle had the same associations; among the Germanic races it was the bird of Odin; among the North American Indians and the early inhabitants of Central and South America the eagle played a prominent role as a totemic animal, associated with sky- and sun-gods.

The eagle may have acquired solar qualities, Wittkower suggests, when the solar deities replaced the early fertility gods during the third millennium in Babylonia:

This would explain the fact that on the seals of the Sargonid age (c.2500 B.C.) a bird of prey, probably an eagle, appears as the monster Zu . . . side by side with the lion-headed eagle as representative of the "good" side. This would give us the historical starting point for tracing the solar conception of the eagle which then migrated from Babylonia to many other civilizations.

Large eagle statues belonging to the second and first millennium have been found in various civilizations of western Asia, and such statues, reduced in size, appear in Hellenistic and Roman times. The bird's identification with the sun is particularly evident in seals and early sculpture of Hittites, Assyrians, Persians, Phoenicians, and of the Levant during the Graeco-Roman period where the eagle actually replaces the usual solar disk. In India the eagle became Garuda, the golden-winged bird of the sun, an emblem of Vishnu. In Egypt the same symbolism was assigned to the hawk, the bird consecrated to Horus, the rising sun, and symbolized the rebirth of the god.

From early times the eagle was a symbol of military power. Ezekiel, in a parable, saw the eagle as the Babylonians persecuting the Jews. According to Xenophon, the Persians carried the eagle as their ensign. Etruscan and Roman rulers, claiming divine origin, displayed scepters with eagles on them. The eagle, adopted as the standard of the Roman legions under the second consulate of Marius, was so well known that Dante was able to use it as a symbol of the Roman persecution of early Christians in his *Purgatorio* without explication.

The sacred associations of the bird were maintained in many cults. It was the bird of apotheosis and resurrection. Tombstones with eagle representations occur in both Levantine and Arabic art; in the Mithraic liturgy, the initiate entered Heaven as an eagle; on the death of a Roman emperor an eagle was let loose to carry the soul to Olympus. On Roman coins the deified emperor appeared above the eagle of Jupiter. Of wide and persistent currency was the idea of the soul of the king appearing in the form of an eagle to watch over his people.

Many of the early symbolic values have persisted through the centuries. Most widespread are the notions of the eagle as representative of majesty, victory, and courage. But in the Christian era other values accrued, many of them deriving from Biblical text and from earlier misstatements of the natural historians such as Aristotle and Pliny. The psalmist's cry, "your youth is renewed like the eagle's," was taken by the bestiarists to imply that the eagle had discovered some kind of elixir of life:

When the eagle grows old its eyes are covered with mist and its wings become heavy. It seeks a fountain, then flies above it into the region of the sun where its wings are burned and the mist consumed. Descending, the eagle plunges three times into the fountain and is wholly renewed.

"Do the same, O man," said the moralist,

you who are clothed in the old garment and have the eyes of your heart growing foggy. Seek for the spiritual fountain of the Lord and lift up your mind's eyes to God—who is the fountain of justice—and then your youth will be renewed like the eagles.

Aristotle's story of the eagle's fabulous eyesight was repeated and developed. The bird was said to look unblinded into the sun, force its offspring to do the same, and reject those who turned away. This eagle was Christ looking directly at His Father, and just as the eagle lifted its young toward the sun, so the angels carried souls to

God who received only the most worthy. The eagle flying high above the sea was supposed to be able to spot fish in the water below. Philippe de Thaon and others saw this eagle as Christ coming from high to conquer men's souls. Also adapted for exegetical purposes was Aristotle's statement that an old eagle died because its upper beak grew too long for it to be able to eat. To save its life, said the Christian writers, the eagle broke its beak with a stone, and to the wise man that stone was the rock of salvation. On behalf of the Egyptians, however, Horapollo suggested a more prosaic symbol for the same condition. The old eagle signified an "old man dying of hunger, for as he grows old his beak becomes extremely hooked and he dies of hunger."

The Church Fathers discovered further symbolism in the alleged habits of the eagle. Good works, they said, were tested in the same way as the eagle tested its young, by holding them to the sunlight; the souls of the just were like eagles because they sought the heavens and were immortal. To Honorius d'Autun the eagle testing its young represented the Last Judgment. Christ kept the good Christians with Him in Paradise. The sinners He threw into the infernal abyss. Rabanus Maurus, taking as his text Deuteronomy xxxii.2 ("the eagle summoned its young to take flight"), identified the eagle with Christ

The eagle is a symbol of Christ.

53

because "Christ never ceased to teach His disciples, that they might advance from virtue to virtue." The eagle in Job xxxix.27 and Matthew xxiv.28 signified the souls of the elect and the promise of resurrection. St. John the Baptist was the eagle because he spoke of the divinity of Christ, and, like an eagle, fastened his eyes on the sun. Conversely, the way of the eagle in Proverbs xxx.19 was the way of the Devil; only with difficulty, said Rabanus Maurus, could his tricks be detected by the righteous.

In art and sculpture the eagle depicted both Christ and St. John. In some illustrations the bird with its eaglets and the risen Christ are side by side. In a sculpture in a Gloucestershire church, only the two feet of the ascending Christ are shown, with the eagle underneath them. St. John is represented as a nimbed eagle or has an attendant eagle which sometimes holds a pen or ink-horn in its beak. A popular motif on baptisteries and fonts was the eagle plunging into the sea, the symbol of regeneration.

The eagle, as Vincent de Beauvais and others pointed out, was *rex avium* (king of birds), and both its dominant rank and its possession of many fabulous characteristics ensured its continued symbolic use. In an early thirteenth-century representation of the fourteen joys of the body and soul in heaven depicted on the north porch of Chartres Cathedral, circa 1215, the eagle was the attribute of Longevity. In a late medieval tapestry representing the war between the Virtues and the Vices, the eagle was the at-tribute of Pride, as it was again in an engraving by Henri Aldegrever. In the iconography of the Four Elements in certain late medieval manuscripts, as the bird of Jove who lived in the heavens and as the symbol of St. John who, according to exegetes such as Christianus Druthmarus stood for *coelum* (the sky or the air), the eagle represented the element Air. In the presentation of the Five Senses, the eagle was the attribute of Sight. Isidore had claimed that even the eagle's name *aquila* derived from *acumine*, the acuteness of its eyes, and as late as 1652 Bernini chose an eagle flying towards the sun as the frontispiece for a scientific work on optics.

The emblem writers connected the bird's high flight with lofty thoughts and found the bird a praiseworthy symbol: in an illustration by Ripa a young man, who wears a crown on his head, singles out an eagle as the symbol of a desire for knowledge. In other emblems the eagle was a good augury, the symbol of success, an attribute of hope, generosity, and sublimity. As Chew notes, the eagle pulled the chariot of Faith. Even the eagle gnawing Prometheus' liver on Mount Aetna was a good bird: the fault lay with Prometheus who, as a symbol of impious curiosity, was justly punished for trying to bring fire from heaven to earth. Rouillé's device was an eagle on a sphere, the attribute of Fortune with the device *In virtute et fortuna*. The illustration itself reminds one of a painting on an early Christian tomb, referred to by Creuzer, where an eagle on a sphere, holding a laurel crown in its beak, symbolized apotheosis.

From antiquity, the eagle was associated with inspiration. To Pindar, the Greek poet, the eagle was a symbol of the poetic mind contemplating higher truths. Like St. John with his vision of the Apocalypse, and like eagle-sighted Beatrice, who was Dante's guide to the Empyrean, this eagle was close to the central power of creation. The divine bird of Zeus became a fitting symbol for an aristocratic kind of poetry. In Roman times, possibly because of a resemblance between aquiline and oratorical flight, the eagle also came to represent rhetoric. For this reason a late Roman rhetorician was given the title *Aquila Romanus* (Roman eagle). In Chaucer's *House of Fame*, the eagle, as the divine messenger bringing the poet a new vision of his art, is part of a very old tradition. Later, Deschamps addressed Chaucer himself as "O lofty eagle!" and in the seventeenth century, the French bishop Bossuet, renowned for his oratory, was called the Eagle of Meaux. The eagle's literary association may be among the reasons for its appearance as a lectern. In medieval Latin the word *aquila* had by itself the sense of lectern.

Although tests have shown that the eagle cannot lift more than eleven pounds in weight, mythological and literary eagles were expert at carrying people. The earliest victim was the attractive boy Ganymede, whom Zeus in the form of an eagle picked up to serve as a kind of bar-tender for the gods. This myth was extensively explicated. Plato believed that it was a Cretan invention to justify pederasty; later, when the fables of Ovid were given a Christian significance, Ganymede became a prefiguration of St. John, and the eagle was Christ or the "sublime clarity" which enabled St. John to read the secrets of heaven. In the Renaissance, Ganymede was interpreted as the human mind beloved by Jupiter, the Supreme Being. A famous drawing sent by Michelangelo to his young friend Cavalieri shows Ganymede in a state of ecstatic trance, passive in the iron grip of a gigantic eagle. According to Panofsky, the drawing symbolizes the neoplatonic *furor amatorius* and expresses the "all-pervasive and all-effacing passion which had shaken Michelangelo's life when he had met Tommaso Cavalieri."

Dreams of flying can often have a sexual significance in literature as well as in life, even in medieval poetry and prose. When Chaucer claims to dream that a golden eagle carried him up to the House of Fame, he poses as a hopelessly unsuccessful lover whose knowledge of romance comes from books instead of from experience. When his heroine Criseyde dreams that a white eagle descends and replaces her heart with his own, the eagle is the perfect symbol for the noble Prince Troilus, and the heart-exchange symbolizes falling in love. In the medieval romance of Octavian, a dream in which the empress sees an eagle snatch up her children, as she is grabbed by leopards and lions, foreshadows her own arraignment as an adulterer. Saints often come from heaven in the form of eagles. As in Criseyde's dream, an eagle does some heart surgery on St. Mary of Oegines while she is weeping for her sins: "She sawe an egil upon hir brest, that as in a welle plonged the bile [bill] in hir brest." This eagle turns out to be St. Benedict and he manages to make her stop crying. Another eagle, flying over the head of the mother of St. Eloy of Limoges, signified that she would give birth to a holy man.

The eagle and the snake, the most powerful of birds fighting the most dangerous of reptiles, possessed an ancient and global significance, as Wittkower has so ably shown. Basically the struggle represents the opposition of light and darkness, good and evil. The figures occur in dreams with such a meaning and survive in dream books of the Middle Ages. The creatures also signify two of the greatest cosmic entities, the sun and the sea: the one can be identified with the sky powers and the other with darkness, the underworld, and water. The early Christian exegetes provided an obvious symbolism for the figure: the eagle according to a sermon attributed to St. Ambrose was Christ overcoming Satan. The eagle's nest was the church. The interpretation was supported by Biblical reference to Christ's victory over the forces of darkness, and the tradition persists to this century. A modern lectern in Peterborough Cathedral depicts the eagle still trampling on the Old Serpent.

The eagle attached by a string to the tortoise, the two-headed eagle, the eagle and the dove, the eagle and the phoenix, the eagle's feathers, all have symbolic significances. The first symbolized in Agrippa's view the relation between the divine and the natural; the second was a heraldic device transmitted to Europe from the East and adopted by Ivan the Great (1462-1505), the ruler of Muscovy, and later appropriated by various other empires. The eagle and the dove, obvious contrasting symbols of strength and weakness, were alchemical terms for processes leading to the rise of phoenix, a stage in the transmutation of metals, and John Donne made use of the symbolism in his witty love poem "The Canonization."

> And we in us find the eagle and the dove.
> The phoenix riddle hath more wit
> By us: we too being one, are it.

Less complex is the meaning of the eagle's feathers. "The Indian," observed Jung, "takes on something of the sun-like nature of this bird when he adorns himself with its feathers. . . . the feather crest is a crown which is equivalent to the rays of the sun."

Almost throughout history the eagle has been a sign of awesome power that might be either good or bad. Camerarius pointed up the polarities of the various traditions when he made the eagle a symbol not only of the pious and compassionate king, but also of the evil demon. The eagle had one habit which caused a notable disaster. "Eagles," said Aelian, the natural historian, "seize tortoises and then dash them on rocks from a height, and having smashed the tortoise's shell they extract and eat the flesh." This activity, as Aelian observed, was said to have killed Aeschylus, the Greek playwright who for years had shunned buildings and trees because he had been told that he will be killed by something falling on his head. According to Guillim, the writer on heraldry, while Aeschylus was sitting on a rock "in deep meditation, an Eagle thinking his bald head had been a stone, let fall a *Tortois* on it, and so made a *Tragicall* end of that noble *Tragedian*."

Aeschylus' fate is not without irony. His most famous drama tells of the eagle sent by Zeus to torture Prometheus. Even the worst student of Greek has no difficulty with Prometheus' favorite expletive. "*Ai! Ai!*" (alas! alas!), cries Prometheus throughout the play, and well he might, for his liver is renewed each day for the eagle to chew on.

Of symbolic eagles in recent literature, the eagle at the center of Tennessee Williams' *The Roman Spring of Mrs. Stone* probably displays the most traditional characteristics. In her youth, Mrs. Stone is accused of behaving like an imperial eagle; in marriage, her husband is her victim, carried off, against medical advice, to Athens to die; as a widow, hovering on the lofty terrace of her Roman palazzo, she appears to the young man to whom she will eventually surrender as a bird of prey; but this eagle is deprived of all nobility. When her lover tells her that she is "interested only in the golden excrement of the American eagle," Mrs. Stone is clearly linked with the American way of life, an existence which the novelist sees as predatory, sterile, and unsavory.

Aelian, ii.26, 20; v.48; vii.16; Alciatus, pp. 144–47, xxxiii; Ambrose, *PL*, 16, col. 519; Anderson, p. 128; Aristotle, *H.A.* ix.32; Augustine, *PL*, 36, col. 1666; 37, col. 1327; Bennett, pp. 50–51; Berry, pp. 290–93; *Bestiary* (ed. Morris), pp. 3–4; Cahier & Martin, ii, 165–66; Calder, pp. 196–99; Chaucer, *Tr*, ii.925–31; Chew, p. 128; Christianus Druthmarus, *PL*, 106, col. 1265; Creuzer, iv.ii.2, lxviii, cxlix; Duchaussoy, pp. 148–51; Evans, 116–20; Gérard, pp. 145–53; Guillim, p. 159; Harrison, *They Tell of Birds*, p. 18; Horapollo, p. 144; Hulme, p. 54; Isidore, xii.7.10; Jung, *Symbols*, 1.183; Katzenellenbogen, p. 78n; Kantrowitz, pp. 10–11; Kiernan, pp. 518–22; Lanoe-Villène, s.v. *aigle*; Leyerle, p. 253; Panofsky, *Studies*, pp. 215–16; Paradin, p. 210; Philippe de Thaon, ll. 2013ff; *Physiologus*, pp. 22–25; Pliny, x.iii; *Prosalegenden*, p. 174; Proverbs xxx.18; Rabanus Maurus, *PL*, 112, col. 862; Ripa, ii.ii.338–39, 345, 441–42; Steadman, "Chaucer's Eagle," pp. 153–59; Topsell, p. 9; Twining, pp. 69–70; Vincent de Beauvais, *Spec. Nat.* xvi.xxxii–xxxiii; Wilson, pp. 157–58; Wittkower, pp. 293–325.

The white gerfalcon works for its royal master.

Falcon

Those chintzy, high-priced little residences tucked away in cobblestone alleys behind old Victorian houses in the heart of London may not seem to have much connection with falconry. Most people think of them as an odd but very superior kind of row housing which has become a fashionable address for the aristocracy and the nouveau riche. Yet the mews, as they are called, were once the place in which hawks were kept in the moulting season. The word *mew* itself comes from the French *muer*: to change (Latin, *mutare*). Falconry may seem a meaningless and even barbarous activity to us today, but from its beginnings in China some two thousand years before Christ it was for centuries one of the chief sports of the upper classes. Even today, people who have never seen a hawk will readily say that a watchful person has "eyes like a hawk"; "a hawk-like mien" still has connotations of superiority and aloofness traditionally associated with the bird.

In the Middle Ages, John of Salisbury accused the aristocracy of going on long hawking expeditions, wearing the medieval equivalent of blue jeans, camping out or sponging on their wealthier friends in order to economize on household expenses. Women, he implied, were better at hawking than men because the worst people

58

were always the most predatory. Certainly, whether through meanness, love of exercise or of poultry, the English ruling classes were ardent falconers at the time, especially the women. Edward III, according to Froissart, had thirty falconers in his army when he invaded France and he either hawked or hunted every day. The Bishop of Ely excommunicated those who stole his hawk from the cloisters in Southwark during divine service. An elaborate ritual was laid down for training various kinds of hawks to fly at pheasant, partridge, quail, landrail, duck, teal, woodcock, snipe, heron, rook, crow, gull, magpie, jay, blackbird, thrush, lark, hare, and rabbit. A gentleman would carry his favorite hawk everywhere, even to church, and if it fell sick he would offer a candle for its recovery. The month of May was represented iconographically as an elegantly dressed youth on a magnificent horse riding, hawk in hand. He might also have a dog with him, for "haukes and houndes" were the symbol of wealth and cultivated leisure.

The word *hawk* in medieval times was used to denote any kind of bird of prey, and no one familiar with the class structure in England will be surprised to learn that various kinds of birds were assigned according to rank. To an emperor were allotted the eagle and the vulture; to royalty the gerfalcon, a bird fierce in the air but tractable on the perch, capable of catching large birds by virtue of the striking power of its wings; to an earl the peregrine, a smaller bird but capable of taking grouse and pigeons with great dash; to a lady the merlin, again a very courageous bird and capable of killing a partridge at a single pounce. A priest was given the sparrowhawk, cunning, handsome, with a propensity to attack larger birds; a yeoman the goshawk, which preferred hares and rabbits to birds. The last two birds, according to some experts, were more difficult to train than other hawks, but all had their place in the aristocratic hierarchy. To the peasant, however, was assigned the kestrel, "useless" as the *Encyclopaedia Britannica* scathingly observes in its article on falconry, although the kestrel does, in fact, destroy mice and cockchafers. It seems odd that Gerard Manley Hopkins should give this bird knightly connotations in "The Windhover" and make it the symbol of Christ.

It is the eagle, the largest bird of prey, which we encounter most frequently as the ancient symbol of the divine. Nevertheless the hawk was universally admired and used as a totem. In Egypt it represented Horus, the god of day. Horapollo said that it was also the symbol of aristocracy, of excellence, of blood and victory. In equatorial Africa, according to Lévy-Bruhl, a chieftain gave the claws or head of a falcon to his son in order that he might inherit the bird's predatory skill.

In the Middle Ages allusions to falconry abound not only in the hunting treatises but in all kinds of literature. The Church Fathers found the hawk (*accipiter*) both a good and a bad symbol. They compared the hawk to the monk, at the same time demonstrating their own familiarity with the training of the bird:

> The hawk is a type of holy man, the one who, so to speak, lays violent hold on the kingdom of God, about which it is written in Job "doth the hawk get her plumage by thy wisdom and stretch out her wings towards the south?" that is "is there any one of the elect to whom thou hast given understanding?" . . . In order that the tamed hawks may grow fine plumage enclosed warm quarters are found for them. The quarters are enclosed by bars, and when the wild hawk has been placed inside, it is kept shut up in order that it may become tame. There it moults its old feathers, and acquires new ones. In like manner anyone in a cloister, being stripped of his old sins, becomes adorned with the virtues of the New Man. When the hawk has become steady in flying . . . it comes back to the hand. Likewise, if any brother come out of the cloister, he is bound to come back to the hand of good works.

Another writer used the figure of the hawk and the dove to represent monks.

> *Ecce in eadem pertica sedent accipiter et columba. Ego enim de clerico, tu de militia ad conversionem venimus ut in regulari vita quasi pertica sedeamus, et qui rapere consueveras domesticas aves, nunc bone operationis manu silvestres ad conversionem trahas id est seculares.*

(Behold upon the same perch sit a hawk and a dove. For we have come, I from clerking, you from military service, to become monks, in order to live the life of the Rule, as it were, sitting upon a perch. And you, who were accustomed to capture tame birds, may now by the hand of good work draw in wild birds, that is, those from outside into the monastic life.)

On the other hand, while Rabanus Maurus could refer to the hawk as the chosen one (*electus*), when he referred to the hawk in connection with Nebuchadnezzar, he found the bird a symbol of greed.

Secular literature tended to stress the aristocracy of the bird. In dreams, especially if they belonged to a young girl, the hawk was a prince or future husband: "I dreamed that I saw a beautiful hawk upon my arm, and his feathers were the color of gold," said Guthrun in the *Volsunga Saga*. The hawk is the Volsung himself whom she marries. As Kelchner observes, in the Old Norse sagas the hawk in a dream was always associated with the nobility. In ballads the hero's unconfessed soul might take the form of a hawk. Even in Sir Walter Scott's day, country folk used to point to a certain stone and say that it was the favorite perch of a blue hawk which, according to the popular ballad, was the soul of Percy Reed. A favorite symbol for the knightly lover, as used for Erec by Chrétien de Troyes and for Troilus by Chaucer, was the sparrow-

60

hawk which, according to ornithologists, "swoops over
a bird and as it passes it drops a foot and picks the victim
up, with absolutely unerring skill." Appropriately, when
the young prince Troilus and the beautiful, golden-haired
widow, Criseyde, consummate their love affair, Chaucer
asked:

> What myghte or may the sely larke seye,
> Whan that the sperhauk hath it in his foot?

> (What can or may the foolish lark say,
> When the sparrowhawk has it in its foot?)

As Chauncey Wood observes, the sparrowhawk is associated elsewhere with sexual activity. The Nun's Priest
for his presumed virility is compared to a sparrowhawk.
In the same poet's "Parliament of Fowls," the birds of
prey, "foules of ravyne," played the leading roles among
the birds. They were the aristocrats, and the poet cited all
those which are named above, with the exception of the
kestrel. But while these birds seem to symbolize various
attitudes to love, the meaning of the poem still eludes us.
Equally baffling is the significance of the hawk in Skelton's "Ware the Hawk." In this poem Skelton, an uncon-
ventional rector by all accounts, told with indignation of

The heraldic falcon symbolizes chivalry.

61

a sporting parson who broke into his church at Diss and let his hawks kill a pigeon and desecrate the altar with blood and dung. Some critics have suggested that the hawk here symbolized heretics.

In the art of the period, the hawk's appearance is more comprehensible. In religious art the hawk symbolized the pleasures of the chase and the secular life as opposed to life in the cloister. In processions of the Seven Deadly Sins the hawk was often the attribute of Pride; in those macabre encounters between the dead and the living, between three corpses and three hunting noblemen, the hawk usually perched on the fist of the living. Here it illustrated both the pride of life and the truth that death was the great leveller.

In the Elizabethan period the hawk was still the sign of the nobility. In Shakespeare's *Macbeth* the falcon which, contrary to nature, "was by a mousing owl hawked at and killed" foreshadowed the murder of Duncan, the king. Giovio, Symeoni, Paradin, and other emblem writers made the hawk a symbol of *noblesse du coeur*: just as all other birds yield to the hawk so should men yield to one who relies not on worldly goods or physical force but on the nobility of the heart.

Of pejorative references to the hawk in Shakespeare, the most striking concerns the peregrine falcon or haggard. According to ornithologists, peregrine falcons are "unattached females [who] appear to wander in search of mates, while unmated males occupy suitable cliffs and on appearance of the female seek to attract her by flying excitedly from one ledge to another." *Haggard* can mean untamed. In *Much Ado About Nothing* the lively heroine Beatrice is said to be "as coy and wild / as haggards of the rock." In *The Taming of the Shrew*, Bianca is called a "proud, disdainful haggard" by her injured lover, and Petruchio in an extended use of falcon imagery says of Kate, "Another way I have to man my haggard, / And make her come and know her keeper's call." When Othello suspects Desdemona of unfaithfulness, the implication is more severe and the hawking figure itself is more complex:

"If I do prove her haggard,
Though that her jesses were my dear heart-strings,
I'd whistle her off, and let her down the wind,
To prey at fortune."

Jesses are the strips of leather to which the leash is fastened. To fly a bird downwind instead of against the wind was to dismiss a useless bird. Thenceforth she had to shift for herself and was said "to prey at fortune."

The hooded falcon had a special symbolic value. The hood was the cap or cover from the hawk's head. The hood was only removed when the quarry was started, in order to prevent the hawk from flying too soon. In the emblem books, the hooded falcon was a symbol of hope,

62

illustrating the phrase *post tenebras spero lucem* (I hope for light after darkness). As such it was a famous printers' mark and also was included in a series of the Seven Virtues to symbolize Hope.

Chaucer, *NPT*, 3457; *PF*, 330–40; *Tr*, iii.1191–92; Child, iv, 521; *EB.*, x, 141; *Erec*, p. 216; Garner, *PL*, 193, col. 81; Giovio & Symeoni, p. 41; Horapollo, pp. 14–16; Kelchner, p. 143; Lévy-Bruhl, pp. 257–58; Panofsky, *Pandora*, p. 142; Paradin, p. 311; Rabanus Maurus, *PL*, 112, col. 853; Shakespeare, *Much Ado* iii.i.35–36; *Othello* iii.iii.260–62; *Macbeth* ii.iv.13; *Taming* iv.i.180–81; iv.ii.39; Swaen (ed.), *passim*; Tervarent, cols. 162–64; Whitney, p. 207; Williams, p. 141; Witherby, iii, 11; Chauncey Wood, p. 399.

Finch

"This bird is of many kinds," said Albertus Magnus, and indeed individual consideration by writers and artists has given some members of the finch family a separate symbolism. Aelian said that finches were cleverer than men in predicting the future: "for instance, they can tell when winter is coming, and they take the most careful precautions against an impending snowfall." In general, however, the finch is more celebrated for its song than for

A finch watches a game of chess.

its prophetic powers. In Italy the poet Robert Browning, thinking of April in England, longed to hear the bird sing on the orchard bough. In Scotland the finch used to be known as "drunken sow" because it was supposed to sing, "drink, drink till you're full wee drounken sowie."

Probably no other bird has been more mistreated. Picinelli in one of his emblems referred to the practice of blinding the bird to improve its song—*caecitate perficitur* (it is made perfect by blindness). Even today in western Flanders the finch is the major participant in a regular Sunday betting game involving some thirty thousand people. The finches, shut up in glass-fronted boxes, are judged on the number of times each utters the distinctive note which marks the end of its song. "A good bird can be worth more than one thousand pounds, and everything is done to stop the birds' singing and to make them repeat just the end of their song. This includes the use of drugs." In medieval times *finch* was a slang term for "chick" or "bird." For a bribe of a quart of wine, Chaucer's syphilitic Summoner, the archdeacon's assistant, would allow a priest to have a mistress and, as far as he himself was concerned, "ful prively a fynch eek koude he pulle." The implication is that the Summoner also kept a wench on the sly. The same significance occurs with reference to "birds" in another Middle English tale, *Piers of Fulham*. In Shakespeare's *Troilus and Cressida* when Thersites calls Achilles' friend Patroclus "a finch-egg," his meaning is not clear. James Harting, the Victorian ornithologist, in commenting on this passage, simply stated: "what species of Finch the poet had in view, it is not easy to determine. It may have been the Bullfinch, but it is more likely to have been the Chaffinch, which has always been a favourite caged-bird with the lower classes." Thersites' remarks are frequently obscene, and here he is either using a synonym for another popular expression of his—"son of a whore"— or alluding to the small size of a finch egg in order to imply that Patroclus is himself insignificant.

Aelian, 1.60; Albertus Magnus, *Animal.* II.1452; Browning, "Home Thoughts, From Abroad," l. 7; Harting, p. 144; Liddell & Scott, s.v. σπίζα; Picinelli (ed. 1678), IV.xxxii; Piers of Fulham (ed. Hartshorne), pp. 1–7, l. 6; Shakespeare, *Troilus and Cressida* v.i.35.

Goldfinch

The brightest of songsters, no bird has been more cruelly treated than the goldfinch. Even today it is caged and sold in European street markets. In the last century, according to Bechstein, because the period of singing was short, the finch as well as the nightingale and the lark was blindfolded in order to prolong its song. In London goldfinches represented one-tenth of the sale of singing birds on the street markets. "The demand for goldfinches especially among women," said Mayhew, "is steady and regular." Whereas the caged nightingale, as the season for migration approached, would show "symptoms of great uneasiness, dashing himself against the wires of his cage or his aviary, and sometimes dying in a few days," the goldfinch was longlived and was known to have lived twenty-three years in a cage. In the thirteenth century, according to Dante, one of the objects most longed for by Italian children was a little bird. Children were given a live bird on a long string and would amuse themselves by letting it fly around, holding firmly to the other end of the tether to prevent its escape. The goldfinch seems to have been the most popular toy, and its popularity was probably enhanced by the belief that the bird possessed curative powers. Friedmann, pointing out that a number of childrens' portraits from various countries also show a child playing with a tethered goldfinch, comfortingly observes "the birds became tame quite readily and seemed not to mind familiar handling."

Nevertheless the goldfinch in the plump hand of the infant Christ in medieval iconography is more than a reminder that the captive bird was long considered a suitable plaything for children. Friedmann, who provides a symbolic explanation, lists nearly five hundred paintings containing goldfinches and states that there are many more. The finch appears frequently in paintings of the Madonna, either with the Child or with the Child and St. John (except when the Child is being suckled), the Nativity, the Adoration of the Shepherds and of the Magi, and occasionally in secular paintings. In Friedmann's view this bird is a conscious representation of the soul which Christ has come to save. Sometimes the dove is substituted as a more explicit symbol, but the goldfinch's tradition makes it, in itself, an admirable symbol. Jacques Schnier, approaching the figure from a psychological point of vew, sees the bird as the unconscious representation of the breast. He states:

In accordance with the unconscious mechanisms of symbol formation, the bird, a form commonly experienced by most people, is selected as a representative of the lost and longed for object. Since in the *Madonna lactans* compositions the Child is depicted in actual possession of the lost object, i.e., the mother's breast, it therefore becomes a superfluous gesture, a redundancy, so to speak, to also show the Child with the lost object in the form of a bird in Its hand.

Schnier points out the abundant evidence for the bird as a mother symbol and observes that in life as well as in art the string to which the bird is tethered assures the child of control over his mother's return.

The goldfinch had other significances which supported its role in Christian iconography. Pliny's *carduelis* and *acanthus* are commonly identified as the same bird, the goldfinch, which fed on thistles. This bird was said to have twelve offspring and to be the symbol of fertility. Possibly Raphael's *Madonna del Cardellino* in which St. John presents the Christ Child with a goldfinch was intended to convey this significance. Certainly in the Renaissance the bird on its nest was a symbol of fertility. In Ripa's emblem of *Fecondita* a woman holds a goldfinch on its nest in her hand. At her feet are a hen and a rabbit, each with its young. The goldfinch was the symbol of fertility for another reason. One of the medieval Latin names for goldfinch was *lucina* or *lucinia*, the "bringer of light." The word seems to have been borrowed from the ancient nightingale (*luscinia*), possibly because the goldfinch's bright plumage made it the natural symbol of light. As such, it was associated with Lucina who was the goddess of childbirth in medieval as well as in ancient times.

As the symbol of light the goldfinch was the image of the dawning day of grace, and this significance may also account for the goldfinch in paintings of the Madonna and Child, especially when the bird is in a free-standing or flying position. Sometimes the bird even appears with the earthly paradise in the background, the pastoral arcady to which man can return because of the birth of the Christ Child.

At the same time, despite its widespread use in paintings, the goldfinch was capable of pejorative interpretation in secular literature where its gay coloring, sprightliness of movement, and tinkling sound made it the symbol of frivolity. Whether Chaucer was thinking of the symbolic significance when he described the young store clerk Perkyn Revelour as being "gaillard . . . as goldfynch in the shawe [grove]" is debatable. Today, except for his apparent enjoyment of Newgate hangings, Perkyn's behavior would be socially acceptable. With a welfare check in his pocket, he would have no need to dip into his boss's till. Perkyn was a good dancer, especially at weddings, skillful gambler, and guitar player. Any woman who met him was fortunate because he was full "of love and paramour [sexual passion]." He was generous with money and when kicked out by his employer quickly found a place with a friend whose wife was a prostitute. But Chaucer's comparison of Perkyn to a rotten apple suggests that he may have been aware of the pejorative symbolism attached to the bird. In *The Floure and The Leafe*, a slightly later poem but one which uses many older conventions, the goldfinch is associated with the medlar, a fruit which according to popular expression "had to be rotten 'er it was ripe," and which was the subject of many ribald puns, particularly in Elizabethan and Jacobean drama later. In the poem the goldfinch leaps prettily from bough to bough of the medlar tree, eats the buds and flowers, and sings. Here the bird symbolizes indolence and worldly pleasure, and as such is a perfect symbol for Perkyn Revelour.

By Grose's time the goldfinch was slang for "one who had commonly a purse full of gold," and goldfinches meant guineas. In the nineteenth century the goldfinch's nest, like the cuckoo's nest, was slang for the female pudendum.

Aelian, x.32; Bechstein, p. 218; Chaucer, *CkT*, 4365–422; *The Floure and The Leafe*, pp. 36, 87; Friedmann, *passim*; Mayhew, II, 59–60; Pliny, x.xl, xlvii; Ripa, I.i.239; Row-

66

land, *Blind Beasts*, pp. 58–59; Schnier, pp. 95–98; Witherby, i, 58.

Goose

Today there is little left of the goose's prophetic powers. Transferred to the battery chicken, even the "lucky" wishbone has lost its meaning; who now even thinks of looking for it among the greasy relics of the Colonel's Kentucky fried? Yet the traditional goose feasts at Michaelmas—when the bone called "Merry Thought," close to the breast of the fowl, was examined for portents of future events or weather conditions—derive from forgotten rituals in which the goose was a sacred bird. Aphrodite and many of the mother goddesses in their capacity as "the Lady of the Beasts" either were the goose, or rode on it, or carried a cloak decorated with the symbol of the goose. In India the white goose was the symbol of the soul and of the sun: Brahma rode on a white goose or assumed its forms; Agni, the god of fire, had goose attributes. The wild gander (hamsa) was a free wanderer. It was the symbol of divine essence, and also of sovereign freedom attained through spirituality. "That is why," writes Zimmer, "the Hindu ascetic, the mendicant monk or saint who is supposed to have become freed from the bondage

The goose is a watchful bird.

of rebirth, is said to have attained the rank of gander (hamsa), or 'highest gander' (paramahamsa). These are epithets commonly applied to the orthodox teacher-saints of present-day Hinduism." In China the goose was associated with *yang*, the principle of light and masculinity. In ancient Egypt the goose was associated with the worship of Ra, the sun god. On a diorite statuette from Ur the creative divinity Gula rides four geese. In Siberia, Ortiki, the youngest son of god, was called the goose spirit and often traveled in the shape of a goose or sat on its wings. The cackling white geese which warned the Roman Capitol of the advancing Gauls were oracular birds, and the quality of vigilance for which the goose remained a symbol for centuries points to its earlier associations.

The restless goose who thinks nothing of wandering into a lady's bedroom in "Goosey Goosey Gander" seems to have little in common with the divine bird, yet its origins are the same. The goose was an erotic symbol for both sexes, because it was the bird of creation, whether in the male solar form of the gods or the female lunar form of the mother goddesses. The goose carved on Greek tombstones stood for marital love; in Rome the goose represented sexual union, fertility, and conjugal fidelity, a symbolism also given to the goose and mandarin duck in China. Eros chases a goose on an Apulian red-figured flask (300–320 B.C.): on Etruscan vessels the goose appears in scenes of ritual plowing and copulation; goose fat in Pliny's view was an aphrodisiac; heretics had amorous relations with the devil in the form of a goose; in the *Bedford Book of Hours* the goose-like creature watching Adam and Eve being driven from the Garden appears to symbolize sexual temptation. Aldrovandi stressed the bird's medicinal and aphrodisiacal properties. The goose was also associated with woman in the scatological rhyme —"There ben women, there ben wordis; / There ben gese, three ben tordys"—and by the Elizabethan period goose was a common name for prostitute. In particular, the Winchester goose, such as Pandarus alludes to in *Troilus and Cressida*, was applied to women in the ancient Southwark establishments whose earnings in the sixteenth century were part of the revenue of the landlord, the Bishop of Winchester. According to Ben Jonson, Shakespeare's contemporary, "The Wincesterian [sic] goose [was] bred on the banks in the time of Popery when Venus there maintain'd her mystery . . . ." Less light-hearted were the references to venereal disease, also termed "Winchester goose" or "Winchester measure."

Chaucer used the word "goose" to mean a foolish person. The proverbial expression "to shoe the goose" meant to do something impossible and, therefore, foolish. The proverbial goose who fell victim to the preaching fox was also a helpless or stupid person, and Chaucer used the word *goosish* meaning "silly." Not surprisingly the goose appears in Brant's *Ship of Fools*. An engraving shows a fool with three geese, one between his legs, one flying away, and one returning to his hand. No matter how far they travel some people never learn, said Brant:

> For every goose when once let loose
> Returns and still remains a goose.

Much later in D.H. Lawrence's short story "Goose Fair" the geese driven to market for sale and slaughter symbolized the slow-witted suffering masses, "weary," their "poor feet . . . dipped in tar for shoes."

The goose appears in representations of the Ages of Man. Shakespeare divided life into seven ages, but from antiquity life was divided anywhere from two parts (youth and age) to sixteen parts. In some of the longer series the goose accompanies old age, an association not, apparently, pointing to the foolishness of old age but indicating that death will pluck a man, like a goose, of all he possesses. Samuel Chew thought that this goose might have some connection with the goose which made the flesh creep by flying over one's future grave—the goose of ill-omen in Graham Greene's *The Confidential Agent*: "A goose went winging by somewhere above his grave—where? He shivered." Old age and the goose are also associated in the proverb "The older the goose the harder to pluck." The explanation given by Brewer (1900) was: "Old men are unwilling to part with their money." He added "the reference is to the custom of plucking live geese for the sake of their quills. Steel pens have put an end to this barbarous custom." Riddell, writing on the same custom, said that feathers from the left wing were best "because their curvature bent away from the eyes of right-handed writers."

Chaucer's Wife of Bath, repeating a statement that every woman however ugly will find a mate, said:

> Ne noon so grey goos gooth ther in the lake
> As, sëistow, wol been withoute make [mate].

In recent times the gray goose has acquired a very different value as a figure for social and political protest. Whatever its antecedents, the ballad of "The Gray Goose," when sung by convicts in the prison camps in the Ameri-

An angry goose cackles at a fox which is gobbling a gosling.

can south, was a means of expressing defiance. In the ballad the gray goose is shot:

> Last Sunday mornin', Lawd, Lawd, Lawd,
> Daddy went a-huntin', Lawd, Lawd, Lawd.
> He carried along his shotgun, Lawd, Lawd, Lawd,
> Along come a gray goose, Lawd, Lawd, Lawd.

The bird causes so much trouble in the plucking and cooking and turns out to be so tough that he is put in the hog pen where he breaks "Ol' Jerry's sawbone, Lawd,

Lawd, Lawd," and then in the saw-mills where he breaks the saw's teeth.

> Well the last time I seed him, Lawd, Lawd, Lawd,
> He was flyin' across the ocean, Lawd, Lawd, Lawd,
> With a long string o' goslins, Lawd, Lawd, Lawd,
> All gwine quink-quank, Lawd, Lawd, Lawd,
>
> They was all gwine quink-quank, Lawd, Lawd, Lawd,
> Along went the gray goose, Lawd, Lawd, Lawd.

According to the folk singer Huddie Ledbetter, the man who could last out, despite the brutality and misery of prison life, was the indomitable goose, a creature who could be shot, plucked, parboiled, thrown to the hogs, put through the sawmill, and yet fly off with his children, honking in derision. This goose seems to be of the same breed as the "wild geese"—the 120,000 Irishmen who left their country to fight in various armies as a result of the penal laws of 1691. In a noble lament with the haunting refrain: "Romantic Ireland's dead and gone,—It's with O'Leary in the grave," W.B. Yeats uses the same symbol:

> Was it for this the wild geese spread
> The grey wing upon every tide;
> For this that all that blood was shed
> For this Edward Fitzgerald died,
> And Robert Emmet and Wolfe Tone,
> All that delirium of the brave?

> Romantic Ireland's dead and gone,
> It's with O'Leary in the grave.

What of the goose that laid the golden egg? Here undoubtedly is the solar goose which laid the cosmic egg. A creation myth describes how, at the beginning of things, the "Great Cackler" or Chaos Goose cackled loudly to the Chaos Gander and laid an egg which was the sun. In contemporary slang this egg has lost all value. It is now a zero, either for the score of a game, or for a grade in school.

Aldrovandi, III, 141–43, 159; Armstrong, *Folklore*, pp. 25–47; "Symbolism," pp. 54–58; Brant (tr. Zeydel), p. 41; Chaucer, *WB*, 269–70; *Tr*, iii.584; Chew, p. 172; Crooke, 343; Greenway, 171–73; Neumann, p. 217; Pliny, x.xxvi; Valeriano, f.174v; Williams, p. 180; Yeats, "September 1913"; Zimmer, pp. 48–49.

Griffin

This creature was always associated with gold. Pliny did not believe in its existence, but Aelian was more credulous:

I have heard that the Indian animal the Gryphon is a quadruped like a lion; that it has claws of enormous

70

strength and that they resemble those of a lion. Men commonly report that it is winged and that the feathers along its back are black and those on its front are red, while the actual wings are neither but are white. And Ctesias records that its neck is variegated with feathers of a dark blue; that it has a beak like an eagle's, and a head too, just as artists portray it in pictures and sculpture. Its eyes, he says, are like fire . . . . And the people of Bactria, who are neighbors of the Indians, say that Gryphons guard the gold in those parts.

Because it was made up of the eagle and the lion, the symbols of dominion and destruction, the griffin was from the beginning an ambivalent figure. The griffin's interest in gold was interpreted in two ways. As a creature who knew where gold was, the griffin was made the emblem of *scientia* or knowledge and as such appeared in the medieval cycle of the virtues and vices. Its alleged habit of building its nest of gold was sometimes construed as generosity, as Henkel notes. Aldrovandi was among those who stated that the ancients regarded the griffin as an image of a magnaminous and generous spirit. Yet the same association with gold also brought the griffin into disrepute. Batman, translating the twelfth-century encyclopedia of Bartholomaeus Anglicus, commented on the griffin as a symbol of the money lender, and Thomas Lodge and other prose writers stressed its covetousness.

In medieval England this strange hybrid figure cap-

The griffin tears people to pieces.

tured the imagination in several ways. Not only did the griffin appear in travel books, lapidaries, and romances as a creature supposed to actually exist, but in both fiction and fact it was a favorite decoration, either sculptured or embroidered in gold. King Arthur possessed a magnificent

The griffin symbolizes the Devil.

both in manuscripts and in sculpture as being airborne by two griffins. Possibly Dante may have been influenced by this motif when he made the griffin a symbol of Christ. Or he may have been thinking of Isidore's account of the griffin which includes, in the same chapter, a reference to Christ as both lion and eagle. Dante put the griffin in his *Purgatory*, where it pulled a car among old men and dancing maidens, quoted the Bible, and magically vanished.

When the griffin is not associated with Alexander, its appearance in ecclesiastical architecture suggests less favorable connotations. In cathedrals in Wells, Chester, Boston, Gloucester, Beverley, Durham, Carlisle, and other places the griffin is frequently represented either fighting a man or clutching a man or animal in its claws. Here the griffin appears to have symbolized the Devil. Purported eyewitness accounts did, indeed, depict the griffin as a terrifying monster. That imaginative traveler John Mandeville said that bows for archery were made from the ribs of a griffin, and the animal was so strong that he could carry off to his nest two oxen yoked together at the plow. The same opinion was shared by Batman, writing in the sixteenth century: "The Gripe and [griffin] hath so great clawes & so large of them bee made cups that bee set uppon boordes of kings," and he then added that there were griffins in England "that devoure more men by usury, then [than] all the Gripes [griffins] in India, the

shield with a griffin on it; his knight Gawain was dressed in a green robe decorated with gold griffins; wills and inventories cited the griffin as a device in vestments, coverlets, and arms. The griffin also appeared in the legend of the hero who took an aerial flight. Probably the introduction of the griffin in such stories was very old. Creuzer referred to a Greek sculpture showing Apollo being drawn by two griffins, and another in which he was metamorphosed into a griffin. The popular medieval version concerned King Alexander, and he was frequently depicted

72

fetchers of golde." Legh, Batman's contemporary claimed to have proof of the griffin's size: "I have a claw of one of their paws, which should showe them to be as bygge [big] as two lyons."

Despite its ambivalent values in literature and art, in heraldry the griffin was much admired. At an early date the griffin *rampant*, that is, the animal erect, looking forward with one hind paw on the ground and with tail and the other three paws upraised, was used in the arms of the House of Montagu. Picinelli refers to Sorbello who used the griffin heraldically with the motto *nec vi, nec vitio* (neither by violence nor by vice). Guillim, explaining the significance of the griffin in heraldry, stated:

> The Griffin having attained his full groweth, will never be taken alive: wherein hee doth *Adumbrate* or rather lively set forth the propertie of a valorous Souldier, whose Magnanimitie is such as he had rather Expose himselfe to all dangers, and even to death it selfe, then [than] to become captive.

Aelian, iv.27; Aldrovandi, i, 608; *Batman uppon Batholome*, f.363; Boutell, p. 79; Creuzer, ii.ii.lxi, lxxx; Dante, *Purg.* xxix.106–14; Greene (ed. Grosart), iii, 224; Guillim, p. 181; Henkel, col. 797; Isidore, xii.2.17; Katzenellenbogen, p. 78n; Legh, f.106v; Lodge (ed. Hunterian Club), ii.ii.38–39; Mayer (ed.), p. 412; Mandeville, l.179; *MED.*, s.v. *griffoun* n.(2); Picinelli (ed. 1698), iv.xxxix; Pliny, vii.ii; x.lxx.

Gull

Gulls are the soaring, buccaneering birds of the ocean which bring a touch of beauty to the city. They were not always in London: they came in one of the bitter winters of the 1890s and have stayed, the lineal descendants, perhaps, of those who once fished marsh and river when London was a small, walled city. Not that gulls are all of one type. There are many species, as Newton and others point out. But we think of them as sea birds, and their eerie, echoing and unmistakable cry has contributed to the widespread superstition that seagulls are the spirits of the dead, especially of those drowned at sea.

The popularity of the gull as a soul bird may have contributed to the success in the early 1970s of a much publicized, undistinguished piece of writing in which the seagull, as the hero, symbolized the spirit of man, yearning to be free. Chekhov's use of the seagull in his famous play of that name is more subtle and complex. At the beginning the bird represents young Nina's illusions about the artistic life. Shot by Treplev and laid at her feet, the bird is the creative spirit which Treplev has now destroyed in himself. As Jackson observes, "the fallen bird defines man's fate only so long as he bases his freedom and happiness upon illusions, deceptions, evasions of reality; at the moment he frees himself of his illusions . . . it is the soaring bird that becomes emblematic of man's ultimate destiny."

In Elizabethan times the word *gull* was used very frequently to mean "a fool, a rogue." The adjective "gullible" is a reminder of such use. This gull has a different derivation. It is from Middle English *golle*, meaning an unfledged bird, and it was used figuratively even then to mean a silly fellow. One of the most famous Elizabethan pamphlets was called *The Gull's Hornbook* (1609). Written by Dekker, it was an ironical manual of instruction purporting to initiate the young country gallant into London society. Not that the sea gull (*larus*) enjoyed a good reputation at the time. Various proverbial expressions suggested that gulls were *rapaces et furaces* (rapacious and thievish). Turner thought that the stern (the black tern), smaller than the sea *lari* and blacker, was the bird "whose vile garrulity gave rise to the old Proverb 'Larus parturit' (the gull is in labor)." He added that "it makes such an unconscionable noise that by its unrestrained clamour it almost deafens those who live near lakes and marshes." Aldrovandi and others saw the gull as the symbol of the insatiability of the merchant class. It also symbolized the man who fell short of expectations because, as the fowler

discovered, there was very little flesh on the bird. Even now the proverbial expression "the gull comes against the storm" points to the bird's unfavorable connotations, suggesting that it foretells disaster.

Aldrovandi, III, 67–70; Armstrong, pp. 211–13; Harrison, *They Tell of Birds*, p. 106; Jackson, pp. 42–44; Newton, *EB.*, XII, 714–15; Shakespeare, *King Henry The Fifth* III.vi.56–58; Turner, p. 79; Valeriano, f.167; Witherby, V, 79ff.

Harpy

An exceptionally ferocious eagle is called a harpy, but of more importance in this study is the mythological monster which gave it its name. In ancient Greek myth, Harpies, as their name derived from *harpazein* implies, made a snatch—often totally disposing of anyone whose sudden disappearance was required by the gods. The various names given to harpies indicate that they were personifications of winds and storms, not unlike the Maruts of the Vedas. In Homer's *Odyssey* these vulture-like creatures with women's heads and breasts were called *harpuiai* (the spoilers). Hesiod said that there were two of them, and they were winged goddesses with beautiful

hair. They kept pace with the winds and birds in flight—
"as quick as time they dart along." Later their number
increased and their appearance deteriorated. Harpies had
hideous faces of old women, ears of a bear, crooked talons,
and hanging breasts. They were tortured with insatiable
hunger. They swooped down from mountains contami-
nating everything with their excrement, fouling the air
with their stench, and carrying off whole tableloads of
food. Virgil's hero, Aeneas, was attacked by harpies on
the Greek island of the Strophades where they lived.
Virgil wrote:

> No monster is grimmer than the harpy; no stroke of
> divine anger ever more cruel; and no demon soaring up
> from the waters of the Styx was ever more wicked. They
> are birds with girls' faces, and a disgusting effluvium
> comes from their bellies. Their hands have talons and
> their faces are always white with hunger.

In the Middle Ages the harpy appears in *The Tretyse
of Love*, an anonymous work which describes remedies
against the Seven Deadly Sins. Here the harpy has a face
like a man, and her nature compels her to kill the first
man that she finds. Then she goes to some water, looks
at her reflection, and becomes very upset when she realizes
that she has killed someone like herself. According to the
moralist, this harpy is the symbol of the soul. The soul,
through sin, kills Christ. Then when the soul remembers

This Harpy has griffin-like features.

Christ's sacrifice, it is sorry. The same story is given as a
fact of natural history by Vincent of Beauvais.

The famous naturalist Gesner seems to have been sceptical about these creatures. Scholars he said had variously
interpreted them as winged feminine demons, swift winds,

or ravenous dogs. Aldrovandi noted that to the Church Fathers harpies were prostitutes. He regarded them himself as symbols of avarice and rapine. As a heraldic device, according to John Guillim, the harpy "should be given to such persons as have committed manslaughter, to the end that by the often view of their *Ensignes* they might be moved to bewail the foulness of their offence." Two years later in *Minerva Britanna* (1612) Henry Peacham maintained that harpies inhabited the royal courts. In accordance with tradition there were three of them:

> The first is he, that carries tales untrue,
> The second, whom base bribing does maintain,
> The third and last, the Parasite I find . . . .

To illustrate his point he shows a mean-looking harpy perched on a table. She has the shape and appearance of a robin except for her very womanly face, long hair, eagle's talons, and large protruding breasts.

Psychologically these malevolent creatures are not hard to explain. In the British Museum on a monument of the harpies which once decorated the tomb of Xanthos in Lycia, a flying harpy holds a child in a suckling position in her arms while she clings to the child's lower limbs with her talons. As we know, the bird symbolizes motherly attributes, but, as Schnier observes, the child's tendency to project on to the mother its own destructive wishes caused by weaning turns the dove-like maternal figure into a sadistic, eagle-like, predatory creature. Like the Sphinx, the Gorgon, and the Sirens, who also have bird attributes, the Harpies bring death and destruction. They are psychompomps which carry off the soul to the underworld, the personification of human guilt and fundamental fears. At the same time, like Medusa and even Demeter herself, they can give birth to horses, and this equine association points clearly to their extraordinary sexual potency. But while these creatures embody a double conception, being the givers of life as well as of death, their destructive capacity is emphasized and they represent the most terrifying aspects of the Mother Goddess.

Turned into allegory, harpies first became courtesans, bringing financial ruin to their lovers, and then they developed into a symbol for avarice in general. Even at the end of the last century Brewer quoted as a common expression: *he is a regular harpy*, meaning "one who wants to appropriate everything; one who sponges on another without mercy." Today the word *harpy* is applied only to a woman. Influenced by the verb "to harp," and by "harridan," the epithet suggests shrewishness rather than greed.

Aldrovandi, 1, 611–21; Bunker, pp. 421–24; Gesner, II.ii.544–66; Guillim (quoting Upton), p. 183; Hesiod, *Theog.*, 265; Homer, *Il.* VI.346; XVI.150; *Od.* I.241; XIV.371; XX.77; Peacham, p. 115; Ripa, II.ii.501; Schnier, pp. 111–12;

Seznec, p. 85; Thompson, pp. 55–56; *Tretyse of Love*, p. 113; Vincent of Beauvais, *Spec. Nat.* XVI.xciv; Virgil, *Aen.* III.212ff.

Hen

To some early writers the hen with her little chickens symbolized the weak but loving and protecting mother:

We do not recognize any other bird as a mother unless it is on its nest with its young. But the hen is so weakened with its young, and is so dirty with its drooping wings and feathers and hoarse cry, and is so miserable that you cannot see its brood or its nest; yet you understand that it is a mother.

Just as the hen defended her brood from the wolf or vulture so the good Christian must defend himself against the Devil. The imagery was associated with the words of Christ as He approached Jerusalem for the last time:

O Jerusalem, Jerusalem, killing the prophet and stoning those who are sent to You! How often would I have gathered your children together as a hen gathers her brood under her wing, and you would not!
(Matthew XXIII.37; Luke XIII.34)

The hen looks after its chicks.

Medieval theologians such as St. Augustine, Garner, and Rabanus Maurus said that this hen was the intelligence or wisdom of God which led the elect to salvation. To St. Chrysostom the hen was the church and the wandering chickens were the people of God following evil pleasures and worldly desires.

In ecclesiastical sculpture the hen and chickens appeared as an emblem of God's providence. As noted in connection with the cock, the image of the rooster and a hen kissing each other upon the tombs of prominent people in ancient times indicated, according to Aldrovadi, a legitimate marriage: "The fervent love of the rooster towards his family . . . admonishes us to love our wives and to reject all prostitutes, who are nothing more than

77

The hen was sometimes used in medicine.

the pestilence and destruction to husbands." On the other hand, Aldrovandi observed, a representation of a hen which erects crest and tail and has small spurs on its feet is a woman who attempts to dominate her husband or, even worse, "entices the other hens as if she were really able to perform as a male and wearies them by leaping on top of them."

Capon, according to Cotgrave, meant a "love letter" or "love message." Shakespeare, writing in the same period, gave two meanings. Cloten, the loutish step-son of Cymbeline, was said to be "cock and capon too," meaning that he behaved timorously as if he were castrated. On the other hand, when the princess in *Love's Labor's Lost* exclaimed, "Break up this capon," she meant that she wanted a love letter opened.

Hen, which in Shakespeare means "wife" or "bed-partner," takes on a bawdy significance comparable to that of "stewed cock" when cooked. *The Interlude of the IIII Elementes* has a scene in which the innkeeper acts as a pimp:

Taverner: Though all capons begone what then
Yet I can get you a stewed hen
That is redy dyght.
Humanyte: Yf she be fat yt wyll do well.
Taverner: Fat or lene I cannot tell
But as for this I wot well
She lay at the stewes all nyght.

78

Hens often had a bad reputation: in the farmyard they were said to be snack-eaters, very choosy about their food. Here, they resembled the man who spent his time chasing women and running into debt. The image of a hen feeding on gold coins symbolized the man who wasted either his own money or the family property. On the other hand, to dream of a flock of hens coming toward you and entering your house meant that you would receive money and distinction, unless the hens were exceptionally small, in which case you would remain poor.

The emblem writers, on the whole, praised the hen. Whereas Ripa regarded the cock as a symbol of jealousy, as well as of divine wisdom, *sanità*, and other commendable qualities, the hen was consistently praiseworthy as the symbol of *fecondità*. To Camerarius the hen represented fecundity, health, and security. John Guillim, the writer on heraldry, had a curious observation to make about the capon. Because the bird grew fatter from being castrated, it was used as "one of the Arguments to proove the *single life* the *happiest*: and that *Celibes* are *Caelites*: the single life, the Saint-like life."

Aldrovandi, II, 269–270; see also Lind, pp. 240, 243; Augustine, *PL*, 38, col. 623; Camerarius, III.lii; Chrysostom, *PG*, 58, cols. 682–83; Garner, *PL*, 193, col. 75; Guillim, p. 164; Rabanus Maurus, *PL*, 112, cols. 939–40; Meyer (ed.), p. 400; Ripa, I.i.239; II.ii.286; III.iii.37, 41; Shakespeare, *Cymbeline* II.i.23; *Love's Labor's Lost* IV.i.56.

Heron

The Hundred Years' War between England and France was supposed to have started because of this bird. The heron was thought to have little courage: if attacked in hawking, it never showed fight but sought to escape by flying higher and higher. Swashbuckling Robert of Artois was outlawed by his brother-in-law King Philip of France and went to Edward III of England for help. According to a French poem written about 1340, when the king was uncooperative, Robert served him a roasted heron at a public banquet, declaring that the most cowardly of birds was fit food for the most cowardly of kings. Edward and his guests immediately made vows on the heron to invade France.

There is some confusion over the name. The identification of the Greek bird *erōdios* which, according to Homer, brought luck when seen flying on the right-hand side, is uncertain. D'Arcy Thompson equates it, for the most part, with the heron, Latin *ardea*. The same word appears in

The heron flees from rain storms.

one of the Vulgate readings of Psalm ciii.17: *Herodii domus dux est eorum* (their leader is of the house of the heron). Rabanus Maurus, commenting on this passage, states: *Herodius est Christus ... quod Ecclesia, quae est habitatio Christi, electos ad vitam perducit. Herodius, perfectus quilibet, ut in Job: "Penna struthionis similis est pennis herodii," [Job xxxix.13] quod talem aliquando hypocrita publice actionem ostendit, qualem exercet ille qui in omnibus perfectus est.* (The heron is Christ ... because the Church, which is Christ's habitation, leads the elected into life. A heron is each perfect one, as in Job: "The feather of the ostrich is like that of the heron," because however much the hypocrite displays his actions in public, the one who is perfect in all things is always busily occupied.)

Elsewhere in the Middle Ages the bird was favorably regarded. The bestiaries extolled the heron for its wisdom, and the *Physiologus* linked it with the pelican of piety in its attitudes toward its young. Isidore said that the Latin word for heron, *ardea*, came from *ardua* (steep places) because of its lofty flight. According to the writer of *De Bestiis*, the heron flew above the clouds to avoid rainstorms; a heron flying away signified a storm.

The belief that the heron was an augury of the weather continued into the Renaissance in the works of both naturalists and emblem writers. Aldrovandi added that the heron was considered a friend to sailors because its

80

presence was said to signify fish in the sea; Camerarius said that it was the symbol of a prudent man who made provision against misfortune. At the same time the derivation of the name caused problems. Aldrovandi observed that while the bird had been regarded as sacred to Minerva because of its lack of sensuality, other authorities considered that *erōdios* was associated with *eros*. Early natural historians said that coition was so painful to the heron that it discharged blood, or even, according to Pliny, wept bloody tears. In consequence, while some writers said that the bird was moderate in its love making, others regarded it as a symbol of a man exhausted through too much sex. John Swan in his *Speculum Mundi* (1635) found the bird similarly reprehensible, though on different etymological grounds:

> This bird is *Avis furibunda, a furious bird*, and so in Latin she is called *Ardea*, of ardeo to burn; chiefly because she is an angrie creature, or because she is greatly inflamed with lust; or else because the dung of this bird doth as it were burn or consume what it toucheth.

Aldrovandi, III, 370–75; Brown, p. 260; Camerarius, III.xlii; Homer, *Il.* x.74; Isidore, xii.7.21; McCulloch, pp. 125–26; *Physiologus*, pp. 31–32; Pliny, x.lxxix; Rabanus Maurus, *PL*, 112, col. 953; Swan, p. 400; Thompson, p. 102; *Political Poems* (ed. Wright), I, 1-25; 363–66.

Hoopoe

The hoopoe is a very beautiful bird, about the size of a thrush, and has black wings striped with white. It possesses a distinctive erectile crest of cinnamon-colored feathers tipped with black, a reward, so the story runs, of King Solomon whom hoopoes once saved from sunstroke. The bird's name derives either from this crest or, as is more likely, from its "hoop! hoop!" sound which, according to Yarrell, "is breathed out so softly, yet rapidly, as to remind the hearer of the note of the dove." Like most crested birds, the hoopoe was venerated by primitive people. In common with the stork, the bird was believed to look after its parents in sickness and old age, and in Egypt it was the symbol of gratitude and filial piety. The hoopoe was placed on the scepter of the god Horus who had waged war against the murderers of his father Osiris. The bird also foretold a good wine harvest. "If this bird sings before the season of the vines," says Horapollo, "it is a sign of a good vintage." In Arabia the bird not only symbolized filial piety but was called "Doctor" because its heart and head were believed to possess magical properties useful either as medicine or as a aphrodisiac.

The bird's alleged family virtues persisted in the medieval bestiaries. Here was a bird which obeyed the Fifth Commandment:

Fisiolocus dixit: est avis quae dicitur uppa; horum filii quum viderint parentes suos senuisse, neque volare posse, neque videre [ob?] caliginem oculorum, tunc filii eorum evellunt vetustissimas pennas parentum suorum, et diligunt (delingunt?) oculos eorum; et fovent parentes suos sub alas suas, donec crescant pennae eorum et reluminent (sic) oculi eorum . . . .

(Physiologus says: "There is a bird which is called the hoopoe; whose sons, when they see their parents growing old, unable to fly and unable to see because of the mist of their eyes, pull out the oldest feathers of their parents, care for[?] their eyes; and warm their parents under their wings until their feathers grow and their eyes become clear again . . . .")

When the parents express their thanks, the children reply that they are simply repaying the kindness shown to them in their youth. The lesson from this is: if unthinking birds honor their parents so well, certainly men who have the gift of reason should.

The bird also possessed a very different value as a result of an erroneous belief expressed by Aristotle, Aelian, and others that the hoopoe built its nest with its excrements. *Sale comme une hoppe* (dirty like a hoopoe) was an old French proverb, and the bird was supposed to sing *mon nid pute* (my nest smells). Often repeated was the folktale of the hoopoe who asked Noah what material it should use to build its nest. "Gold," said Noah. Not understanding, the bird asked again. "Silver," said Noah. Again the bird did not understand, and when it repeated its question Noah gave a brief impatient exclamation which the bird took literally. In fact, the hoopoe's nest smells unpleasantly for several reasons: the bird's tail glands give off an offensive odor; the hen in incubation rarely leaves her nest; the parents do not remove the feces of their offspring as most birds do.

Because of its unsanitary habits, the bird could represent baseness as opposed to everything that is good. It was the form which the gods gave to wicked Tereus after his rape of his sister-in-law, and in Greek myth, he cried "pou? pou?" for his lost womenfolk. The cuckoo and the hoopoe associated together were symbolic of an incestuous relationship; the nightingale and the hoopoe were contrasted with one another. The homilist Odo of Cheriton in the story *De Uppupa et Philomena: contra luxuriosos et de religiosis qui eos fugiunt* (Concerning the Hoopoe and the Nightingale: against the voluptuous, and concerning religious men who flee from them) made the symbolism explicit: the nightingale represents the devout praising God in nightly chorus, while *uppupa . . . significat mulierem fornicariam* (the hoopoe signifies the fornicating woman). A rhyming bestiary contrived to combine the bad characteristics with the good but Bartholomaeus Anglicus found the bird inexecrable. Its heart, he said, was used by criminals in their deeds, and he repeated Isidore's statement that *cuius sanguine si quis se inunxerit dormitum pergens, daemones in somnis se suffocantes videbit* (whoever smears himself with the blood [of a hoopoe] on going to sleep, will see demons suffocating him in his dreams). In a Breslau-Lüben manuscript, dated 1349, the proverb *est avis ingrata, que defedet sua strata* (it is an ungrateful bird that soils its own nest) is specifically applied to the hoopoe and the bird is said to signify fornicators and adulterers: *talis est upupa per quam significantur fornicarii et adulteri* . . . . The proverbial expression "it's an ill bird that fouls its own nest" probably refers to the hoopoe, in Kunstmann's view, because among nest-befouling birds, the hoopoe is distinctive for fouling its own nest rather than someone's else's. In Germany the bird was used in proverbial invective, *in sein eigen nest hofieren wie ein widhopf* (to defecate in his own nest like a hoopoe). Among the numerous scatological expressions used by Martin Luther the hoopoe appears twice: *er stinket wie ein wiedehopfnest* (he stinks like a hoopoe's nest). Today, probably because of its comparative rarity, the hoopoe has lost its significance, although in the last century "uneducated rustics" in England thought the bird was unlucky and the Swedes were said to be terrified of the bird; they thought it was a portent of war because its crown looked like a helmet.

The hoopoe is kind to its parents.

Aelian, III.26; Aristotle, *H.A.* IX.15; Bartholomaeus, XII. xxxvii; *Best Divin.*, pp. 217–19; Brehm, II, 31; Cahier & Martin, II, 178–79; Horapollo, p. 142; Ingersoll, p. 153; Isidore, xii.7.66; Kunstmann, *passim*; Odo of Cheriton, IV, 213–14; Pliny, x.xliv; Wood, *Bible Animals*, 460–63.

Ibis

The ibis is a rare bird related to the stork family. It was sacred in ancient Egypt but found little favor in western Christendom. Herodotus gave a detailed description of the bird and said that it killed flying snakes:

> The ibis is a bird of a deep-black color, with legs like a crane; its beak is strongly hooked, and its size is about that of a landrail. This is a description of a black ibis which contends with the winged serpents. The commonest sort, for there are two quite distinct species, has the head and the whole throat bare of feathers; its general plumage is white, but the head and neck are jet black, as also are the tips of the wings and the extremity of the tail; in its beak and legs it resembles the other species. The winged serpent is shaped like the water snake. Its wings are not feathered, but resemble very closely those of the bat . . . .

> I once went to a certain place in Arabia, almost exactly opposite the city of Buto, to make inquiries concerning the winged serpents. On my arrival I saw the backbones and ribs of serpents in such numbers as it is impossible to describe . . . . The place where the bones lie is at the entrance of a narrow gorge between steep mountains, which there open upon a spacious plain communicating with the great plain of Egypt. The story goes, that with the spring the winged serpents come flying from Arabia towards Egypt, but are met in this gorge by the birds called ibises, who forbid their entrance and destroy them all. The Arabians assert, and the Egyptians also admit, that it is on account of the service thus rendered that the Egyptians hold the ibis in so much reverence.

The bird's habit of standing on straddled legs, with its long beak lowered, formed a triangle, in Plutarch's opinion, which enhanced its sacredness. Horapollo, on the other hand, saw the bird's shape as resembling a heart. The ibis symbolized the heart because the animal was consecrated to Hermes or Thoth—"the lord of every heart and of reasoning." The ibis was also the symbol of the morning, and typified perseverance and aspiration.

For the early natural historian Aelian the bird had less pleasant associations:

> The ibis is a very hot-blooded creature; at any rate it is an exceedingly voracious and foul feeder if it really does eat snakes and scorpions. And yet some things it digests without difficulty, while others it easily expels in its excrement. And very rarely would one see a sick ibis, yet it thrusts its beak down in every place, caring nothing for any filth and treading upon it in the hope of tracking down something even there.

Such observations were developed by the bestiarists. The

ibis cleaned out its bowels with its own beak, fed on corpses, and spent its time walking at the water's edge looking for dead fish or a corpse; the bird was afraid to enter deeper water where the clean fish were because it did not know how to swim. In almost every explication of the ibis's revolting habits, the bird was a symbol of the sinner. "The man seeking redemption enters the deep waters," said the preacher, "but if you choose not to enter the depths to seek the food of His grace then you have chosen to gather dead things and the most defiled corpses for your nourishment . . . ." A typical bestiary illustration shows the ibis feeding its young with snakes' eggs. This notion that snakes' eggs were part of the ibis's diet persisted for many centuries. Sir Thomas Browne remarked that the Egyptians destroyed the eggs of the ibis "for an opinion it was of that Nation, that the Ibis feeding upon Serpents, the venomous food so inquinated their oval conceptions, or eggs within their bodies, that they sometimes came forth in Serpentine shapes."

Despite the opinion of the bestiarists, the ibis was an ambivalent figure. Even Aelian, after commenting unfavorably, added that "when the ibis turns to rest it first of all washes itself and purges." Aldrovandi concluded that the bird could signify both *immunditia* (filth) and *salubritas* (wholesomeness). The emblem writers, who seem to be among the last to use the ibis symbolically, differed in their opinions. To Alciatus the ibis purging

The vile ibis feeds its young on snakes' eggs.

itself had an unfavorable significance, while to Valeriano it was the symbol of health or cleanliness.

Aelian, x.29; Alciatus, p. 295, lxxxvi; Albertus Magnus, *Animal.* II.1499; Aldrovandi, III, 318; Browne, III, 7; *De Bestiis, PL*, 177, col. 55–56; Cahier & Martin, II, 205–206; *EB.*, XIV, 218; Herodotus, II, 75–76; Horapollo, p. 56; McCulloch, pp. 132–33; Pliny, VIII.xli; x.xl; Valeriano, f.127v.

Jackdaw

Like the magpie, the jackdaw was associated with thieving and hoarding. The *monedula* (jackdaw), said Pliny, was a bird whose unique fondness for stealing, especially silver and gold, was remarkable. Although Gesner seems sceptical, he and many other ornithologists repeated a false etymology in illustration of the jackdaw's propensities. "The jackdaw by the Latins is named *monedula*, as if it were *monetula*, from *moneta* (money) which alone of birds, as Pliny says, it steals." Not surprisingly, the bird appeared with a merchant to illustrate the sin of Avarice in a medieval procession of the Seven Deadly Sins.

In earlier times the usual term was daw. Jack, which in the Middle Ages was a name applied familiarly or contemptuously, later came to be used as a prefix to indicate the daw's worthlessness. There was some confusion over the names used to denote a chough and a jackdaw, both of which were popularly regarded as gossips and thieves. A chough in medieval word-books was called a *monedula*, and a jackdaw was sometimes known as a *graculus*. Gesner and Aldrovandi, however, translated *graculus* as chough, and used the name which the Alpine chough has today. Aldrovandi compared the jackdaw to an avaricious man, and this jackdaw commanded more respect than the garrulous one. The latter was the symbol of a fool or simpleton. The usual derogatory term was "daw" or "dawcok." "A daucock ye be, and so shall be styll," remarked Skelton, attacking his great enemy Cardinal Wolsey. Shakespeare found the image of the daw useful: "Where dwell'st thou?" a servant asks Coriolanus. "I' the city of kites and crows," replies Coriolanus, referring disparagingly to Rome which he has left in disgust. The serving man cheekily replies: "Then thou dwell'st with daws too?" "No," snaps Coriolanus, "I serve not thy master." In *Troilius and Cressida* the rabble are "crows and daws"; the heroic Trojan princes are "eagles."

The jackdaw is rarely used in symbolism today. One exception is its appearance as the title of a series of case books on various topics. Since each publication is a folder stuffed with maps, facsimiles of documents, and other useful items culled from many sources, the name seems appropriate.

Aldrovandi, I, 772; Gesner, II.ii.520–27; Greene (ed. Grosart), XL, 74; Lodge (ed. Hunterian Club), II.ii.29; Pliny, x.xli; Shakespeare, *Coriolanus* IV.iv.37–44; *Troilus and Cressida* I.ii.229; Swann, p. 130; Witherby, I, 22.

Jay

Goldsmith called this bird "one of the most beautiful of the British birds," and said that "its behavior was extremely docile." Other naturalists, however, single the bird out for its "harsh, grating voice, and petulant, restless, disposition." Probably Goldsmith was thinking of the caged jay. Jays congregate in small noisy communities. They are very alert and utter piercing screams when danger threatens. The ordinary voice of a jay is soft, but the bird is a very skillful imitator. According to J.G. Wood, the caged jay soon learns to talk and displays "its imitative powers with considerable success, mocking the bleating of sheep, the cackling of poultry, the grunting of pigs, and even the neighing of horses, with wonderful truth."

In earlier times there appears to have been some confusion between this bird, the chough, and the jackdaw, all members of the crow family. In the illustration (*above*) from a late twelfth-century bestiary in the Bodleian Li-

The jay is a garrulous bird.

brary, the text describes a *graculus—graculus enim garrulos significat et gulosos* (for the *graculus* signifies

87

garrulous and greedy people). In the bestiaries *graculus* is usually regarded as the jackdaw, but a scribe has written in the top margin of this manuscript that in English the bird is a jay.

In the Middle Ages to "jangle like a jay" was a popular expression, especially when applied to women. Occasionally the jay is used in a complimentary way. In a love lyric a young woman is said to be as gentle and playful as a jay. To Chaucer, however, the jay appears to have symbolized mindless chattering and repetition. By Elizabethan times the term jay, when applied to women, was even more derogatory. In Shakespeare's *Merry Wives of Windsor*, Mrs. Ford says she will teach the old rascal Falstaff "to know turtles from jays," that is, to distinguish honest women (as represented by the faithful turtledove) from women of ill-repute. At this time, because of its bright plumage, the jay also represented any gaudily dressed person. Petruchio in *The Taming of the Shrew* makes this implication when he remarks: "Is the jay more precious than the lark / Because his feathers are more beautiful?"

The term "to jay-walk" does not come from the bird; it derives from jay, medieval Latin *gaius* meaning foolish. Brewer has another explanation for the jay's association with stupidity. According to his dictionary compiled toward the end of the last century, the jay is "a plunger; one who spends his money recklessly; a simpleton. This is simply the letter J, the initial letter of Juggins, who, in 1887, made a fool of himself by losses on the turf."

Chaucer, *Gen. Prol.*, 642; *MlT*, 774; *RvT*, 4154; *CYT*, 1396; *PF*, 346; Goldsmith, II, 98; Halliwell, II, s.v. jay; Harting, pp. 121–22; McCulloch, p. 134; *MED.*, s.v. *jai*; Shakespeare, *Merry Wives* III.iii.34; *Taming* IV.iii.172–73; Wood, *An. Creat.*, III, 280.

Kestrel

Kestrel is the English name for one of the smaller falcons. Writers of early hunting treatises despised this bird and stated that it could only be used by persons of inferior rank for hawking purposes. Transferred to men, as Robertson points out, the kestrel was associated with the lowest social order, and became a term of opprobrium. One revealing epithet for the bird was windfucker, possibly derived "from its manner of hovering with its head against the wind." Thomas Nashe (1567–1601), in a scurrilous piece of invective, refers to a woman who "thought that, instead of a boye (which she desired) she was delivered

The kestrel (bottom right) looks at the Apocalyptic angel.

and brought to bed of one of those kistrell birds, called a winged-fucker." Writing in the same period Spenser uses the bird to signify baseness:

> No thought of honour ever did assay
> His baser breast, but in his kestrel kynde
> A pleasant veine of glory he did find.

Greene (ed. Grosart), II, 155; Nashe (ed. McKerrow), III, 62; Robertson, *Preface*, p. 411n; Spenser, *FQ*, II.iii.4.

Kingfisher

Halcyon days are calm days, so called because, according to popular belief, when the kingfisher or halcyon hatches her eggs no storm can arise at sea. Originally these days referred specifically to the winter solstice. "For seven days before the winter solstice," said Pliny, "and for the same length of time after it, the sea becomes calm in order that the kingfishers may rear their young." This fable was constantly repeated. Cicero wrote a long poem in praise of the bird, and the Church Fathers saw the halcyon as an exemplification of the magnanimity of the Creator:

Behold the little bird, which in the midst of winter, lays her eggs on the sand by the shore. From that moment the winds are hushed; the sea becomes smooth; and the calm continues for fourteen days. This is the time she requires; seven days to hatch, and seven days to foster her young. Their Creator has taught these little animals to make their nest in the midst of the most stormy season, only to manifest His kindness by granting them a lasting calm. The seamen are not ignorant of this blessing; they call this interval of fair weather their halcyon days; and they are particularly careful to seize the opportunity, as they then need fear no interruption.

Associated with the belief that the kingfisher nested either on the shore or in the sea during mild weather is the story of a devoted married couple called Ceyx and Alcione. When Ceyx was accidently drowned Alcione sought to join him in the sea. The gods out of pity changed them both into kingfishers. Ovid, who told this story, continued:

Still do they mate and rear their young; and for seven peaceful days in the winter season Alcione broods upon her nest floating upon the surface of the waters. At such a time the waves of the sea are still.

Robert Graves thought that the kingfisher was originally a manifestation of the moon-goddess and that the word derived from "princess who averts evil."

The circumstances of Ceyx's death show that the Aeolians, who were famous sailors, gave the goddess the title "Alcyone" because as Sea-goddess she protected them from rocks and rough weather . . . . I have twice (with an interval of many years) seen a halcyon skimming the surface of the same Mediterranean bay, on both occasions about midsummer when the sea was without a ripple: its startlingly bright blue and white plumage made it an unforgettable symbol of the Goddess of the calm seas.

Certainly the kingfisher's bright coloring and distinctive appearance have made it an object of veneration and legend in many countries. Still current in France in the last century was the belief that the kingfisher acquired its brilliant feathers after being freed from Noah's ark. Its upper surface took on the color of the sky above it, and its breast became a rich chestnut color because it was scorched by the setting sun beneath.

The saint that sometimes accompanies the bird is St. Martin who, according to some accounts, was ground to pieces in a mill, and died on November 11. Joan of Arc tells the admiring Dauphin at the beginning of Shakespeare's trilogy of *King Henry VI*,

"Expect Saint Martin's summer, halcyon days,
Since I have entered into these wars."

She meant that with her help the French could expect

success against the English troops besieging them.

Commonly the bird was a praiseworthy symbol. To Gerald of Wales, the kingfisher signified saintly men because it did not putrify after its death; to the anonymous homilist in the late fourteenth century it symbolized St. Anne who gave birth to the sinless Virgin; the sea represented the readiness to sin "which overwhelms many men." The customary presentation of the kingfisher by the emblem writers had little to do with the actual bird. The kingfisher makes its nest on land, at the end of a kind of tunnel which it bores with its bill. According to Newton, while the nest forms a pretty cup-shaped structure during incubation, excreta and decaying fish soon turn it into a dripping, fetid mass. Nevertheless the halcyon of Valeriano, Alciatus, and Ripa squats comfortably on its nest in the middle of a calm sea. Giovio and Simeoni show two halcyons on one nest sailing safely through the Straits of Messina with Scylla on the one hand and Charybdis on the other. The emblematic halcyon stood for tranquility, peace, often with the motto *ex pace ubertas* (abundance from peace). Aldrovandi referred to various proverbial expressions associated with the kingfisher's peace and noted that the bird was also a symbol of the contemplative man. Ripa also made the halcyon the symbol of Benevolence and Matrimony, and Valeriano the symbols of *iustitium* and *consuetudinis rarae homo* (suspension of business and the man of rare custom). The

91

The kingfisher brings calm days.

two halcyons with the motto *nous savons bien le temps* (we know well the time) formed a device for someone who knew how to choose the right moment for action. The monument at Delft to William the Silent who was shot dead in 1584 just after his fourth marriage was decorated with a halcyon on its nest and the words "peaceful among furious waves," referring to the prince's guardianship of the Netherlands against the threat of Spanish domination. Picinelli regarded the kingfisher as the symbol, among other things, of the virginity of Mary. He also noted that many noble families took the bird as their badge with such mottoes as *certa quies* (assured quiet) and *omnia tuta* (all things safe).

The bird was supposed to possess other qualities, especially the gift of prophecy—"vertue prognostick," as Sir Thomas Browne called it. The kingfisher's dried body was said to avert thunderstorms, and if the body was hung by a thread to the ceiling of a room it would point its bill to the quarter from which the wind blew.

> "But how now stands the wind?
> Into what corner peers my halcyon's bill?

exclaims Marlowe's Barabas as he gloats over his gold in his counting house and anticipates further trading profits. In Shakespeare's *King Lear*, Lear's faithful servant Kent, denouncing the sycophants at court, declares that such rogues:

> "Turn their halcyon beaks
> With every gale and vary [varying wind] of their masters."

Here the implications are pejorative: instead of being the usual augury of happiness, the bird signifies cunning or obsequiousness.

Oliver Goldsmith scorned such beliefs: "The only truth which can be affirmed of this bird, when killed, is, that its flesh is utterly unfit to be eaten; while its beautiful plumage preserves its lustre longer than that of any other bird we know." Yet, throughout the centuries, the kingfisher has remained, as Swan described it in the seventeenth century, "a strange bird and as it were nature's dearest darling." Even Christina Rossetti, who liked to write poems urging her friends to remember her when she went away into a silent land, declared on her birthday that her heart was "like a rainbow shell / That paddles in a halcyon sea." Nor has the bird yet lost all figurative meaning. According to psychiatrist J.A. Hadfield, the term halcyon days "refers to the lovers destined to float in one another's embrace over a calm, warm, and tranquil sea."

Albertus Magnus, *Animal.* II.1443–44; Alciatus, pp. 506–509, clxxviii; Aldrovandi, III, 514–15; Ambrose, *PL*, 14, col. 238; *De Bestiis, PL*, 177, col. 95; Browne, III.x; Gerald of Wales, V, 5; Gesner, II.iii.89; Giovio & Simeoni, p. 197; Goldsmith, II, 237–38; Graves, 187–88; Hadfield, p. 170; Lanoe-Villène, s.v. l'alcyon; Marlowe, *The Jew of Malta* 1.i.38; *M.E. Sermons*, pp. 327–28; Newton, *EB.*, xv, 808; Ovid, *Met.* XI.745–48; Picinelli (ed. 1678), IV.iii; Pliny, X.xlvii; Ripa, I.i.83; Shakespeare, *Lear* II.ii.73–74; I *King Henry VI*, 1.ii.131–32; Swan, p. 417; Valeriano, ff.180v–181.

Kite

A kite was last seen flying over Piccadilly on June 24, 1859. In London, according to an Italian visitor in 1500, kites were so numerous that they would swoop down and snatch bread and butter from children's hands. Today the kite, as a rare species, is flatteringly described as "one of the most graceful and beautiful of birds." In early times it was the symbol of greed, cowardice, and deceit.

The bird was already despised as "the thieving watcher" when Aristophanes wrote *The Birds*. It is true that Peisthetaerus, a character in the play, astonishes the chorus by claiming that the kite once ruled Greece and that, as a result, people still bowed before it. Apparently in pre-Homeric times its presence around the altars at time of sacrifice was regarded as that of the god himself. But by Aristophanes' time, the bird was so disreputable that the thought of its former divine associations was amusing. Theognis subsequently emphasized its ruthless qualities, and Plautus and other writers regarded the bird as a synonym for greedy men. In the Middle Ages, Dante made the bird a symbol of petty tyrants; Jean de Meun, describing in the *Roman de la Rose* the world of amorous intrigue, regarded as kites the amateur bawds and pimps, the chambermaids and servants who act as go-betweens for lovers, clamoring for rewards such as robes, cloaks,

The kite was a symbol of greed.

gloves, or mittens. They were like kites ravishing all that they could seize—*E ravissent come uns escoufles / quanquil en pourront agraper*. In a story told by the homilist Odo of Cheriton, *De pullo galline et milvo* (concerning

93

the chicken and the kite), the kite was the Devil and its prey signified all those who did not hear the Lord's voice. To other men of the church such as Rabanus Maurus and Garner the kite stood for the Devil and for rapacity itself:

Milvus est diabolus, ut in Zacharia: "Et habebant alas quasi milvi," [Zach. v.9] quod reprobi ad instar diaboli in superbiam se extollunt. Milvi, rapaces, ut in Levitico: "Milvum et vulturem non comedetis," [Levit. xi. 14] id est, rapaces et invidos non debetis imitari.

(The kite is the devil, as it says in Zachariah: "And they had wings like a kite's," because, condemned by their resemblance to the devil, they elevate themselves in pride. Kites are the greedy ones, as in Leviticus: "Do not eat the kite or the vulture," that is to say, you should not imitate the rapacious nor the envious.)

In the fourteenth century John Gower, in describing a procession of the Seven Deadly Sins, made Gluttony a woman riding on a wolf and holding a kite on her wrist. The kite could also represent the deadly sin of Sloth. When Isidore contended that the *milvus* took its name from *mollis*: soft or supple, he may have meant that the bird was flexible rather than soft. (He subsequently called the bird *rapacissimus*.) Other pseudo-etymologists, however, including the preacher Bromyard, said that the bird's name came from *molliter volans*, meaning "flying weak-ly," hence the imputation of laziness. Present ornithologists declare that the kite is a very lively and fearless bird, but according to Bartholomew, it was cowardly and fearful among great birds, and Vincent of Beauvais stated that three kites would flee from one sparrowhawk. Chaucer called the bird a coward, and Alan of the Isles when he observed *illic venatoris induens personam milvus, veneratione furtiva, larvam gerebat accipitris* (the kite putting on the guise of the hunter, in secret veneration, takes the mask of the falcon) probably referred obliquely to its reputed cowardice as well as to its pretentiousness. Only in medicine does the kite appeared to have enjoyed a favorable reputation. According to Albertus Magnus, its head "borne before a man's breast . . . giveth to him love and favour of all men and women." A stone found in the kite's knees reconciled enemies if given to them to eat in their meat.

In Elizabethan times the kite was often associated with Cressida; not with Chaucer's gentle heroine but with the disillusioned prostitute stricken with leprosy, portrayed in the moralistic sequel by Henryson, a Scottish schoolmaster, about 1492. "What constancy is to bee hoped for in kytes of Cressid's kinde," asked Pettie. "May one gather Grapes of Thornes, Suger of Thistles, or Constancy of Women?" "Fetch forth the lazar kite of Cressid's kind," yells Pistol in *King Henry V*, meaning Doll Tearsheet, the prostitute at the inn. Here the allusion is probably to disease rather than to fickleness because leprosy was commonly thought to be venereal. The word *lazar* or *leprous* also extended to the kite's prey. According to Harting:

> Although a large bird, and called by some the royal Kite (*milvus regalis*) it has not the bold dash of many of our smaller hawks in seizing live and strong prey, but flies about ignobly, looking for a sickly or wounded victim, or for offal of any sort.

Frequently Shakespeare associated the kite with death or violence. Cassius feels that the kites are hovering about Caesar's murderers, as though they were "sickly prey"; the defeated enemy is a prey for "carrion kites"; Gloucester is said to have been murdered by a kite; Lear calls his daughter a "detested kite" and then invokes Nature to make her sterile. In support of his thesis that the bird is both a breast and penis symbol, Wormhoudt notes various word clusters associated with the kite in Shakespeare's plays and adds:

> we have here a group of images which express the double aspect of the bird symbol. The kite-food refers to bird-breast, kite-bed to bird-penis; kite-death-spirits to the masochistic attachment and aggressive defense directed at breast and penis, that is, to oral and phallic castration. These translations, of course, cannot be applied to specific contexts mechanically, but if taken in the light of each play's total meaning will be seen to be significant.

Among other Renaissance writers the symbolism of the kite varies. Whitney makes the kite the symbol of the greedy man to illustrate the proverb *male parta, male dilabuntur* (badly gotten, badly scattered):

> The greedie kyte, so full his gorge had cloy'de
> He coulde not brooke his late devoured praie:
> Wherefore with griefe, unto his damme hee cry'de,
> My bowelles lo, alas doe waste awaie.
> With that quoth shee, why doste thou make thy mone,
> This losse thou haste is nothinge of thy owne.
> By which is mente, that they who live by spoile,
> By rapine, thefte, or gripinge goodes by mighte,
> If that with losse they suffer anie foile,
> They loose but that, wherein they had no righte?
> Hereof, at firste the proverbe oulde did growe:
> That goodes ill got, awaie as ill will goe.

Ripa, on the other hand, shows a woman holding the helm of a ship in her right hand and a sail in the left while she looks at a kite over her head. Referring to Pliny, Ripa states that the ancients directed the helms of their ships by watching the various movements of the tail of the bird. Valeriano uses the same device for *navigatio* (navigation), but he also makes the bird the symbol of rapacity. In

Swan's *Speculum Mundi* the kite becomes the emblem of an envious person "who rejoiceth in the fall of others." Natural historians of the period support the low opinion of the bird. Both Gesner in 1555 and Aldrovandi in 1599 state that the kite is a symbol of greed and audacity. It is not only in London that the bird snatches food from the hands of children, according to Gesner, but in the towns and cities of England generally. The same statement was made even earlier by Turner.

Alanus, *PL*, 210, col. 435; Albertus Magnus, *Secrets*, p. 58; Aldrovandi, 1, 401; Aristophanes, *Birds*, 865ff; Bartholomew, xii, 27; Bromyard, *Sum. Praed.*, art. 4; Cahier & Martin, ii, 26; Chaucer, *PF*, 349; Cicero, *Q. Fr.* 1.2.2.6; Dante, *Conv.* iv.vi.187–90; Garner, *PL*, 193, col. 82; Gesner, ii.iii.609–14; Gower, *Mirour* 1.914–16; Greene (ed. Grosart), ii, 230–31; iv, 43–44, 61, 132, 314; Harting, p. 43; Holbrook, p. 253; Hudson, pp. 289–90; Isidore, xii.7.58; Jean de Meun, iv.ll.13716–17; Odo of Cheriton, iv, 208–209; Pettie (ed. Hartman), p. 231; Plautus, *Poen.* v.5.13; Pliny, x.xii; Rabanus Maurus, *PL*, 112, col. 999; Ripa, ii.ii.508; Shakespeare, *King Lear* i.iv.253; *Hamlet* ii.ii.563–65; *Henry VI*, pt. 2, iii.i.248–50; iii.ii.191–93; v.ii.11; Sneyd, pp. 10, 62n.10; Swan, p. 395; Theognis, *Frag*, 1302; Thompson, pp. 119–21; Turner, p. 117; Valeriano, ff.129v, 130; Vincent de Beauvais, *Spec. Nat.* xvi.cviii; Whitney, p. 170; Wormhoudt, p. 179.

Lapwing

"A foul and villainous bird" is what Caxton, the first English printer, called the lapwing. This bird owes its reputation to the ingenious tricks it uses to protect its young from predators. "In Wales as a boy," wrote Robert Graves,

> I learned to respect the lapwing for the wonderful way in which she camouflages and conceals her eggs in an open field from any casual passer-by. At first I was fooled every time by her agonized *peewit, peewit*, screamed from the contrary direction to the one in which her eggs lay, and sometimes when she realized that I was a nest-robber she would flap about along the ground, pretending to have a broken wing and inviting capture.

In medieval England the bird's reputation was not improved by the fact that *lapwing* stood for both the hoopoe and the peewit. Tereus, the wicked king of Thrace whose story of rape and involuntary cannibalism is described elsewhere in this book, was turned into a hoopoe. John Gower who retold the story declared that Tereus became a "lappewincke" (hoopoe) because the bird was the "falseste of alle." Chaucer, on the other hand, referred to the native bird as "the false lapwynge, ful of trecherye." A flock of lapwings was called a "deceit of lapwings."

In Europe the bird seems to have had a bad reputation

both in fact and fiction. In France, according to the great naturalist Aldrovandi, women who misbehaved were called lapwings as a sign of reproach. In southern Scotland its screams were said to have betrayed the Covenanters when they were hiding from their pursuers. "To seem the lapwing and to jest tongue from heart" and "To cry most where the nest is not" were proverbial expressions for dissimulation. "A querulous bird" Swan called it in his *Speculum Mundi* (1635). The belief that the lapwing's young were in such haste to be hatched that they ran out of their eggs with part of the shell sticking to their heads gave the bird additional pejorative significance. The expression "shell on its head" became proverbial, and the precocious fledgling was said to symbolize presumption. In Webster's *White Devil*, Brachiano, listening to the youthful boasts of his son, declares: "Forward lapwing! He flies with the shell on 's head!"

The lapwing's protective strategies earned the bird more respect in earlier times. According to the Koran, the bird was the most intelligent of the prophetic birds which attended King Solomon and it guarded his secrets.

Aldrovandi, III, 527; Chaucer, *PF*, 347; Gesner, II.iii.765–66; Gower, *CA*, v,l.6046; Graves, p. 54; *MED*, s.v. lap-wink; Greene (ed. Grosart), III, 78; v, 192–93; IX, 102; X, 77; Lyly, *Euphues* (ed. Arber), II, 214, 416; Nashe (ed. McKerrow), III, 58; Swan, p. 416; Witherby, IV, 396.

Lark

Soaring flight, flute-like song, and inconspicuous appearance have all contributed to making the lark a distinctive literary symbol. Yet it acquired its predominant symbolism as the result of a mistake. The lark is the bird that chants "tirra-lira" at the gates of heaven. Shakespeare and Milton said the lark sang hymns there; Drayton, hallelujahs; Spenser, the liturgical matins. Lyly thought the bird clapped its wings at the same place; Blake declared that the lark was itself a "mighty angel"; Coleridge said that its voice was like one; Wordsworth called it the "ethereal minstrel," singing at heaven's gates; in a Darwinian universe, Elizabeth Barrett Browning could still write of "the holy lark."

These religious connotations accrued as a result of false etymology. Some medieval writers, such as Alexander Neckam, thought that the Latin name for lark, *alauda*, derived from *laus*, meaning praise. They did not realize that *alauda* was of Celtic origin from *al*, meaning high or great, and *aud*, meaning song. The lark, said the Church Fathers, sang hymns of praise to the Creator. A group of larks was called "an exalting of larks." A fifteenth-century English treatise, the *Pilgrimage of the Soul*, states explicitly that larks are birds "that in Latyn han the name of praysyng and of worshepyng, and be called 'alaude' . . .

and purely they prayse God with hire mery song." In the "Devotions of the Fowles," a poem once attributed to Lydgate, the lark sings appropriately of the Ascension; in Jean de Condé's "La Messe des Oisiaus" the larks sing the *Introit*.

Whether the lark was a symbol of joyous gratitude to the divine in more ancient times is uncertain. Lanoe-Villène, noting that the lark was honored on the Isle of Lemnos, consecrated to Hephaestus, conjectures that the bird signified hymns and prayers rising to the throne of the deity. Certainly the lark's association with the divine persisted in folk belief for many centuries. Aldrovandi (1522–1605), the noted natural historian, while pointing out the mistake in derivation, told of the widely accepted belief current in his childhood that every day the lark flew aloft seven times to sing hymns to its Creator.

In addition to being an ardent hymn singer, the lark was the herald of the day. Milton found the bird an appropriate symbol on this account:

> and now the Herald Lark
> Left his ground-nest, high towring to descry
> The morns approach, and greet her with his Song:
> As lightly from his grassy Couch up rose
> Our Saviour.

Even the lark flies down to listen to Orpheus.

98

Milton's morning lark is a *topos* as used by many other poets to indicate time and transitions. It is a device analogous to classical poets' use of rosy-fingered Dawn leaving the couch of Tithonus. As Priscilla Bawcutt observes, "the lark's salutation of the dawn . . . was an ornate and ceremonial way of indicating the time, or in narrative poetry of marking a fresh stage in the action."

The association with the dawn also made the lark a love bird. The Virgin herself is addressed as "O larke of lo[u]e" in Lydgate's "Balade in Commendation of Our Lady." In the secular bird service the lark sang lauds to Venus or the God of Love instead of to the Creator. In the *Court of Love*, a parody of matins and lauds, while the eagle cries "*Venite!*" (come!), the falcon "*Domine, Dominus noster*" (O Lord, Our God), the popinjay "*Celi enarrant*" (the heavens declare), the goldfinch "*Domini est terra*" (the earth is the Lord's), in honor of the God of Love, the lark played its customary role: "laudate! sang the lark with voice full shrill." Like the nightingale, the lark was the bird of lovers, but whereas the nightingale was primarily associated with the night and with the consummation of love, the lark was the bird which brought the dawn and forced the lovers to part. The lark is an *aubade* translated by Dronke plays the traditional role:

Last Tuesday night, in a wood by Béthune,
my love and I went to play

all night by the light of the moon,
until it was day,
and the lark sang 'Beloved, away!'
and he gently replied
'It is not yet light, my adorable one –
so help me Love, the lark has lied!'

Then he drew close, and I did not resist –
he kissed me a good three times,
more than once I also kissed!
(what harm was in this?)
We wished that night hundred times multiplied –
just those words left aside:
'It is not yet light, my adorable one –
so help me Love, the lark has lied!'

The lark not only awakened lovers but tried to get them out of bed. It was in token of the bird's energy, so some scholars have claimed, that Caesar, after his conquest of Gaul, chose the crested lark for the insignia of the superior new legion which he raised there. Alexander Neckam, always anxious to point a moral, spelled out the lesson to be learned from the bird: *Haec igitur avis desides arguit somnolentiae* (This bird reproves the idle for their sleepiness). With good reason, Chaucer called the bird "the bisy larke, messager of day." As such, the bird was the symbol of hope, happiness, and good luck, and found its way into proverbial expressions in many countries.

The caged or trapped bird, on the other hand, was a symbol of suffering humanity. "Didst thou ever see a lark in a cage?" the villain Bosola asks his doomed mistress in Webster's *Duchess of Malfi*:

> Such is the soul in the body; this world is
> like her little turf of grass, and the heaven
> o'er our heads, like her looking-glass, only
> gives us a miserable knowledge of the small
> compass of our prison.

These poignant lines, according to Bridges, were the starting point for Hopkins' "Caged Skylark," but as far as I know a possible significance of Webster's allusion to the lark's looking-glass has not been noted. In Spenser's *Faerie Queene*, the chaste goddess Diana, who had an unfortunate gift for attracting *voyeurs*, saw Faunus peeking at her through a bush; she streaked after him and took him "like darred Larke, not daring up to looke / On her whose sight before so much he sought." Spenser was using a pun here: in addition to its modern meaning, *dare* meant to fascinate, daze, paralyze. A *dare* was a circular board studded with bits of glass which was used to trap larks—hence the expression to *dare* a bird. Hopkins' own phrase, "As a dare gale lark," suggests that he was familiar with the term. Webster appears to imply that humanity is trapped: what the mirror is to the lark so

heaven above is to the soul. John Bunyan, writing in the same century, found the lark's mirror an emblem of "sinful Pleasures." The lark was "a shadow of a saint," and the fowler who used the snare was, needless to say, the Devil. In the nineteenth century, John Ruskin, sociologist, philosopher, and art historian, used the figure more eloquently to attack those who, like Newman in 1845, had rejected the Anglican for the Roman Catholic Church:

> But of all these fatuities, the basest is the being lured
> into the Romanist Church by the glitter of it, like larks
> into a trap by broken glass; to be blown into a change
> of religion by the whine of organ-pipe; stitched into a
> new creed by gold threads on priests' petticoats; jangled
> into a change of conscience by the chimes of the
> belfry.

With the Romantics, the lark became a symbol for various human experiences. The lark in Blake's "Milton" inhabited a landscape of private mythology and was the embodiment of inspiration. Los was poetry and the lark was Los's messenger. Similarly, Wordsworth, Coleridge, and Shelley saw the skylark as the symbol of spiritual transcendence and of creativity in its highest form. In his famous poem, Shelley disclaimed the notion that the skylark was a bird: it was the soul, fully winged, in its totality and perfection as described in Plato's *Phaedrus*; it was also the symbol of the poet and an apostrophe to the power of poetry itself. Implicit in the poem is the contrast between the joy of the spirit of the ideal poet embodied in the bird and the unhappiness of the earthly poet despairing of man's regeneration. In Hopkins' "The Sea and the Sky-lark" the skylark is one of the symbols of eternity: the joyous song of the lark and the unchanging sound of the tide are contrasted with the ephemeral condition of man.

A different tradition which associated the lark with Scylla—who, according to Ovid, betrayed her father and was turned into a ciris—did not have much currency. This tradition, as Droulers points out, made the lark the symbol of treason. Henry Peacham, however, likened the mavis and the lark, "who cheerily warbled their delicious strains," to vain pleasure seekers. He considers they would have done better to be like the turtledove and withdraw to "shadows and solitariness." Mrs. Beeton, the famous cookery expert, preferred to have larks baked in a pie, and today millions of larks that sang all summer long on the English downs are snuffed out by trappers on the sand dunes of Les Landes and sold as gastronomic delicacies on European markets.

The crested lark, *chalaundre* in Middle English and *chala[u]ndre* in Old French, probably gets its name, so Littré suggested, from Latin *calautica*, meaning "head-dress," with reference to the bird's crest. This bird should not be confused with the *caladrius* or *charadrius*, a bird of different feather that sings like a thrush, perches on the beds of invalids, and makes a diagnosis with a speed and infallibility unknown in the medical profession. The lark which we have been describing had no power to cure jaundice or to tell by a look whether a sick man would die. It was the soul itself, joyous and immortal.

Albertus Magnus, *Animal.* II.1443; Aldrovandi, II, 831; Allen, p. 603; Blake, "Milton," II.xxxv, xxxvi, 36; Browning, "Aurora Leigh," i.l.953; Chaucer, *KnT*, 1491; Coleridge, "The Ancient Mariner," l.365; "Fears in Solitude", *Court of Love*, pp. 445–47, esp. l.1415; *Devotions of the Fowls*, pp. 6–7; Drayton, *Noah's Flood*, l. 397; Dronke, p. 182; Droulers, p. 10; Harrison, *They Tell of Birds*, p. 71; Hopkins, p. 455; Harting, pp. 132–36; "La Messe des Oisiaus," p. 1; Lanoe-Villène, s.v. *l'alouette*; Lydgate (ed. Norton-Smith), p. 27; Lyly, *Alex & Campaspe* v.i; *MED*, s.v. *larke / lerke / laverok*; Milton, *PR* ii.279–82; Neilson, pp. 216–17; *OED*, s.v. *dare*, v. 2, 5; Neckam, p. 115; Ovid, *Met*. VIII.11ff; Peacham, p. 110; *Pilgrimage of the Soul*, 5.1.87a; Pliny, XI.xliv; Ruskin, *Stones of Venice*, I, append. 12; Shakespeare, *Cymbeline* II.iii.22; Spenser, *Epith*. 80; *FQ*, VII.vi.47; Webster, *Duchess of Malfi* IV.ii.127ff; Wordsworth, "To A Skylark"; "Gold and Silver Fishes in a Vase."

Magpie

"No other bird," observes one ornithologist, "has such a look of infinite cunning and devilment." Despite the magpie's handsome appearance, its dazzling combination of snowy white and black, shot through with iridescent green, purple, and red, the expression "flekked as a pie" (spotted or variegated like a magpie) seems to have had unpleasant connotations even in Chaucer's day. The predominant trait which contributed to the bird's evil reputation appears to have been its ability to talk. Not that it was thought to talk well. Oliver Goldsmith declared that "its songs were too thin and sharp to be an exact imitation of the human voice" and that sometimes its tongue was cut in an effort to improve its speech. It was said to have been the only bird which refused to enter the Ark, preferring instead to perch on the roof and gabble over the drowning world. In ancient Rome its vocal reputation was perpetuated in the legend of the nine sisters called the Pierides who challenged the Muses to a singing contest. So objectionable were they when they were judged the losers that they were turned into magpies as a punishment.

Magpies are not liked by everyone.

102

They looked at each other, watching their faces narrow into horny beaks, as a new addition was made to the birds of the forest. When they tried to beat their breasts, the movement of their arms raised them, to hover in the air. They had become magpies, the scandalmongers of the woods. Even now, as birds, they still retain their original power of speech. They still chatter harshly and have an insatiable desire to talk.

In Rome also the bird was sacred to Bacchus and therefore was a symbol of drunkenness and garrulity. Its verbosity, especially its tattle-telling, entered into folktales and became proverbial. The word *gazette* probably derives from dialectal Venetian, *gazeta*: a coin, originally the price of the publication. But claims have been made that the newspaper or *gazzetta*, inasmuch as it divulges secrets, must derive from *gazza*, the Italian for magpie. To medieval writers women were "pies" because of their "jangling," and a babbler of either sex was a "pie." *Plus jangleresse qu'une pie* or *garrulior pica* (more garrulous than a pie) were common expressions. A whole group of poems appeared at the end of the thirteenth century entitled "De la Femme et de la Pie." In one of the most spirited of these, edited by Jubinal, the woman and the magpie are assailed as vain, gossipy, proud, argumentative, and vengeful, and always looking for personal profit. Even their jealousy is blameworthy. Just as the magpie spies on its mate wherever it goes, so the wife also:

Espie son mary
Par gelosie qu'ele a . . . .

(Spies on her husband
Because of her jealousy . . . .)

Chaucer's use of the comparison is more lighthearted. The merchant's wife who is seduced by a monk is as "jolif" as a pie; the Wife of Bath describes herself as being "joly" as a pie, and the miller's wife is described as being proud and pert as a pie. The unpleasant cackling magpie is alluded to only once. Ornithologists seem to agree that magpies are not as faithful as turtledoves, and, according to Wood, if one magpie of a pair is shot, the survivor never fails to find another mate within two or three days. "Sometimes the period of widowhood exists only for some twenty-four hours, and there have been instances where a magpie has found another mate within a few hours after the decease of its former spouse." The association of the magpie with women is seen in the name itself. Originally it was a pie (Latin *pica*). The prefix is an abbreviation of Margaret. Maggot and Madge are among the names given in England to the pie; in France, Margot and Jacquette.

The magpie's incorrigible addiction to pilfering has no doubt contributed to its unpopularity. It is an audacious robber of other birds' nests, driving its bill through their eggs to carry them away, or pulling out their unfledged young. It will tackle all kinds of small household objects.

103

Wood gives an account of a tame magpie which carried off the reading glasses from the nose of an elderly gentleman who had fallen asleep. Persecuted for its kleptomania, the bird altered its habits early in this century, according to Newton. Instead of being "the merry, saucy hanger-on of the homestead," it became "the suspicious thief, shunning the gaze of man, and knowing that danger may lurk in every bush." Gunston, however, writing more recently, stated that the trend had reversed: "where one or two were seen in the past, five or six now occur in all their conspicuous arrogance." The bird's compulsive thievery appears to have given rise to the medical term *pica*, a craving for unusual foods, not uncommon in pregnancy. This female complaint had already been given a technical name in ancient Greek medicine. It was called *kissa*, apparently deriving from the chattering, mimicking, and greedy bird of the same name which Liddell and Scott identify as the jay.

The bird's characteristics contributed to its being regarded almost universally as a symbol of ill-omen. In Scotland the magpie was known as the Devil's bird, and a magpie flying near a window portended death. "Trust not the pie's chattering—many men are deceived thereby . . . . Put not your trust in witchcraft. Whenever it is true, that is merely through the Devil's craft to make men believe what is hateful to God," said Robert of Brunne in 1303. In Germany witches rode on magpies' tails; in Perth-shire until the end of the eighteenth century magpies were believed to have the power to transform themselves into human form. Unless you were in Yorkshire where you crossed your thumbs to avert the magpie's evil, you should wear a hat; on meeting a magpie in Sussex you raised your hat and bowed; in the West Country you spat on it. The number of magpies you saw was important too, and there were many rhymes about it. According to J.H. Owen, the rhyme in Wales was:

> One for sorrow, two for joy,
> Three for a burying, four for a wedding.

Armstrong who gives this information provides a curious addendum: "Mr. Owen's brother-in-law, a highly qualified doctor, always saluted any magpie he might see on his rounds." Perhaps this polite physician was thinking of the bird's knowledge of herbs. The magpie, like the woodpecker, used a special herb to uncover its nest, should the entrance be blocked. Albertus Magnus stated rather cryptically that the herb was useful "to loosen bonds" and gave instructions how to attain it:

> Go into the wood, and look where the Pie has her nest
> with her birds, and when thou shalt be there, climb up
> the tree, and bind about the hole of it wheresoever thou
> wilt. For when she seeth thee she goest for a certain herb,
> which she will put to the binding, and it is broken
> anon and that herb falleth to the ground upon the cloth,

which thou shouldst have put under the tree, and be thou present and take it.

In the Vedic hymns, the magpie was associated with disease, according to Gubernatis. The association was persisted in folklore, possibly strengthened by the fact that the magpie does have a knack of smelling out a lurking sickness and will attack and tear out the eyes of an ailing sheep or lamb. Perhaps this association as well as a reputation for greed and gossip contributed to making the bird a symbol of dissipation and vanity. As such, it appears in Flemish paintings of the sixteenth century. In those of Jerome Bosch, the caged magpie is a symbol of the *maison close*. On the other hand, according to Ripa, a young woman holding a magpie represented docility: "In a domestick state, the magpie is said to be a more docile bird than any of the feathered tribe, and is not only easily taught to imitate the human voice but delights in it." The Chinese regarded the bird with similar favor. It was said to be a bird of joy and sacred to the Manchus. The chattering of magpies before a house indicated the imminent arrival of guests.

Martial, the Roman satirist, made the magpie the symbol of the poet: "I, a loquacious magpie, greet you with intelligible speech, my lord, and were you not to see me you would refuse to believe that I was a bird." According to the bestiaries, magpies were like poets because they could imitate words in a distinct voice like men. Hanging from tree branches, they chattered annoyingly. If they were unable to speak they could at least copy the sounds of the human voice. At the present time, when anyone with sufficient presumption and flair for public relations can be a poet, surely such an appropriate symbolism should be revived.

Albertus Magnus, *Secrets*, p. 99; Armstrong, *Folklore*, p. 243; Chaucer, *CYT*, 565; *Tr*, iii.527; *RvT*, 3950; *ShipT*, 1399; *WB Prol*, 456; *PF*, 345; *MerchT*, 1848; *De Bestiis*, *PL*, 177, cols. 95–96; Gesner, ii.iii.698; Goldsmith, ii, 97–98; Gubernatis, ii, 258; Gunston, pp. 338–41; Jennison, p. 118; Jubinal (ed.), ii, 326–29; Latham, p. 9; Liddell & Scott, s.v. Κίσσα; Martial, xiv.76; Matheolus, ii.52; Newton, *EB.*, xvii, 393; Ovid, *Met.* v. ll. 300–678; Pliny, x.xxxxi, lix; Ripa (ed. Richardson), p. 97; Robert of Brunne, pp. 12–17; *Seven Sages of Rome*, ll. 2193–2292; Swainson, p. 76; Swann, p. 151; Thompson, pp. 146–48; Williams, p. 228; Witherby, i, 26; Wood, *An. Creat.*, iii, 303–304; Wulff, pp. 117–19.

Nightingale

Among those jolly songs that English ex-undergraduates like to sing as they gather round the piano and clink mugs of strong ale is one about a young man who invites his girl to come out and

> Hear the fond tale
> Of the sweet nightingale
> As she sings in the valley
> Be-low! O-O-O! O-O-O! O-O-O!
> As she sings in the valley be-low!

The form of this song is really very old. It is a *demande d'amour*: the young man asks and the young woman refuses. The persistency of his request and her uncompromising rejoinder tell us that this invitation has more to it than Tennyson's simple injunction to Maud to come into the garden now that the black bat, night, had flown. Listening to the nightingale is a euphemism, a euphemism which in a cruder age has been replaced by a four-letter word.

The beautiful young wife in a twelfth-century verse romance by Marie de France listened to the nightingale. She was married to an old man and fell in love with a handsome knight who was her neighbor. Unable to meet, the two looked longingly at each other from their windows, and she knew that her passion was returned. One night her husband woke up as she was going to the window and asked what she was doing. She replied that she had a passionate desire to hear the nightingale sing. The husband flew into a rage; he got up, caught a nightingale, and wrung its neck in his wife's presence. Sorrowfully she sent the little bird to her lover in secret. He put it in a small, jeweled casket which he carried with him wherever he went. They both knew that the death of the nightingale meant the end of their love. The nightingale's song symbolized sexual happiness. Nearly two centuries later Boccaccio was more explicit. In one of the stories of the *Decameron* a young girl, Caterina, wants to meet her lover secretly. She asks her parents to let her sleep on the balcony to enable her *udir cantar l'usignuolo* (to listen to the nightingale). Here the phrase is a humorous euphemism for making love, and the nightingale itself is finally identified with the male organ. The last meaning, according to Farmer in his *Vocabula Amatoria*, persisted in the French underworld to the late nineteenth century.

As a symbol the nightingale is complex. The love with which it is traditionally identified may be unhappy or happy. Associated with the ancient story of rape and revenge, the bird sings a lament; associated with the spring and the May morning, the nightingale sings simply of happy love; associated with the poet, it can express either personal ecstasy or pain; in a further meaning, exclusive to the Middle Ages and directly opposed to the secular interpretation already illustrated, the nightingale sings of Christ's death and resurrection and is itself the symbol of the greatest love.

"Why should I speak of the nightingale? The nightingale sings of adulterous wrong," said King Edward III, who was planning to seduce a married countess. The adulterous wrong done to the nightingale is gruesomely recounted by Homer, Virgil, and others. In Ovid's version, Tereus, king of Thrace, raped his sister-in-law Philomela and tore out her tongue in order that his wife Progne should not learn what had happened. Philomela managed to tell her story by weaving a tapestry depicting the rape. Progne avenged herself on her husband by serving up her son Itys *en casserole*. Finally the gods intervened; Tereus was turned into a kite, hoopoe or lapwing, Progne into a swallow, and Philomela into a nightingale. Some medieval interpreters took the tale as a reminder of the dangers of love and, like members of an old-fashioned vice squad, regarded Philomela less as a victim than as a temptation to sexual love. The attitude is most obvious in *Ovide Moralisé*, a twelfth-century allegory of the myth. Progne is the soul, Tereus the body, their son Itys *le bon fruyt de sainte vie* (the good fruit of a holy life), while Philomela stands for the world and its pleasures. Progne longs to see her sister and sends Tereus for her, but he cannot resist her because she signifies *amour decevable et faille* (deceitful and treacherous love). We find a similarly censorious tone in less didactic works, where the nightingale is a symbol of incitement to lust rather than of betrayed virtue. The nightingale in the twelfth-century bird debate "The Owl and the Nightingale" appears to be

107

The nightingale brings dreams of lust.

the symbol of earthly pleasures. Whether the poem is also a political satire with King Henry II as the nightingale and Thomas à Becket as the owl is open to question, but certainly the nightingale maintains her erotic associations, and the owl eloquently condemns her for encouraging lust and adultery. The same Philomela, though more contrite, appears in the poem by Chaucer's contemporary, John Gower. The reddish markings on the plumage of the nightingale are blushes of shame, and the nightingale's traditional song of *oci, oci!* (usually interpreted as kill, kill!) becomes a lament for lost virginity:

> Oh why
> Why ne were I yet a maid!

Despite the fact that the male bird is the singer, this myth made her female, and in numerous poems it is the female nightingale who sings, especially when a young woman is succumbing to love. Chaucer's heroine, the young widow Criseyde about to fall in love with Prince Troilus, hears the nightingale sing "a lay / of love, that made her herte [heart] fresh and gay." When she consummates her love she becomes the nightingale, timid at first and then, as she gains confidence, making "hire vois out rynge." The same nightingale is often depicted as singing with a thorn against her breast. Possibly the idea began in Persian poetry where the nightingale is associated with the rose. Thus Hafiz writes:

> At dawn, the Nightingale said to the East Wind,
> "How I suffer with yearning for the cheek of a rose!
> Because of that cheek's hue, the blood gathers in my heart;
> As I cling to the rose tree, I am pierced by the point of
> a thorn."

John Lydgate was one of the earliest English poets to mention the thorn, but by the sixteenth century the prick of the thorn carried obvious sexual implications. Pliny had said that the nightingale often died at the end of its song, and this dying was used in the traditional metaphorical sense to mean coition. The myth of Tereus's violation was still responsible for the theme, and the *jug, jug*, which turns up as a refrain in many of these poems was, as T.S. Eliot declared, "a song for dirty ears." The Elizabethan poet Gascoigne spent more than a hundred lines explaining the meaning of the syllables which he claimed to hear in the bird's song. Jug was for *jugum* (the yoke of matrimony broken by Tereus) or for *jugulator* (the murderer, Progne). John Lyly in *Alexander and Campaspe* (1584) tells the story of the nightingale in five lines:

> What bird so sings, yet so does wail?
> Oh, 'tis the ravished nightingale.
> *Jug, jug, jug, jug, Tereu!* she crys,
> And still her woes at midnight rise. Brave prick-song!

Barnabe Barnes is wittier and briefer:

> I'll sing my Plain Song with the turtle dove
> And Prick Song with the nightingale rehearse.

There were many happy nightingales in early English poetry, singing to the point of exhaustion as heralds of Maytime and love. "Merry as a nightingale" was a stock phrase. Nevertheless, from early times, the bird's song was often called melancholy, a veiled allusion, in Thompson's

108

opinion, to the melancholy seasonal ritual associated with Adonis or Atys. To the good Christian, the idea of the song as a dirge foreboding the singer's death cried out for some kind of allegorical interpretation. Garrod, wrongly in my view, thought that Aldhelm regarded the bird as prophetic of death and resurrection. Many centuries later, however, two poems by John Lydgate, apparently based on a Latin poem by John Peckham which had many imitations, show an elaborate development of the nightingale's symbolism. The prose introduction describes how the nightingale before her death flies to a treetop and there, at the hours of divine service, *prime, tierce, sexte,* and *nones,* sings mournful notes. She dies in the tree at *nones.* These songs are meant to commemorate Christ's passion. The poem concludes by spelling out the allegory:

> this nyghtingale, that thus freshly can
> Bothe wake and singe, as telleth us scripture,
> Is Crist hym-self ande every cristen-man . . . .

In Lydgate's second poem, the nightingale, like Philomela, sings *oci, oci*! but her cry is not for vengeance on false lovers or rapists but on those who do not appreciate Christ's salvation. In other religious lyrics the nightingale sings praises to God, personifies man's soul, or is the Virgin Mary herself, as Dunbar declares:

> Hail, glorious Virgin, hail . . .
> Hail, gentle nightingale!

The nightingale sings as she sits on her eggs.

In some bestiaries, the nightingale singing incessantly in forest and garden is the soul waiting throughout the night for the coming of the Lord; or the nightingale sitting on her eggs, warbling while she works, is the poor but honest wife singing as she toils at her spinning to get bread for her infants.

To the Greeks, as Garrod pointed out, nightingale and

poet had the same name, *aedon* or singer, and in the choruses of their tragedies, the nightingale was "the stock symbol of unassuaged grief." Centuries later both values are combined in Keats's magnificent ode. The immortal song of the bird that

> Charmed magic casements, opening on the foam
> Of perilous sea in faery lands forlorn,

becomes that of the heartsick poet. To him and to other romantics, the nightingale was above all the creative experience of the dedicated artist. "A poet is a nightingale," said Shelley,

> who sits in darkness and sings to cheer its own solitude with song; his auditors are as men entranced by the melody of an unseen musician, who feel that they are moved and softened, yet know not when or why.

Yet the nightingale continues to be associated with grief rather than with gladness. Elizabeth Browning's *Bianca*, the victim of unhappy love, attacks the nightingale's song with surprising ferocity:

> Oh, owl-like birds! They sing for hate, they sing for
> doom,
> They'll sing through death who sing through night,
> They'll sing and spurn me in the tomb –
> The nightingales, the nightingales!

T.S. Eliot's nightingales singing near the convent of the Sacred Heart are even more sinister. Perhaps they are those two strange young women who fiddle with their stockings or tear grapes with murderous paws earlier in the poem. Like Philomela they are associated with death, for in the end "their liquid siftings fall / To stain the stiff dishonoured shroud." Or should we apply the meaning for nightingale given by that military gentleman Captain Francis Grose in 1785?

> It is a point of honour in some regiments, among the grenadiers, never to cry out or become nightingales while under the discipline of the cat-of-nine-tails; to avoid which, they chew a bullet.

Are these nightingales informers, revealing secrets that put an end forever to the laughter of ape-necked Sweeney? The sense of nightingale as "squealer" is still current; it may even have been current in Chaucer's day: when the Wife of Bath boasts that she could sing like a nightingale after drinking a draught of sweet wine she may have been thinking less of her musical talents than of her tittle-tattling about her fourth husband who was not only a "revelour" but "had a paramour." In their *Dictionary of Slang*, Farmer and Henley give yet another meaning for nightingale which may also be relevant. They regard the bird as a synonym for "barrack hack" and "tart."

The song of the nightingale is still admired. In the last

century the famous singer Jenny Lind delighted in the title "The Swedish Nightingale." But, like everything else, nightingales are not what they used to be. Pliny tells of two nightingales who spoke fluent Latin and Greek, and Gubernatis with a somewhat vague reference to the *Ornithologus* writes of two nightingales which, in 1546 at Ratisbon, disputed as to which of them spoke the best German. Even the famous thorn at the breast, whether it represented the pangs of love to the nightingale as lover or, as Hawkins claimed, the passion of Christ to the nightingale as the Virgin, may not be what it seemed. Hawkins' contemporary, Sir Thomas Browne, was already asking "whether the nightingale's sitting with her breast against a thorn be any more than that she placeth some prickles on the outside of her nest, or roosteth in thorny and prickly places, where serpents may least approach her," and since that time zoologists have claimed to find a thorn not only in the nest of the nightingale but in that of a sparrow—no doubt the result of accident rather than design.

Aldhelm, *Aenigmata*, xxii; Armstrong, p. 247n; Baldwin, pp. 207–29; Boccaccio, v, 4; Browne, *Pseudodoxia*, iii.xxviii; Cahier & Martin, ii, 159; Chandler, "The Nightingale," *passim*; *Larks, passim*; *Chant du Roussigneul, passim*; *De Bestiis, PL*, 177, col. 96; Clanvowe, p. 232; Du Méril, *Poésies Pop.*, p. 278; Garrod, pp. 134, 136; *Gesta*, clxvii; Gower, *CA*, v, ll. 5551–6047; Grose, s.v. *nightingale*; Gu-bernatis, ii, 236; Harting, p. 127; Hawkins, p. 151; Lampe, "Tradition," p. 52; Lazar, p. 185; Lydgate, *Minor Poems*, pp. 4, 5, 19; Marie de France, pp. 146–51; Neckam, pp. 102–103; Ovid, *Met.* vi. 412–674; *Ovide Moralisé*, vi, 2217–3840; Peckham, *Analecta Hymnica*, l. 602ff; Pliny, x.xliii, lix; Raby, pp. 435–48; Shippey, p. 60; Swainson, pp. 18–22; Telfer, pp. 25–34; Thompson, pp. 16–22, 30–31.

Ostrich

Those indiscriminate hearty eaters in TV commercials have probably never heard of "ostrich stomach," the proverbial expression which might accurately describe their remarkable digestive powers. Yet the ostrich's capacity to swallow rocks, metal, and other objects to aid its gizzard, in addition to its other curious traits, has singled it out for many curious symbolic interpretations. The most common representation shows a long-legged bird with an iron nail or horseshoe hanging from its beak, and even comparatively recently in Britain this figure, symbolizing an excellent digestion, advertised a beer with the well-known slogan "Guinness is good for you!"

In earlier times, the symbolism deriving from the bird's dietary habits varied. Gluttony is depicted by the head of an ostrich in a representation of the Seven Deadly Sins

The ostrich covers its eggs with sand.

in the form of the apocalyptic beast on a stained-glass window of St. Nizier at Trier. In the Renaissance, Ripa also assigned the bird to *Gula*, gluttony, in one of his emblems. On the other hand, its symbolism was favorable

in heraldry. The ostrich, collared, chained, and holding a nail in its beak, was the badge of Queen Anne, wife of Richard II, and, as Nichols observes, is depicted on the gown of the effigy in Westminster Abbey. The bird with nails, key, and horseshoe was also the crest of the King of Hungary and of Bohemia. Here the bird appears to have symbolized the appetite of the valiant warrior for the cold steel of battle, a meaning perhaps influenced by the fact that the German for ostrich, *Strauss*, also means a fight or scuffle.

In the Renaissance, the association of valor or endurance was applied in a more general sense. In the *Sententiosa Imprese* of Giovio and Symeoni the nail-eating bird was festooned with a scroll which read *spiritus durissima coquit* (courage digests the hardest things). The explanatory verse runs:

> *Divora il struzzo con ingorda furia*
> *Il ferro & lo smaltisce poi pian piano,*
> *Cosi . . .*
> *Smaltir fa il tempo ogni maggiore ingiuria*

> (Devour does the ostrich with eager greediness
> The iron, and then very easily digests it,
> So . . .
> Time causes every injury to be digested.)

Camerarius gave a different meaning: *magno animo fortis perferre pericula suevit, / Ullo nec facile frangitur ille metu* (the brave man with a great spirit grows accustomed to endure dangers. Nor is that man easily broken by fear).

Other facts of natural history gave rise to further symbolic interpretation. The ostrich digs her nest in the sand, and of her clutch of twenty-five eggs she is only able to hatch about fifteen. Occasionally the female leaves the nest during the day and covers the eggs with sand, allowing the sun to do the hatching. A verse in Job xxxix.13–16 attributed this habit to forgetfulness: "God has made her forget wisdom." To the early Christian Fathers this ostrich stood for dilatory preachers, the synagogue, and *simulatores* (hypocrites). The ostrich's supposed negligence was made a fact of natural history:

> The wings of the ostrich wave proudly, but are they the pinions and plumage of love? . . . For she leaves her eggs to the earth, and lets them be warmed on the ground, forgetting that a foot may crush them, and the wild beasts may trample them. . . . She deals cruelly with her young, as if they were not hers; though her labor be in vain, yet she has no fear; because God has made her forget wisdom, and given her no share in understanding.

In the bestiaries, on the other hand, the forgetfulness of the ostrich was praiseworthy, indicating that the bird's mind was on higher things. *Li ostriche est example del home qui vit en carite, et est paciens et humles* (The ostrich is an example of a man who lives in charity, and is patient and humble). Some writers combined Job's verse with pre-Vulgate reading of Jeremiah viii.7, *et 'asida' in celo cognovit tempus suum* (the ostrich in the heavens knows its time). They continued: *Quanto magis nos oportet agnoscere tempus nostrum, et elevare oculos cordis nostri semper ad caelum, obliviscere que terrena et sequere caelestia?* (How much more ought we to know our time and to raise the eyes of our heart always to the sky and forget earthly things and follow the celestial?). Others took the ostrich's unusual parturition as a figure for Christ descending to Hell and freeing the souls from Purgatory or regarded the ostrich eggs hatched by the heat of the sun as the image of Christ revived by God the Father. This last interpretation, according to Réau, accounts for the appearance of ostrich eggs in certain churches between Holy Wednesday and Easter morning. Durandus, on the other hand, gives a different explanation for the same custom, which was probably introduced by Crusaders who had seen the eggs hanging in Turkish Mosques:

> Again, some say that the ostrich, as being a forgetful bird, "leaveth her eggs in the dust" and at length, when she beholdeth a certain star, returneth unto them, and cheereth them by her presence. Therefore the eggs of ostriches are hung in churches to signify that man, being left of God on account of his sins, if at length he be illuminated by the Divine Light, remembereth his faults

and returneth to Him, Who by looking on him with His Mercy cherisheth him. As it is written in Luke that after Peter had denied Christ, the "Lord turned and looked upon Peter." Therefore be the aforesaid eggs suspended in churches, this signifying, that man easily forgetteth God, unless being illuminated by a star, that is, by the influence of the Holy Spirit, he is reminded to return to Him by good works.

According to Evans, the ostrich's same incubatory habits, when translated into secular terms, symbolized life-giving inspiration.

Other characteristics attributed to the ostrich gave rise to a pejorative symbolism. The ostrich does not, in fact, bury its head in the sand as is popularly believed; when alerted to danger, the bird puts its head flat on the ground to inspect the source. Nevertheless, its reputation for cowardice, as well as its occasional failure to hatch eggs, made it a symbol of the sin of Sloth and of the idle person. In an emblem ascribed to Ripa the ostrich appears with a young girl who is caressing two doves. The white doves were a symbol of simplicity of manners, and Ripa's translator explained the appearance of the ostrich thus: "[The ostrich] is emblematical of that simplicity of spirit, which participates a little of imbecillity, as it is affirmed by naturalists, that when this large bird is chased, it covers its head in the reeds, and then thinks itself all out of sight." Equally reprehensible was the bird's failure to become airborne. To Richard Rolle, an early fourteenth-century hermit who was very friendly with the nuns of Hampole in Yorkshire, the ostrich which, despite its wings, could not fly symbolized the man weighed down with "affeccyons and othire vanytes." Making a similar point, Whitney showed the bird standing with wings outspread, poised as if ready for flight. Here the bird was the symbol of hypocrisy, as it had been to Rabanus Maurus in the ninth century and Neckam in the twelfth century and to others:

> The Hippocrites, that make so great a showe,
> Of Sanctitie, and of Religion sounde,
> Are shaddowes meere, and without substance goe,
> And beinge tri'de, are but dissemblers founde.
> Theise are compar'de, unto the Ostriche faire,
> Whoe spreades her wings, yet sealdome tries the aire.

Great importance has been attached to the feathers of the ostrich. In ancient Egypt the feather was the constant symbol of the goddess of justice and truth. Sometimes the goddess was represented by a woman with an ostrich feather in place of her head. According to Horapollo, the feather of an ostrich symbolized a man who distributed justice impartially, "for this bird has the feathers of its wings equal on every side, beyond all other birds." In the room of Constantine in the Vatican, an ostrich accompanies Justice. Ripa gives Justice the same emblem not only because of its feathers which signify impartiality, but also because "the ostrich ruminates its food as Justice should the testimony put before her."

Ostrich feathers have been important in English heraldry. They were a royal badge from the time of their introduction in the fourteenth century. Edward III used an ostrich feather on one of his seals, and Queen Philippa had a silver alms dish with an ostrich feather enameled at the bottom, possibly deriving from her association with the House of Hainault. Three feathers also appeared on the shield upon the monument of the Black Prince in Canterbury Cathedral. Associated with the feathers were the mottoes *Ich Dien* and *Houmout*, signifying noble service and magnanimity. The coroneted plume of three ostrich feathers has been regarded as the special badge of the Prince of Wales from the Stewarts to the present day. *Ostrich*, the name of an inn at Colnbrook, Bucks, is a corruption of *Hospice* which, in the twelfth century, was a monastic guesthouse intended for the "welfare of man in this life and his salvation in the next." When Hounslow Heath became such a notorious hunting ground for cutthroats that many crimes went undetected, the original lofty purpose of the inn was forgotten. Selected guests were given a special bed which was placed on a trapdoor above the kitchen. In the dead of night the innkeeper released the latch and the sleeping guest would slide quietly down into a cauldron of boiling liquid. Some sixty met their death by this method. If they were, as was rumored,

brewed into ale, the customers must indeed have had "ostrich stomachs."

d'Ayzac, p. 27; *Best. Divin.*, pp. 272–74; Boutell, pp. 237–44; Cahier & Martin, ii, 197; iii, 260, 261; Camerarius, iii.xix; Chew, p. 138; Durandus, i.iii.43; Evans, p. 94; Garner, *PL*, 193, col. 79; Giovio & Symeoni, p. 115; Gregory, *PL*, 76, cols. 578–84, 593–94; Ham (ed.), p. 236; Horapollo, p. 158; *Medallic Illus.*, iii, 133; Nichols, p. 48; Rabanus Maurus, *PL*, 112, cols. 1061–62; Réau, i.128; Ripa, i.i.182; (tr. Richardson), i.95; Rolle, i, 194; Vincent of Beauvais, *Spec. Nat.* xvi.cxxxviii–cxl.

Owl

It is the wise old owl which has survived into this century. Even the term "owlish," while not intended to flatter, hints at studiousness or at least specious intelligence. Yet all over the world the owl has also been the *avis turpissima*, the most evil bird of all, the prophet of doom, associated with death and evil spirits. The dual symbolism goes back to antiquity.

Early symbolism stressed the owl's sagacity. The bird was highly esteemed in Athens where it was the attribute of Pallas Athene, the goddess of wisdom. The owl's luminous eyes, its ability to remain awake at night and to see in the dark were indications of its supernatural powers. The little owl, *glaux* or *noctua*, was so called because of its glaring eyes, and when Homer described Athene as *glaucopis*, he probably meant fierce-eyed or flashing-eyed rather than the color grey or greenish. On early Athenian coins a chubby, smiling goddess with a plain helmet appeared with a well-groomed, self-confident owl. When the Athenians defeated the Persians at the battle of Marathon in 490 B.C., they thought that Athene flew over them in the guise of an owl. They subsequently depicted the goddess on a large silver coin with her helmet decorated with olive leaves. The owl of Marathon, open winged as though just taking flight, occupied the whole reverse side of the coin. During the period between the Persian and the Peloponnesian wars, when Athens was dominant, the silver mines in the Laureotic regions produced a spate of various coins, and all but the smallest had owls on them. As Seltman observed:

> The mixed sizes of these owls and their varied attitudes are attractive, especially when you consider that the Little Owl lays eggs over a fair period and "staggers" the hatching, so that a nestful of these birds contains owl-chicks of various ages and sizes. This gives point to a neat passage in *The Birds* of Aristophanes. Promises of prosperity are made to the Athenians in the words:

> Little Laureotic owlets
> Shall be always flocking in:
> You shall find them all about you,
> As the dainty brood increases,
> Building nests within your purses;
> Hatching little silver pieces.

"There goes an owl" became proverbial to denote success, and many years later, in 310, Agathocles of Syracuse released large numbers of owls to encourage his warriors to defeat the Carthaginians in Africa. Another proverbial expression used to denote a useless gift was "to carry owls to Athene"; Athene had so many owls that more would be superfluous. The Athenians were so closely identified with the owl that, according to Plutarch, the Samians, taking advantage of a temporary victory, branded the foreheads of their Athenian prisoners with the figure of an owl.

The bird's reputed sagacity and occult powers also caused it to be used for magical purposes. According to ancient belief an owl's heart applied to the left breast of a sleeping woman would persuade her to reveal all her secrets. This belief was not only repeated by Albertus Magnus in the twelfth century but appeared in a modified form in *The Long Hidden Friend*, a strange work published in Pennsylvania in 1863. For centuries, the owl was associated with various pharmaceutical preparations. An owl's heart hung above the head was believed to restore the memory; its eggs induced sobriety. According to Swan's *Speculum Mundi* (1635), "Some say that the egges of an Owl broken and put into the cup of a drunkard . . . will so work on him that he will suddenly lothe his good liquour and be displeased with drinking."

The same occult powers also caused the owl to be regarded primarily as a portent of evil. The owl's natural characteristics, its sudden pounce on its victims, its eerie cry, its preference for darkness, and the carrion smell of its nest made it the sinister messenger of the death goddesses. One of the most notable of these was the Mesopotamian goddess Lilith who was winged, bird-footed, and accompanied by owls. The Romans regarded the bird as a bad omen, foretelling death. Virgil said that an owl hooted from the top of the temple before Dido's suicide. Pliny, without any scepticism on this occasion, told of the consternation in Rome when an owl appeared in the forum. Horace associated the owl with witchcraft and described the use of owl's feathers in incantations; Ovid's Medea put the flesh and wings of the same bird in a ghoulish potion which turned Jason's father into a young man. In China and some Eastern countries the owl was believed to suck the blood like a vampire. When someone was about to die in a Chinese village, the voice of the owl was heard calling "dig, dig!," urging that the grave be made ready. Some said that the bird took away the soul. According to

Horapollo, the sparrow, when pursued by other birds, mistakenly turned to the owl for help. Therefore the ancient Egyptians depicted a sparrow and an owl to represent a man who fled to his patron for assistance but received none. Even to dream of an owl was unlucky: according to Artemidorus, a soothsayer living in the second century A.D., whose book on dream symbolism has been carefully studied by many psychologists including Freud, the traveler who dreamed of an owl would either be shipwrecked or mugged.

Except for the kind of owl called the *nycticorax*, the bird was wholly evil to the Church Fathers. The common view was that the owl signified the Jews who rejected Christ. This unfavorable symbolism applied not only to the *bubo*, depicted as a heavily feathered, slothful bird which hovered around tombs and lived in caves, polluting them with its dung, but to the *noctua*, an owl which derived its name from its night flight, and to *ulula*, the screech owl. As a symbol of the Jews preferring the darkness of error to the illumination of the Gospels, the owl appeared in miniatures, paintings, and carvings on Romanesque capitals and misericords. In some of these representations the bird was tormented by sparrows or doves, birds which, in this instance, symbolized the righteous Christians. Sometimes the owl appeared in scenes of the Crucifixion. At the foot of the Cross in the *Antwerp Crucifixion* by Antonello da Messina (1430–79), for ex-

The owl is attacked by a magpie and other birds.

ample, is a small tufted owl. In his symbols of the cross Typotius links the owl with the bat and the frog as creatures preferring darkness to light. To St. Basil even the owl's eyes were symbolic of evil. Keen-sighted at night but almost blind by day, the owl symbolized the seeker after "vain knowledge," who could never see the truth. In the procession of the Seven Deadly Sins, John Gower makes the owl represent the sin of Sloth.

The pejorative Christian symbolism of the owl was increased when the bird accompanied the ape in medieval illuminations and carvings. Often the ape was presented as a hunter with an owl instead of the customary hawk on his fist; sometimes the ape with the owl rode backward on a goat or an ass, an equestrian position assigned to criminals on their way to execution. A moulding at Bourges Cathedral has crockets formed entirely of owls and apes. The reason for the association of these two creatures is not far to seek. For if the owl was the worst bird, *turpissima avis*, the ape was the worst beast, *turpissima bestia*. The association of the two was strengthened by their physical characteristics. The owl is the only bird whose eyes are turned forward, and with the small, stiff feathers encircling its eyes it has, in some species, a simian appearance. In many of the illustrations, the ape was the Devil, the well-known fowler or trapper of souls, using the owl as its lure. Together they hunted small birds, that is, "those whose spirits are in harmony with God." Sometimes they lurked near the Tree of Knowledge or the tree representing the Seven Deadly Sins, or even by the Crucifix itself.

The favorable significance given to the *nycticorax* was

probably due to the following verse from Psalm ci.7: "*similis factus sum pellicano solitudinis: factus sum sicut nycticorax in domicilio*" (I am like the pelican of solitude: I am like the owl in its abode). Because the pelican was the traditional symbol of Christ, Rabanus Maurus interpreted this owl as Christ. Christ was saying that He was in His sepulchre—"*Idest, mortuus positus sum in sepulcro.*" Similarly the *Physiologus*, ascribed to Epiphanius, likened the *nycticorax* to Christ. Just as the bird preferred darkness to light so "*Christus dilexit nos sedentes in tenebris, & in umbra mortis*" (Christ chose us sitting in darkness and in the shadow of death).

In secular literature and in art the owl's symbolism was ambivalent. Bartholomew repeated Pliny's statement that the owl was ominous and that its appearance in a city signified destruction. Artists such as Hieronymus Bosch (1450?–1516) represented the owl as wholly evil. Similarly, although critics have variously interpreted the early Middle English debate poem "The Owl and the Nightingale" as having to do with religious and courtly poetry, old and new types of music, asceticism and pleasure, gravity and gaiety, philosophy and art, the contemplative and active life, or Thomas à Becket and Henry II, to the nightingale in the poem the owl was a monster, ugly, miserable, ominous, filthy in habits and hated by all other birds. To Chaucer the owl was the portent of death, the prophet of "wo and of myschaunce," and Spenser called

the bird "death's dreadfull messengere" whom men "abhorre and hate." Shakespeare's owl with the "merry note" in *Love's Labour's Lost* is an exception. In *Julius Caesar* the owl that shrieked in the marketplace is the ominous Roman bird. "The owl shriek'd at thy birth, an evil sign," Henry VI tells Gloucester. Guilty Lady Macbeth calls the shrieking owl the "fatal bellman," tolling the bell for the dead—an image which finds its counterpart on stained glass windows and sculpture where an owl raises a bell with its talons. Mad Ophelia's observation, "they say that the owl was a baker's daughter," is a reminder of the girl of popular legend who refused Christ bread on His way to the cross and was turned into an owl as punishment.

To emblem writers such as Alciatus and Valeriano the owl was Minerva's bird. Valeriano also regarded the *noctua* as a symbol of victory for the Athenians and as the hieroglyph of death for the Egyptians. The *nycticorax* was the symbol of the despot and of hypocrisy, and both the *noctua* and the *nycticorax* were symbols of the humility of Christ. In 1603 a eulogy of the bird comes from the owl itself in Drayton's poem of that name where the owl serves as a mouthpiece to criticize the economic, social, and political conditions of the age.

On the other hand, in the same century the owl became an emblem of Melancholy which Henry Peacham personified as a solitary man studying in a dark forest. The hermits' companions were very different from those two lighthearted creatures of Edward Lear's, who later went to sea in a pea-green boat. They were "Madge the Owle and Melancholy Pusse, . . . light-loathing creatures, hatefull, ominous." The owl's association with darkness also gave rise to a curious figurative expression. An owl was, of course, a lady of the night, but *owling* in English law was the crime of smuggling wool overseas at night to avoid paying customs. The first statute against it was passed in 1336–37, and by the statute of 1566 the punishment involved the cutting off of the left hand and nailing it in a public place.

As a symbol in poetry the owl still sometimes retains its sinister connotations. In "The Owl," war-poet Edward Thomas (1878–1917) described how, as a weary traveler, he found comfort in an inn—"All of the night was quite barred out except / An owl's cry, a most melancholy cry . . . ." That cry represented those who could not escape. The owl spoke for "all who lay under the stars, / Soldiers and poor unable to rejoice." Dylan Thomas in "Over Sir John's Hill" used a brilliant image to describe the owl's cry:

> Only a hoot owl
> Follows a grass blade blown in cupped hands
> In the looted elm.

Here the owl's cry meant death and was the culminating symbol of the death imagery in the poem.

Alciatus, pp. 91–94, xix; Artemidorus, III, lxv; Baldwin, 207–29; Basil, *PG*, 29, col. 182; Cahier & Martin, II, 169; III, 235; Chaucer, *PF*, 343; *Tr* v.319–20, 382; *LGW*, 2253; *EB*, xx, 398; Gower, *Mirour*, I, l. 893; Horace, *Ep*, v.19–20; Horapollo, p. 117; Howe, p. 175; Isidore, xii.7.39; Knight, pp. 128–29; Liddell & Scott, s.v. γλαυκῶπις; McCulloch, pp. 147–48; Neumann, pp. 236n, 272; Ovid, *Met*. VII, l. 269ff; Peacham, p. 126; Philippe de Thaon, ll. 2789–2802; *Physiologus*, p. 83; Pliny, x.xvi, xliii, xcv; xxxix.lxxxii; Plutarch, *Pericles*; Rabanus Maurus, *PL*, 112, cols. 1006–1007, 1084–85; Rowland, *Blind Beasts*, pp. 37–40; Seltman, p. 18; Shakespeare, *Hamlet* IV.v.42–43; *Henry VI*, pt. 3., v.vi.44; *Julius Caesar* I.iii.26–28; *Macbeth* II.ii.3; *Love's Labour's Lost* v.ii.908; Spenser, *FQ* II.xii.36; Swan, p. 404; Topsell, p. 14; Typotius, p. 8, xii; Valeriano, f.146v; Virgil, *Aen*. IV.462; Williams, p. 264.

Parrot

The Maharajah of Nawanagar had a parrot, one hundred and fifteen years old, which traveled in a Rolls Royce and possessed an international passport; George V's parrot, Charlotte, used to peruse state and confidential documents over his master's shoulder; Humboldt, the German explorer, met an aged parrot in South America which was the sole possessor of the language of the Atures, an Indian tribe which had itself become extinct. That the bird should often be depicted reading a scroll is therefore not surprising. As early as Ctesias, the parrot was praised both for its bright plumage and its ability to speak. The Romans domesticated the bird, training it with some cruelty. "Its head is as hard as its beak," wrote Pliny, "and when it is being taught to speak it is beaten with a rod of iron." A fine-looking parrot, wearing a collar and evidently a household pet, still remains on the walls of Pompeii.

As in the case of Rome itself, wine and women were said to be the parrot's downfall. Pliny observed that the parrot was extremely lascivious when drunk—*in vino praecipue lascivia*—and early in medieval times two distinct kinds of parrots developed. The Waldensian bestiary described only the good parrot which loves purity—*ama totavia la purita*—and urged men to emulate the bird. According to another bestiary, however, there were two varieties: the *villain* which had only three toes and the *gentil* which had six. The parrot's facility with language was sometimes praiseworthy. Salimbene told of a parrot which as it was snatched up by a kite uttered an invocation which was dear to its mistress: *sanct Thoma, adjuva me* (St. Thomas, aid me!) and was miraculously rescued. On the other hand, the story which homilists told to illustrate the text "Ye mountains of Gilboa, let there be no dew upon you!" (2 Samuel i.21) exemplified craftiness. Par-

The parrot with three toes has a mean disposition.

rots, explained the homilists, are susceptible to dampness and therefore prefer dry places. A knight who had a parrot in Britain for many years went on a crusade and happened to go to Mount Gilboa where he saw a parrot which so strongly reminded him of his own that he said: "Our parrot, which is just like you, in his cage at home, sends you greetings." No sooner had he uttered these words than the strange parrot fell to the ground, to all appearances dead. The knight was astonished, and when he returned home he told his family of the incident. His own parrot listened attentively and when the climax was reached uttered a loud cry and fell over, again to all ap-

A parrot can talk like a man.

pearances dead. Greatly distressed, the family took the bird out of its cage and laid it down in the open air on the chance of its recovery. To their dismay the parrot instantly spread its wings and flew off, presumably to rejoin its companion on Mount Gilboa. Bestiarists also claimed that the parrot hated rain because water spoiled its colors. Possibly the parrot was being confused with the West African turaco which has a crimson pigment in its feathers that is indeed soluble in water. The point that the bestiarists wish to make was that the parrot which avoided the rain symbolized the good Christian.

In Middle English the bird was called popinjay from the French *papegai*. Usually it was a term of contempt. The popinjay in Chaucer's *Parliament of Fowles* is "ful of delicasye" (full of wantonness). Chaucer's old merchant goes home as "murie as a papejay"—he is stupidly cheerful, not knowing that he has been cheated of both his wife and his money. The pejorative sense was reinforced by the fact that the usual target in archery was a painted representation of a popinjay, swinging from a high pole. By Shakespeare's time a popinjay had come to mean a fop, or a conceited, empty-headed person. In satire the parrot fared better. In "Speak, Parrot," Skelton used a very learned bird to expose the evils of Henry VIII's court and to attack Cardinal Wolsey. The parrot becomes both a symbol for the poet and for the poetic faculty.

"Parrot is no woodcock, nor no butterfly,
Parrot is no stammering stare, that men call a starling.
But Parrot is my own dear heart and my dear darling . . .
I pray you, let Parrot have liberty to speak!"

122

David Lyndsay's "The Testament and Complaynt of Our Soverane Lordis Papyngo" is an amusing though less subtle attack on abuses in the church. Here a magpie, raven, and kite, representing a Canon Regular, a Black Monk, and a Holy Friar respectively, each claim to give a dying parrot absolution and be responsible for its earthly goods. At its death they ignore the will and devour the bird.

In emblem books and didactic works of the sixteenth and seventeenth centuries the parrot represented various values. Both Ripa and Valeriano regarded the parrot as the symbol of an eloquent man. Thynne depicted a parrot on a sea-tortoise for the same purpose. In a *Booke of Christian Prayers* (1578), in an illustration of five women representing the senses, Touch has a parrot on her wrist biting her thumb. In *A Worke For None But Angels and Men* (c.1655) by Thomas Jenner a parrot bites the hand of a woman who represents Feeling. The verse reads:

When Hearing, Seeing, Tasting, Smelling's passed;
Feeling (as long as life remains) doth last.
Mayde, reach my Lute, I am not well indeede:
O pitty-mee, my bird hath made mee bleede.

In the Far East the bird had other values. In folktales especially, the talking parrot was like the tell-tale crow, warning the deceived husband. Among the Kols and minor castes in the northwestern provinces of India the bird seems originally to have been a kind of marriage totem of the Dravidian races. It was a sacred bird, and images of it made of wood of the cotton tree or of clay were hung up in the marriage shed. As the symbol of love, the parrot was also the vehicle of Kama, the Indian god of love. In China a representation of a parrot used to be a symbolic warning to women to be faithful to their husbands. It pointed back to the legend of a pearl merchant in the province of Kiangsi who was on the point of being ruined by the intrigues of his faithless wife, when the state of affairs was made known to him by a talking parrot.

Ascham (ed. Giles), III, 116; Cahier & Martin, II, 186; Chaucer, *PF*, 359; *ShipT*, 559; Chew, pp. 194–95; Crooke, p. 344; Greene (ed. Grosart), III, 50; IX, 243–44; X, 238; Harvey (ed. Grosart), I, 229; II, 8; Howe, p. 36; Nashe (ed. McKerrow), III, 116, 344; Pliny, x.lviii; Ripa, 1.i.214; Thynne, pp. 36–37; Valeriano, f.166v; *Waldensian* (ed. Mayer), pp. 403–404; Williams, p. 275.

Partridge

Many modern ornithologists claim that the partridge's sexual habits are unusual. Some two or three hundred partridges will hold a kind of convention lasting for at least three successive days, and there is "much running about, occasional fighting and 'love making,' and departure of pairs at intervals." According to the ancient natural historians, however, partridges were so lustful that they only had to get near each other in order to conceive. "If the females stand facing the males," said Pliny,

> they become pregnant by the afflatus that passes out from them, while if they open their beaks and put out their tongues at that time they are sexually excited. Even the draft of air from males flying over them, and often merely the sound of a male crowing makes them conceive.

"When the partridge is about to lay her eggs," said Aelian, "she tries to hide them from her mate for fear that he may crush them, because he is lustful and tries to prevent the mother from devoting her time to rearing her young. So incontinent is the partridge." Deprived of female company, male partridges fought and practiced sodomy.

Ancient historians also allowed the partridge some virtues: the mother bird decoyed the fowler away from its nest by behaving like the lapwing, feigning a broken wing; the male partridge was a tenacious fighter, especially when the female was present. Nevertheless, for centuries the partridge not only continued to be the symbol of incontinent lust but had further bad habits assigned to it. On Biblical evidence, the bird was said to steal the eggs of others. "Like a partridge hatching eggs which he has not laid is the man who amasses wealth which he has not justly earned; in the midst of his days he must leave it, and at the end he will prove himself a fool" (Jeremiah xvii.ɪɪ). In actual fact, according to Evans, the partridge is very benevolent and even adopts orphans of other partridges; its reputation for pilfering may have arisen from the old belief that people who stole clothes were destined to be reborn as gray or speckled partridges, according to the color of the clothing taken. However unjustly maligned, the thieving partridge was regarded by the Church Fathers as the symbol of envy, and by bestiarists as the symbol of treachery or of the Devil himself. The bestiarists added that the bird received no reward for its greed because the young birds, on hearing the voice of their true mother, flew off to her. Similarly, God's offspring, on hearing Christ or the voice of the Church, flew away from the Devil. Nor did the female partridge's protection of her young by feigning a broken wing improve her reputation. St. Ambrose appeared to sympathize with the frustrated hunters and saw the bird as a symbol of deceit. "Partridges," he said, "lead hunters astray by their trickery and thus keep them from their nests and from their young." Bersuire, noting the smallness of the partridge's wings and its consequent inability to fly far, gave fearfulness as its dominant characteristic. Chaucer gave *partriches wynges* (partridges' wings) to

Lady Fame. He may have misread *pernicibus alis* (with swift wings), but he may have wished to imply that fame, like the partridge, was treacherous. The association of the partridge with treachery may have been strengthened by the practice of using a lame and therefore easily tamed partridge to decoy other birds. In Ecclesiasticus xi.30 this captured partridge became an allegory of the proud man who rejoiced in the disasters into which he had lured his neighbors.

Robert Graves, on the other hand, finds a totally different symbolism in the characteristics assigned to the partridge, seeing in them a reference to the sacred hobble dance of ancient mysteries. The partridge was sacred to the love-goddess because of its reputation for lust, and the Arabic word for "hobble" derives from the word for partridge. The love dance of the partridges is performed by the male. He becomes very absorbed in it, fluttering around in circles with hobbling gait, one heel always poised ready to strike at a rival's head. The hens watch, quaking with excitement. The sacred dance must have mimicked this sexual dance of the partridges. Noting that Pliny observed that "in no other animal is there any such susceptibility in the sexual feelings" and that when the female is sitting on her eggs the cocks relieve their tensions by practicing sodomy, Graves suggests that such remarks might have been inspired by the organized sodomy in the temples of the Syrian moon-goddess.

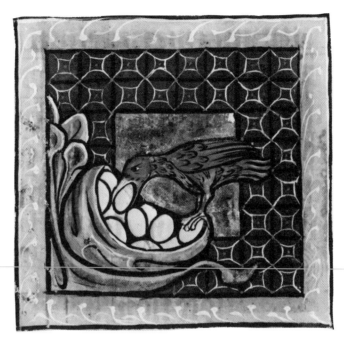

The partridge steals eggs of other birds.

It is as a sexual symbol that the partridge is most conspicuous. Isidore called it *immunda* (impure); Brunetto Latini said it was *luxurieuse* (lustful). Emblem writers such as Valeriano agreed with the ancients that the bird signified *amor turpissimus* (most wicked love) and *im-*

125

moderata nequitia (excessive wantonness), as well as avarice. Titian gave a glimpse of the partridge through the window of a room occupied by a naked love-goddess. Ripa personified lust as an overdeveloped young woman caressing a partridge and sitting on a crocodile. The commentary assumed that the reader understood the significance of the partridge.

> A young Damsel with her Hair finely curl'd; in a manner naked; sits on a crocodile, and makes much of a partridge. Naked because, Luxury squanders away the Goods of Fortune and destroys those of the Soul. The crocodile, for her fecundity, denotes luxury; and her Teeth, tied to the right arm, excite Lust, as 'tis said.

By 1700 English slang equated partridge with "whore," a significance it retained to the early twentieth century. "Go home, ye fop," says the tavern keeper in an old song, "and for half-a-Crown a Doxey get. But seek no more a partridge here." These partridges turn up in curious places. There are two partridges in the racy fabliau "Des Perdriz." The husband and lascivious priest covet them; the lecherous wife secretly eats them and sets the two men at odds with one another. There is the partridge in the well-known carol beginning "On the twelfth day of Christmas my true love sent to me . . . ," a cumulative song which children sang in the Victorian nursery, paying a "forfeit" for every item forgotten. According to the version used, the partridge is either in, on, or up a pear tree, and the song can be sung in two ways, either beginning with the twelfth day and proceeding in reversed numerical order until the second day is reached, or beginning with the second day and adding the days and gifts until the twelfth day is reached. In the first version the partridge in a pear tree provides the final line; in the second version the partridge is the first gift. Thus, in both, it receives special emphasis. The twelve days are, of course, those between Christmas Day and Epiphany, the great midwinter festival of Yule. Explicators of the carol, while admitting the bad reputation of the partridge, avoid explicitly glossing the partridge in the pear tree. Ornithologically the image is unsound. The partridge does not normally perch. It may rarely do so on a wall but only very exceptionally on a tree. It roosts on ground vegetation and at the bottom of hedgerows. The image becomes more meaningful when one realizes that the pear tree is a well-known phallic symbol. As such it occurs in medieval lyric and in the old fabliau which Chaucer so brilliantly adapted for the *Merchant's Tale*. Paul Olson points out that because *pirum / poire* meant both pear and rod, the pear was traditionally associated with the male genitalia. The variants to "a partridge in a pear tree," such as "part of a juniper tree" or "partridge all in the barley," suggest an attempt at censorship. For in addition to the innocuous and intangible gifts of "twelve ships a-sailing, eleven bulls a-bleating, ten ladies dancing" and so on, the lover of the singer is making a gift of himself.

Aelian, III.5, 16; IV.1; VII.19; Ambrose (ed. Caillou), VIII, *Epist*, xxxii, 1, 6–8; Aristotle, *Generation* II.vii; "Des Perdrix," see Bartsch, pp. 200–201; Cahier & Martin, III, 247–48; Camerarius, III.lxviii; Chaucer, *HF*, iii.392; Eucherius, *PL*, 50, col. 750; Evans, p. 144; Graves, 327–28; Ham (ed.), pp. 235–36; Isidore, xii.7.63; Latini, p. 151; Meyer (ed.), p. 438; Olson, p. 207n; Pliny, x.li; Rabanus Maurus, *PL*, 112, col. 1027; Ripa, II.ii.451–52; (ed. Richardson), I, 50; Robbins, pp. 15–16, 234; Valeriano, f.175v; Witherby, v, 241.

Peacock

Sixty years ago Rudyard Kipling called England "a garden full of stately views . . . with statues on the terraces and peacocks strutting by." Today, if you do not see peacocks in their English sanctuary on Brownsea Island near Poole Harbor, you may have to be content with the marble, wood, ivory, and china peacocks decorating fireplaces, ceilings, walls, tables, and even the royal throne in King Ludwig's fairy-tale castle in Bavaria. For peacocks have become scarce even in the stateliest homes of Europe, and

the proverbial expression "as proud as a peacock" is seldom used. Yet, since antiquity, certain conspicuous characteristics of the male bird—its exotic plumage, its obvious vanity, as well as its delicate flavor on the banqueting table—have combined to give it a rich symbolic history. Just as the eagle, Jupiter's bird, symbolized the apotheosis of Roman emperors, so the peacock, sacred to Juno, symbolized that of Roman empresses. For this reason the bird was carved on tombs and funerary lamps, and from pagan monuments of the dead the motif passed to Christian tombs to denote the ascent of the soul and its union with God. The symbolism was reinforced by the belief that the peacock's flesh was incorruptible. St. Augustine in *The City of God* referred to the peacock's durability as one of the marvels of nature created by God:

> This property, when I first heard of it, seemed to me incredible, but it happened at Carthage that a bird of this kind was cooked and served up to me. I took a suitable slice of flesh from its breast, and when it had been kept as many days as make any other flesh stinking, it was produced and set before me and emitted no offensive smell.

St. Augustine added: *Quis enim nisi Deus creator omnium dedit carni pavonis mortui ne putrescerent?* (For who except God, the Creator of all things, endowed the flesh of the dead peacock with the power of never decaying?). In

the Roman catacombs two peacocks facing each other with a bunch of grapes between them depict the soul quenching its thirst at the eternal fountain of life; peacocks standing upon a small bowl represent the glorified spirit rising above mundane cares; two peacocks with a cross between them on a sepulchral urn again symbolize immortality. Sometimes in Christian as well as in pagan symbolism the peacock is associated with the eagle in which case the peacock usually represents immortality allied to victory and strength. With the phoenix, also a symbol of immortality, it has the same meaning in a thirteenth-century sculpture at St. Pierre, Caen, where Samson, himself a type of victory over death, breaks the jaws of a lion. Since peacocks were reputed to destroy serpents, two birds sometimes flank the Tree of Knowledge.

The tail feathers themselves acquired special significance. In pagan times the eyes in the tail symbolized the stars in the heavens, or were associated with Argus whose hundred eyes were transferred on his death by Juno to her own bird. In Christian Rome, on Easter days when the Pope was carried in state into St. Peter's, he flourished a fan (*flabellum*) of ostrich feathers on which were sewn the eye spots from peacocks' plumes, the latter signifying the vigilance of the Church. Peacock's feathers were used

The peacock has a magnificent tail.

128

for angels wings in art, architecture, and in the mystery plays. Ezekiel's description of the cherubim as having wings "full of eyes" made such use appropriate, and angels' wings made of peacocks' feathers were so commonplace that Chaucer was able to reverse the image and refer to the "pekok with his aungels fetheres bryghte" without explanation. For one pageant presented at London Bridge in 1464 twenty-one pence were spent on "nine-hundred peacock's feathers for making angel's wings." Brooklyn Museum, New York, possesses a fan dating from the eighth or ninth century which bears a cross flanked with seraphim and beasts with peacock feathers in their wings surrounding a large cross.

The moral nature of the peacock was attacked even in classical times. To Aristotle the bird was jealous and conceited; to Pliny, ostentatious, spiteful, salacious, alien, and proud. Small wonder that the medieval Church Fathers disapproved of this showy creature and moralized over the striking contrast between its beautiful tail and ugly feet and strident voice. According to the *Physiologus*, the peacock was said to weep at the sight of its feet and to scream raucously at night when it awoke from sleep, thinking that it had lost its beauty. Here, warns the preacher, was an example of the mortal soul, conscious of its shortcomings, who "in the night of this world" feared it might lose the grace which God had given it. Other homilists declared that the tail represented foresight; a foolish man was like a peacock which had lost its tail.

All down the centuries moralists referred to the proverbial pride of the peacock, and in Elizabethan times the peacock still represented the sin of Pride in depictions of the Seven Deadly Sins. Among the heraldists, meanness was added to the peacock's faults and the bird was said to swallow up his excrements "because he envieth man the use thereof." The peacock could be likened, said Guillim, to those who were proud because they were generally of "such *sluttish* and *dirty qualities*." Noting that the bird becomes bashful and tries to hide itself when it molts, Guillim drew a comparison which had already been very popular among the preachers—"such is the quality of many *Dames*, who being painted and richlie attired cannot keepe within dores, but being *undressed* and in their owne hew they are loath any man should see them." Moralists saw the bird as a type of falsity or of the Devil. It was said to lay twelve eggs, and these eggs represented various sins such as homicide, pride, blasphemy, avarice, and other evils. Often repeated was the idea expressed by earlier natural historians that the peacock destroyed the eggs of its female in order to have more time for sexual pleasure. The peacock, said Aldrovandi, was extremely salacious. It had the feathers of an angel, the voice of a demon, and the movements of a thief. To emblem writers such as Ripa, the peacock was still the symbol of *superbia* (pride).

At the same time, the peacock, garnished with its own brilliant plumage, was highly rated gastronomically, and at many a sumptuous banquet knights took their most solemn oath "on the peacock." The preparation in the kitchen was elaborate. The *Epulario* or *The Italian Banquet*, translated in 1598, gives instructions how to prepare a peacock so that when it is brought to table "it shall seeme to bee alive and cast fire out of the mouth." Apparently camphor, cotton wool, and wine were stuffed into the beak.

In modern times the peacock has taken on a variety of significance. Brewer, writing at the beginning of this century, states that the phrase "let him keep his peacock to himself" means "let him keep his eccentricities to himself." Apparently when mad King George III, partially recovered from one of his attacks, prepared to read the king's speech, a minister coached him to end each sentence with an inaudible word such as peacock in order to secure an appropriate pause. Unfortunately, the king remembered only part of the advice and to the bewilderment of his audience punctuated every phrase with audible peacocks. Sean O'Casey's *Juno and the Paycock* makes use of conventional associations: Juno symbolizes long-suffering motherhood; Jack Boyle, her drunken husband, symbolizes reckless pride. In D.H. Lawrence's first novel, *The White Peacock*, the attributes of the male bird are assigned to woman to symbolize her sexuality and her hostility to the male. The peacock perched on the statue of an angel in an abandoned church reminds the embittered, passionate narrator of his predatory first wife—"the miserable brute has dirtied the angel. A woman to the end, I tell you, all vanity and screech and defilement." Similarly, in the short story "Wintry Peacock," the bird has the "devilish soul" of the female. At the end of the tale, the narrator (and Lawrence) approve of the philandering husband—"a handsome figure of a man"—subjugating the peacock-soul of his wife.

Aelian, v.21; Aldrovandi, II, 12, 21; Aristotle, *H.A.* IX.i; Augustine, *PL*, 41, col. 712; Bartholomaeus, XII.xxxi; Bloomfield, p. 245; Cahier & Martin, II, 161; Chaucer, *PF*, 356; Chew, pp. 3, 96, 109n; Creuzer, IV.ii.lxviii, cclxi; *Epulario*, C; Garver, p. 303; Giffin, p. 50; Guillim, p. 165; Hulme, p. 191; Owst, p. 411; *Physiologus*, pp. 48–49; Pliny, x.xxii; Randall, p. 101; Ripa, I.i.50; Swan, p. 109; *Tretyse*, p. 110; Twining, pp. 49, 50, 190; Valeriano, f.171; De Vitry, p. 114; Wailes, pp. 949–54.

Pelican

That large, grayish, comical-looking bird which squats placidly on every post along the waterways at Clearwater,

Florida—who would associate it with Christ? With its short body, wing span of about seven feet, and a beak measuring sixteen inches, it looks even more grotesque in flight. Yet this is the bird which as a representative of Christ was carved more frequently in churches than any other, often by craftsmen who had never seen the bird in real life. One reason for the symbolism lies in a mistaken conception of how the mother pelican feeds its young. It was believed that she nourished them with the blood of her breast, often dying in the process. In actual fact the mother bird puts the fish which she has caught in a pouch, an elastic fold of skin hanging from its beak, then opens her jaws and lets her young feed. The identification with Christ was assisted by the reference in Psalm ci.7: "I am become like the pelican who dwells in solitude." The verse was commented upon by the Church Fathers, and St. Thomas Aquinas addressed Christ as the Pelican in a hymn which was translated by Richard Crashaw:

> Oh soft self-wounding pelican,
> Whose breast weeps balm for wounded man!
> Ah, this way bend thy benign flood
> To a bleeding heart that gasps for blood.

It was probably due to this symbolism that Dante's Beatrice referred to Christ as "il nostro Pellicano."

Equally ancient as the story which gave rise to the pelican of piety is the account of internecine strife between

The pelican kills and revives its young.

parents and offspring. According to the bestiaries the pelican had excessive love for its young. When the young began to grow, however, they struck their parents in the face. The parents in turn struck and killed them. After three days the mother pierced her side, bathed the dead children in her blood, and revived them. Here the pelican was either a symbol of Christ the Redeemer or of God who sacrificed His Son and revived Him after three days.

The pseudo-natural history of the pelican also provided images in a secular context. In the *Ancren Riwle*, a thirteenth-century conduct book for nuns, the pelican who kills her young is like a bad-tempered female recluse. The young pelicans were her good works which she sometimes destroyed with the bill of sharp wrath. According to the writer, she immediately repents, "and with her own bill pricks her breast: that is with confession of her mouth wherewith she sinned and slew her good works, draweth the blood of sin out of her breast, that is of the heart in which is the life of the soul, and thus shall then quicken her slain birds which are her works." In *King Lear* the young pelican became a symbol of filial ingratitude. Goneril and Regan are called "those pelican daughters" by their suffering father, and he, by implication, is the suffering Christ. In the nineteenth century the sacrificial pelican became a complex symbol for Alfred de Musset. In *La Nuit de Mai* both the pelican and the wolf illustrate the stoicism that the poet must display. The pelican's self-sacrifice also symbolizes the poet probing his own sufferings for the entertainment of his readers.

The emblem writers gave the pelican a varied symbolism. According to Horapollo, in ancient Egypt the pelican signified a fool. It laid its eggs on the ground even though it could have deposited them in higher places. Fowlers surrounded the nest with dried dung and set fire to it. Seeing the smoke, the pelican tried to extinguish the fire with its wings, but only fanned the flames and became itself an easy prey to the fowlers because of its burnt wings. In the sixteenth century Alciatus was among those who made the pelican a symbol of gluttony and garrulity; Reusner and others, using the motto *Pro lege et grege* (for law and for the flock), took the pelican as the emblem of the good king devoting his life to peoples' welfare. Similarly favorable was the symbolism implied in *The Princely Pelican*, a book written about Charles I in 1649. Edward Topsell, the Elizabethan naturalist and translator of Gesner, called the pelican the Alcatraz, taking the name from the Greek *kados*, meaning water pot, a word which, he said, applied to the pelican because of its pouch. He credited the bag under the pelican's beak with an extraordinary capacity: one learned man found a whole Blackamore infant in it; another authority declared that a soldier's coat, a hat, and three pairs of shoes were taken out of a pelican's throat. He too compared the pelican to Christ but noted that it could also symbolize a glutton and a loud, unpleasant talker.

At least once a week medieval clergy would recite Psalm ci.7: *similis factus sum pellicano* (I am become like to the pelican). Nevertheless, according to Kenneth Sisam, the magnificent Eadwine Psalter, written at Canterbury Cathedral in the twelfth century, translates the verse "I am become like to the skin of a dog" (*pelli canis*).

Aelian, III.23; Alciatus, pp. 303–304; xc; pp. 313–14, xcv;

Ancren Riwle, pp. 118–19; Boutell, p. 144; Crawshaw (ed. Turnbull), p. 191, ll. 45–50; Dante, *Parad.* XXIII.113; Garver, p. 314; Graham, pp. 235–43; Ham (ed.), p. 235; Horapollo, p. 74; Meyer (ed.), pp. 437–38; Pliny, x.lvi; Réau, 1.94–96; Reusner, II.xiv.73; Shakespeare, *King Lear* III.iv.73; Sisam, p. 215; Topsell, pp. 29–39; Turner, pp. 151–53; T.H. White, pp. 132–33.

Pheasant

The pheasant, brought into Europe from the banks of the Phasis, a river in Asia Minor, is the most beautiful of birds, next to the peacock. According to Goldsmith, when Croesus, king of Lydia, was installed on his throne with all the barbarous magnificence of eastern splendor, he asked Solon, the austere lawgiver, if he had ever seen anything so fine. Solon replied that having seen the beautiful plumage of the pheasant he could not be impressed by any other displays.

In ancient China the pheasant was regarded as a thunder bird because it was supposed to beat a drum with its wings and make thunder. In the spring young people danced in order to bring the rain, copying the movements of the bird and flapping their arms like wings. The

The pheasant is easily taken.

pheasant was also the symbol of authority.

In England, the pheasant has erotic connotations. In a lyric from a fifteenth-century miscellany the poet goes hawking and raises a pheasant. When he runs to retrieve it he is caught in a briar which bears a message urging him to turn back. Here the pheasant symbolizes pleasure and the hawk youth. In folk metaphor, the pheasant shares the sexual meaning given to game and poultry. Farmer and Henley in their dictionary of slang refer to pheasant as "a wanton," and pheasantry as "a brothel"; and it seems to me that Herman Melville in his short story "Poor Man's Pudding and Rich Man's Crumbs" uses pheasant, along with crumbs, pie, pork, and beef as slang terms for women in the sexual sense.

> "Yes, who knows! . . . his Royal Highness the Prince Regent might have eaten of that identical pheasant."
> "I don't doubt it," murmured I, "he is said to be uncommonly fond of the breast . . . ."

The slang meaning owes more to the pheasant as a tasty dish than to its colorful plumage. As one writer points out: "The females are universally attired in a sober dress of brown, often indeed exquisitely pencilled with spots and zig-zag lines, but totally destitute of the brilliant hues which glistened in their mates." The same writer adds that their flesh "affords to man a wholesome and nutritious food."

Armstrong, *Folklore*, pp. 110–11; Goldsmith, pp. 72–73; Rigg, pp. 51–52; Rowland, "Sitting," p. 80; Williams, p. 284; Witherby, v, 234.

Phoenix

Few fabulous creatures have any popular currency today, but the phoenix, like its myth, never dies: it continues to illustrate maxims which accompanied early printed representations of the bird as a symbol: *semper eadem* (always the same) or *ex me ipso renascor* (I am reborn from myself). Certainly its symbolism has narrowed; in addition to being the symbol of eternity, resurrection, and the attribute of fire and hope, it was once the symbol of Christ, the Virgin, of individuals, and of many abstract qualities. In the eighteenth century, Phoenix men, according to Captain Francis Grose, were firemen belonging to an assurance office, and today the phoenix still gives its name to insurance societies, construction companies, dry-cleaning establishments, and other commercial concerns.

The association with fire indicates that aspect of the myth which caught the popular imagination—the bird as a human torch or voluntary sacrifice from whose ashes a new bird emerges. Herodotus was the first to describe the miraculous bird: he claimed only that it came from Arabia to Heliopolis in Egypt once every five hundred years, bringing its aged parent which it smothered in myrrh and placed in the temple of the sun. The bird was like an eagle in size and was partly red and partly gold. Pliny,

Aelian, Ovid, and others elaborated the story. Tacitus said that the bird appeared in 34 A.D. but was believed to be an impostor. The most familiar form of the legend is that in the bestiaries:

Phoenix, the bird of Arabia, is so-called because of its reddish purple color (*phoeniceus*). It is unique: it is unparalleled in the whole world. It lives beyond five hundred years. When it notices that it is growing old, it builds itself a funeral pyre, after collecting some spice branches. On this pyre, turning its body towards the rays of the sun and flapping its wings, it sets fire to itself of its own accord until it burns itself up. Then on the ninth day afterwards, it rises from its own ashes.

According to some versions, on the day after combustion

the priest finds on the altar a small, sweet-smelling worm. On the second day it has the appearance of a bird, and on the third day the priest discovers a perfect phoenix.

This bird is probably to be identified with the *benu*, the purple heron, which was said to be ceremoniously sacrificed by the priests of Heliopolis every five hundred years. It was one of the sacred symbols of worship from Arabia, representing the sun which died in its own fires every night and rose from them again in the morning. The *benu* also had the alternative meaning of palm tree in Egyptian, the palm tree itself being self-fertile and

135

The phoenix sits on its burning nest.

everlasting. The word *phoenix* means both purple and palm tree. In accounts of Pliny and others the tree in which the bird immolates itself was a palm. According to Lactantius:

Quae postquam vitae iam mille peregerit annos . . .
Tunc petit hunc orbem, mors ubi regna tenet . . . .
Tum legit aerio sublimem vertice palmam,
Quae graecum Phoenix ex ave nomen habet.

(When she has already completed a thousand years of
life . . . she seeks this world where death reigns . . . .
then she chooses a lofty palm tree with its top reaching
to the heavens, which bears its Greek name "phoenix"
from the bird.)

Lactantius' poem, written in the third century A.D.,
shows how naturally the phoenix adapted itself to Christian symbolism. Already a striking symbol of the resurrection because of the Roman practice of cremation, the bird
passed easily from the old to the new religion, sometimes acquiring a halo in mosaic representations. Christian writers may have been more sceptical about the bird's
actual existence than they were about the unicorn's, but
they had no qualms about using its fabled characteristics
in the service of the Church. In general, the phoenix was
Christ; the circumstances of the bird's death and rebirth
symbolized the resurrection, immortality, the mystery of
the Trinity, the birth of Christ, or the penitent sinner. The
most elaborate explications came from the bestiaries. The
perfume which filled the two wings of the phoenix symbolized the sweetness of divine grace, as diffused through
the books of the Old and New Testaments; all these
perfumes were the works of the righteous man whereby
he earned eternal life; just as the phoenix stirred up the
flames by fanning them with its wings, so the saint
"mounting up on wings of heavenly meditation, has his
soul kindled and renewed by the flames of the Holy
Spirit." An eighth-century Anglo-Saxon poet created an
elaborate allegory in which the phoenix symbolized not
only the risen Christ but the chaste monastic recluse
reaching the heavenly kingdom through a purifying fire.
Preachers such as Odo of Cheriton likened the phoenix
gathering spices to the just man who increased his good
deeds as death approached and he embarked on immortal
life. Other writers stressed the bird's uniqueness, solitariness, its sinless self-reproduction, and found the bird
a suitable symbol for the Virgin herself. Albertus Magnus
in *De Laudibus Beatae Mariae Virginis* compared Mary
with the phoenix *quae est unica avis sine patre* (which is
a unique bird without a father). The unknown poet of
the *Pearl* declared (ll. 429–32):

Now, for synglerty o hyr dousour,
We calle hyr Fenyx of Arraby,
That freles fleghe of hyr fasor
Lyk to the Quen of cortaysye.

(Now for the uniqueness of her sweetness
We call her the Phoenix of Arabia

Which flawless flew from her Creator
Like the Queen of Grace.)

Because of its hermaphroditic nature, its regeneration through a combination of male and female natures, the phoenix could also symbolize both Mary and Christ. In Henry Hawkins' poem "The Virgin" (1633) the phoenix has two hearts and they belong to

Jesus and his Mother
So linkt in one, that one without the other
Is not entire.

Horapollo had spelled out the symbolism of the phoenix for the Egyptians: it denoted the soul "because this is the longest lived of all creatures in the world"; it symbolized a man returning home after a long time in a foreign land; it also symbolized the overflowing of the Nile because of its association with the sun, the popular belief being that the Nile overflowed because of the sun's heat. In the Renaissance the phoenix was a symbol of the element of fire, of rarity, rebirth, eternity, solitariness, and hope. As Rosemary Freeman observed, "The phoenix did noble service in and out of emblem books. Its peculiar method of reproduction made its application almost unlimited." Writers of prose tracts, such as Lodge, Greene, and Nashe, and writers of emblem verses, such as Valeriano, Camerarius, Paradin, and Ripa, all used the phoenix for its traditional values. *Unica semper avis* was the most common emblem. Geoffrey Whitney, 1586, was one of the first to apply the bird to a town. Nantwich in Cheshire was almost totally destroyed by fire on December 10, 1583, but within three years, because of the generosity of Queen Elizabeth, "the whole site and frame of the town, so suddenly ruined, was with great speed re-edified in that beautifull manner." Whitney's phoenix stood in the middle of the flames and with outspread wings prepared for a new flight.

Petrarch had used the phoenix in praise of Laura's beauty. Chaucer referred to the Duchess Blanche as the "soleyn fenix of Arabye," and the French sonneteers continued the tradition. But at no time was the phoenix more frequently applied to persons as a commendatory term than in the sixteenth and early seventeenth centuries. Nicholas Breton described Sir Philip Sidney as a phoenix in his epitaph on the dead poet and asked "why death should do so great an injury . . . to kill a phoenix when there were no mo[re]." Paradin, explaining the phoenix device of Eleanor of Austria, stated "just as the phoenix is always alone and the only bird of its kind in the world, so are the most excellent things of marvellous rarity and lightly sown." Especially was the phoenix symbol used at the French and English royal courts where the popular idea that the phoenix was "heir to itself" made the bird the perfect symbol of kingship. Here the bird demonstrated the perpetuity of sovereignty: it illustrated the meaning of the famous maxim current since the sixteenth century, *Le roi ne meurt jamais* (the king never dies), and the English equivalent, the king is dead, long live the king! The Order of the Holy Ghost, founded in 1579 by Henry III, was originally to be named the Order of the Phoenix because, so the courtiers argued, the phoenix was "the only creature of its kind, and without any paragon," and as such resembled the French king who "was the Phoenix of all kings in the world." The symbolism is most clearly expressed in an explanatory note to the design of a medallion which was intended to announce the death of Louis XIII and the accession of Louis XIV. The illustration is of a phoenix on its lofty pyre, illumined by solar rays:

> The phoenix is born and soars from the cinders of his father by the influx sent to him from heaven and the sun.
> In the same way, the king is given to us miraculously from on high; and from his father's *lit funèbre* [funeral bed] he soars to his own *lit de justice* [bed of justice].

As Kantorowicz observes in his splendid study of medieval political theology, "the metaphor was not badly chosen, for we have to recall that the French king made his first solemn appearance in the Court of Parlement [sic] as legislator and supreme judge—that is, held his first *lit de justice*—almost immediately after his accession, and sometimes even before his predecessor [sic] king was buried."

In England the phoenix was an emblem of Queen Elizabeth I. She was *sola phoenix* (the solitary phoenix) on some memorial pieces; *unica phoenix* (the unique phoenix) on the medallion issued in the year of her death, 1603. Another phoenix motto: *semper eadem* (always the same) was applied to her as early as 1578, and in *The Light of Britayne*, 1588, she was hailed as "The Phoenix of the Worlde: The Angell of England." The famous Phoenix Jewel showed a profile of the queen on one side in gold and enamel, and on the other a phoenix in flames. Whenever the queen's portrait was decorated with emblems, the phoenix was usually included.

While the phoenix was an ideal symbol for the Virgin Queen, Chester's "Love's Martyr," a long poem which is described on the title page as "allegorically shadowing the truth of love in the constant Fate of the Phoenix and Turtle [turtledove]," applied the image somewhat gloomily to the ageing Elizabeth:

> This Phoenix I do feare me will decay,
> And from her ashes never will arise
> Another Bird her wings for to display,
> And her rich beauty for to equalize;
> The Arabian fiers [fires] are too dull and base,
> To make another spring within her place.

No such pessimism darkened the observations of Shakespeare when he used the symbolism some ten years after the queen's death, as a compliment to her and, by extension, to the reigning monarch James:

> But as when
> The bird of wonder dies, the maiden phoenix,
> Her ashes new create another heir
> As great in admiration as herself,
> So shall she leave her blessedness to one . . .
> Who from the sacred ashes of her honour
> Shall star-like rise, as great in fame as she was . . . .

Yet Shakespeare's earlier poem "The Phoenix and Turtle," which looks back in form to the medieval Bird Mass, was less sanguinary in tone. It is one of the strange collection of poems by "Ignoto," Ben Jonson, Chapman, Marston, and others published with Chester's "Love's Martyr" in 1601. In most instances, the phoenix appears to symbolize Queen Elizabeth and the turtledove her favorite, Essex, Robert Devereux, who was executed on February 25, 1601.

Not every reference to the phoenix was to Queen Elizabeth, however. The bird was a favorite emblem for women who died in childbirth, and for widows. With the motto *nascitur ut alter* (in order that another might be born), the phoenix was used to honor Jane Seymour who died willingly or, as some said, was deliberately sacrificed in a Caesarean operation to give birth to Edward VI in 1537. It was applied in less regal circumstances to Ann Savage who lies propped up in a huge four-poster bed on a brass memorial at Wormington, Gloucestershire, engraved in 1605. Here the comparison is less appropriate because the swaddled child on the coverlet beside her has a little "chrysom" (baptismal cloth) on its head, indicating that the child did not survive. Lady Bona of Savoy, widowed by the assassination of her husband in 1476, selected as a device for her coins a phoenix surrounded by flames, with the motto *Sola facta, solum Deum sequor* (Being made alone, I follow only God). In a volume almost contemporary with "Love's Martyr," *A Treasurie or Store-House of Similes*, 1600, Robert Cawdray gives the phoenix an even wider significance under *Woman*:

> As the Bird of *Egypt*, which when she is old, purgeth
> al the filthie humors of her body with spice of *Araby*,
> and sendeth forth of her mouth a woundrous sweete
> breath: Even so a Woman, when shee is past bearing of
> children, then should she savour and breath all heavenly
> things, so that she neither doo nor say any thing that
> is not religious and godly, and that may bee an example
> for the yonger Women to follow.

Aelian, vi.58; Albertus Magnus, *De Laudibus Beatae Mariae Virginis*, vii.3.1; Breton, p. 10; Bugge, pp. 332–50; Cahier & Martin, ii, 183–85; Camerarius, iii.c; Cawdray, p. 828; Chaucer, *BD*, 982; Chester, p. 15; Chew, p. 130; Collins, pp. 222–26; *De Bestiis, PL*, 177, col. 48; *EB*, xxi, 457; Free-

The quail comes from Quail Island, the ancient island of Delos.

man, p. 77n; Garver, p. 315; Giovio & Symeoni, p. 4; Greene (ed. Grosart), II, 43, 49; IV, 36; VIII, 182; IX, 128, 207; XII, 24, 252; Hawkins, p. 269; Herodotus, II, 73; Horapollo, pp. 54–56; Hubaux and Leroy, *passim*; Kantorowicz, pp. 389–91, 413, 414; Kantrowitz, pp. 2–13; Lactantius, *PL,* 7, cols. 279–80; Lodge (ed. Hunterian Club), I.v.63; Martigny, pp. 534–36; McCulloch, p. 178; *Medallic Illus.,* I, 90; Meyer (ed.), p. 439; Nashe (ed. McKerrow), I, 5, 182–83; Odo of Cheriton, IV, 187; Ovid, *Met.* xv.392–407; xv.391ff; Paradin, p. 36; Petti, p. 74; *Physiologus,* pp. 42–43; Pliny, x.ii; Réau, I.96–98; Ripa, I.i.208, 210; II.ii.19; Rowland, *Blind Beasts,* pp. 44–45; Shakespeare, *Henry VIII,* v.v.40–44; Sherman, p. 44; Tacitus, *Ann,* vi.28; Tervarent, cols. 304–306; Typotius, p. 3; Valeriano, f.144; Whitney, p. 177; Williams, pp. 286–87.

Quail

In some parts of Great Britain this bird is popularly known as "wet my lips" or "wet my feet" from the cock's peculiar three-syllabled mating cry. Although the males practice polygamy, fighting so fiercely in matrimonial rivalry as to be easily captured, a punishment which, according to Goldsmith, they "richly deserve," it is the females which have acquired a bad reputation. The Reverend Brewer, writing in 1900, said that the bird was "very salacious" and was therefore a name for "a prostitute or courtisan." Most earlier lexicographers, including Nares, Halliwell, and Farmer, gave a similar symbolism apart from Cotgrave (1611) who regarded *caille coiffée* simply as a term for "woman," and Grose (1785) who rather curiously defined quail pipe as "a woman's tongue." In Shakespeare's *Troilus and Cressida* (1602) Agamemnon is described as "an honest fellow enough and one that loves quails." Harting thought that Shakespeare was alluding to the Greek warrior's fighting abilities, but Virgil Whitaker glosses quails as "loose women."

The erotic significance dates from ancient times, when the bird was a symbol of generation and rebirth. Latona, the goddess who gave birth to Artemis and Apollo at Delos, regarded the bird as her own: the Phoenician Hercules, whose death and resurrection were commemorated annually, was revived when the quail, a bird "noted for its pugnacity and lechery," was held to his nose. The same significance may explain the story of the migrating quails in Exodus xvi.13 and Numbers xi.33–34. In the first account the Israelities were able to eat the quail without evil results, according to the Lord's promise; in the second account the good Lord lost patience and after declaring that the Israelites would eat quail for a whole month until it came out of their nostrils, "smote the people with a very great plague"—a punishment for their dissatisfaction and, possibly, a warning of what happened to those who sought to follow alien gods. In the ninth century Rabanus Maurus, Archbishop of Mainz, in commenting on the passage, declared, "by quail is meant the pleasures of the body."

Quails were kept for fighting in ancient Greece and Rome, and were highly esteemed for their courage. Even in recent centuries quail fights have been popular in Italy and in China. According to an early twentieth-century writer, quails exist in large quantities in China: "[The Chinese] carry them about in a bag, which hangs from their girdle, treat them with great care, and blow occasionally on a reed to rouse their fierceness. When the bird is duly washed, which is done very carefully, they put him under a sieve with his antagonist, strew a little millot [sic] on the ground, so as to stimulate the envy of the two quails; they soon commence a fight, and the owner wins the prize." Harting told of similar quail fights in Italy, a country which, according to Pliny, had so many quail that flocks of them would blot out the sun or sink a ship on which they had settled.

Paradoxically, the quail has long had a reputation for cowardice and stupidity, possibly because of the readiness with which the bird allows itself to be captured. According to Goldsmith:

Quails are easily caught by a call; the fowler, early in the morning, having spread his net, hides himself under it among the corn; he then imitates the voice of the female with his quail-pipe, which the cock hearing, approaches with the utmost assiduity; when he has got under the net, the fowler then discovers himself, and terrifies the quail, who attempting to get away, entangles himself the

Quails are attacked by a hawk.

more in the net and is taken. The quail may thus very well serve to illustrate the old adage, that every passion, carried to an inordinate excess, will at last lead to ruin.

Jean de Meun in the *Roman de la Rose* compared a silly quail caught by the fowler's net to a young woman easily duped by a man's flattery. Older women were like the more experienced quail who had been almost caught before:

> Hearing the words that they have heard before
> And seeing the attitudes that they have seen,
> The more they been deceived, the more they're sly
> To recognize, far off, the trick again.

Chaucer's misogynistic Clerk of Oxford pictured shrewish women, like the Wife of Bath, making their husbands cower like quails. In *Pearl*, a poem of the same period, the narrator said that he stood as still as a "dased quayle," and the verb "to quail" was used as early as 1440 in Capgrave's *Life of St. Katherine*. The belief that the quail alone of all creatures suffered from falling sickness or epilepsy may have contributed to the bird's reputation for faint-heartedness. "It is customary to spit at the sight of them as a charm against the disease," Pliny had said.

The Athenians thought that the bird fed on poisonous seeds, and this belief was repeated by Pliny. Many centuries later the same fiction gave Topsell an opportunity for a favorable symbolic application: like the quails who survived their noxious diet, so clergymen and all good people "heare, and see the evils of this wicked world, and are never the worse." Topsell also found another curious characteristic in the quail to use for didactic purposes:

> When they [the quails] fall into the Sea, thorough weariness, they holde up one winge instead of a sayle, and the other they use like an oare to stirre forward, and supporte their Bodies from sinkinge. Such (say the Divines) is the Case of penitent soules, for they could not chuse but perishe betwixt shame, and sorrowe for their sinnes in the bitter and dangerous sea of this world, yf yt were not for the one winge of faithe which they hold up towards Heaven and the other of repentance

142

which keepeth them up, and stirreth them forward to salvation.

When the emblem writers turned to the quail, they had many symbolic significances to choose from. The quail was undoubtedly a symbol of regeneration, and Horapollo's contention that the bone of a quail symbolized permanence and safety no doubt points to its ancient value. But if the quail had been a term of endearment to the Roman playwright Plautus, among moralists the bird was condemned for eroticism. Picinelli reproved it vehemently for its salacity, as did the naturalist Aldrovandi. Although Picinelli was able to find some good values in the quail, the bird was not only lascivious but exemplified envy. Valeriano stated that the quail was the Egyptian hieroglyph of impurity and was used to denote both an evil and an ungrateful man. The bird exemplified *perditissima malignitas* (most profligate malignity).

The quail's pugnacity has already been noted. The Chinese, who admired this quality, also made the bird the symbol of poverty: its flecked plumage was said to be a reminder of patched clothing or of rags and tatters.

Aldrovandi, II, 158; Capgrave, l. 1775; Chaucer, *ClT*, 1206; Goldsmith, II, 85; Graves, p. 133; Halliwell, II, 658; Harting, pp. 218–19; Horapollo, p. 97; McCulloch, p. 160; Morgan, p. 129; Picinelli (ed. 1581), II.308–12; Plautus, *As*, III.iii.76; Pliny, x.xxxiii; Rabanus Maurus, *PL*, 112, col. 904; *Roman* (tr. H.W. Robbins), pp. 457–58; Shakespeare, *Troilus and Cressida* v.i.50–51; Topsell, p. 10; Valeriano, ff.176v–177; Whitaker, p. 1009; Williams, p. 302.

Raven

Readers of Edgar Allan Poe have always wanted to know where he found that raven which came gently tapping on his door one wintry night.

Once upon a midnight dreary, while I pondered weak
   and weary,
Over many a quaint and curious volume of forgotten lore,
While I nodded, nearly napping, suddenly there came a
   tapping,
As of some one gently rapping, rapping at my chamber
   door.
" 'Tis some visitor," I muttered, "tapping at my chamber
   door—
       Only this and nothing more."

Ah, distinctly I remember it was in the bleak December,
And each separate dying ember wrought its ghost upon
   the floor.
Eagerly I wished the morrow;—vainly I had sought to
   borrow

From my books surcease of sorrow—sorrow for the lost
  Lenore—
For the rare and radiant maiden whom the angels name
  Lenore—
      Nameless here for evermore.

Open here I flung the shutter, when, with many a flirt
  and flutter,
In there stepped a stately raven of the saintly days of yore;
Not the least obeisance made he; not a minute stopped or
  stayed he;
But, with mien of lord or lady, perched above my chamber door—
Perched upon a bust of Pallas just above my chamber
  door—
      Perched, and sat, and nothing more.

Lowell in *A Fable for Critics* suggested that the bird was
really the bedraggled pet raven called Grip belonging to
Charles Dickens:

There comes Poe with his raven, like Barnaby Rudge,
Three-fifths of him genius and two-fifths sheer fudge.

Another scholar thought the bird came from a dining-
room chair belonging to Poe's guardian, which had a bird
like a raven carved on its back. The fact is from the time
the gloomy bird perches on the bust of Pallas Athena to
its final "nevermore!" it displays many of the characteristics ascribed to it from early times, especially the raven's

fabled power of ominous prophecy. Poe may have regarded the bird as a symbol of "mournful and never-
ending remembrance," but his raven was the traditional
bird and its function was to perform traditional messenger service, reporting from the Devil to the man who
had sold his soul in a vain attempt to recover his dead love.

Who Leonore was we do not know for certain. She
may have been sixteen-year-old Leonora Bouldin, whom,
according to Braddy, "the poet kissed and urged to re-
form" in Tripolet Alley, Baltimore, one dark night in
1847 or 1848. Whoever she was, the presence of the raven
certainly signified the impossibility of recovering her and
spelled irrevocable doom for her lover. Some carping
critics have smugly observed that the owl, not the raven,
was the bird of Pallas Athena. However, Pausanias at
Messenia saw a statue of the goddess holding a raven,
and other writers stated that the raven was her attribute.
Of more interest is the question whether the raven was
also the symbol of Lenore herself. According to Pliny, the
soul of Aristeas assumed the form of a raven, and Poe here
may have been making use of the widespread idea that the
human soul took the form of a bird as it leaves the body.
Ideas about the raven are very ancient, widely diffused,
and remarkably homogeneous, despite some differences
in detail. As Armstrong observes:

The raven peeps forth from the mists of time and thickets

of mythology as a bird of slaughter, a storm bird, a sun and fire bird, a messenger, an oracular figure and a craftsman or culture hero.

Poe's raven has many ancient characteristics and essentially illustrates the meaning of the Celtic phrase "raven's knowledge." It sees and knows all—about the living as well as the dead:

And the raven, never flitting, still is sitting, still is sitting
On the pallid bust of Pallas just above my chamber door;
And his eyes have all the seeming of a demon's that is
    dreaming,
And the lamp-light o'er him streaming throws his shad-
    ow on the floor;
And my soul from out that shadow that lies floating on
    the floor
Shall be lifted—nevermore!

In ancient times the raven was a divine bird. According to Strabo, two ravens at the command of Zeus, one from the east and one from the west, met at the Delphic oracle. The single raven consecrated to Apollo at Delphi was the symbol of wisdom and science. Similar attributes belonged to Odin's two ravens, Hugin and Munin, in Norse mythology. Among the Romans the raven was the favorite emblem of Juno as an exemplification of continence or widowhood, and according to Aelian, "men of old used to sing the song of the raven at weddings after the bridal song, by way of pledging those who came together for the begetting of children to be of one mind." Pliny told of a young raven hatched on the top of the temple of Castor and Pollux which used to salute the emperor and the populace every day. When it died, it was taken to a funeral pyre along the Appian Way on a magnificent bier carried on the shoulders of two Ethiopians with a flute player in the lead—"All this," added Pliny drily, "in a city in which many leading citizens receive no obsequies at all!" Similarly, among the Egyptians, according to Horapollo, the raven was highly esteemed: two ravens signified monogamy and marital fidelity; one raven was the symbol of longevity because the bird was supposed to live one hundred years.

The raven also had less praiseworthy attributes. Pliny referred to the popular belief that ravens were thought to conceive through their beaks and that a pregnant woman who ate a raven's egg gave birth to her child through her mouth. As a result of such ideas the satirists, Martial and Juvenal, gave the name of raven to the lover who indulged in *fellatio*.

Among the ancient Hebrews the bird's reputation was pejorative for a different reason. It was a *corvus* which Noah sent from the Ark to check the flood conditions, a sensible choice because the raven is a robust bird accustomed to search for its food far from home. According to Hebrew folklore, the raven, originally white, was turned

The raven has a hoarse voice.

black as a punishment for not returning. The account in Genesis viii.6–7 is not explicit— *Noe . . . dimisit corvum; qui egrediebatur, et non revertebatur, donec siccarentur aquae super terram* (Noah . . . sent out the raven which went forth and did not return until the waters dried up above the earth)—but the Church Fathers all assumed the raven to be a shameless defector, a striking contrast to the divine dove which returned with an olive branch in its beak. The raven feeding on corpses was the evil man enjoying the fleshpots. The raven's cry was *cras! cras!* (tomorrow! tomorrow!)—the reply that sinners gave when told to repent. "I tell you," said St. Augustine, "when you make a voice like a raven (*vocem corvinam*) you destroy yourselves." To other exegetes, Noah's raven stood for the Jews who lived on the carrion of the Old Law rather than enter the ship of St. Peter (the New Law).

To Rabanus Maurus the raven was the sinner expelled from the church—*Ut in Genesi: "Emisit corvus, qui non est reversus" quod ejicitur ab Ecclesia procax et contumax, et damnatur* (As in Genesis: "He sent out a raven which did not return," because the shameless and insolent man is cast from the Church and is damned).

Other Biblical references did not necessarily cast the bird in such an unfavorable light. The eye in "The eye that mocks the father and scorns to obey a mother will be picked out by the ravens of the valley" (Proverbs xxx.17) belonged to the sinner suffering the punishments of Hell. The bird's dietary habits, according to bestiarists, constituted the allegorical saving of souls: confession and penance were the ravens which "pulled out the eyes of covetousness from the soul, dead in trespasses and sin." Much later, these same eye-eating ravens become Milton's

146

enemies, the bishops "that would peck out the eyes of all knowing Christians." From the psalmist's assertion that God gave food "to the young ravens which cried" (Psalm cxlvii.9) and Job's rhetorical question "Who provideth for the raven his food?" (Job xxxviii.41) came the curious fable that the parent raven did not feed its young until the ravelets showed their darker plumage. Rabanus Maurus and Garner interpreted this raven as a preacher, and the young ravens as those seeking God; other exegetes thought this raven exemplified the sin of pride.

The raven's supernatural prophetic powers, signs in themselves of the bird's once god-like status, continued to be accredited to it and were even enhanced because of the belief expressed by Pliny that the bird was capable of human speech:

> At the present day there was in the city of Rome at the time when I was writing this book a raven belonging to a knight that came from southern Spain, and was remarkable in the first place for its very black color and then for uttering sentences of several words and frequently learning still more words in addition.

This statement was later elaborated by Bartholomew and others who said that the raven had sixty-four changes of voice and was therefore a symbol of guile. Such vocal powers from the Icelandic sagas to the literature of the present day were associated mainly with death and de-

Ravens croak over ruined cities.

147

struction. Only in the Old English epic does the raven appear as the morning bird of joy and light after Beowulf's victory over Grendel, reversing the traditional symbolism in order to indicate that the warriors can once more sleep safely in the Great Hall. Elsewhere in Old English poetry as well as in Old Norse, the raven eager for carrion was a constant visitor to the battlefield. It was the *wonna hrefn*, the dusky raven, and in Celtic folklore ravens become demons which attacked the warriors. For many centuries it remained the bird of foreboding. To illustrate the Office of the Dead in a Parisian Book of Hours the bird sits on a withered tree croaking *cras, cras*, as Death strides over prostrate victims. In Breughel's picture "The Triumph of Death" a raven perches on the horse which is drawing a wagon load of corpses. A sixteenth-century woodcut shows a raven crowing on an hourglass to which Death points with a grimacing smile. To Shakespeare, also, the raven was the portent of death: "The raven himself is hoarse," says Lady Macbeth, "that croaks the fatal entrance of Duncan under my battlements." The raven was still a symbol of slaughter for Joe Barlow writing his "Advice to a Raven in Russia, December 1812" in which he declared that the carrion of Napoleon's wars was spread all over Europe. The raven has an exceptionally broad wing-span, sometimes extending three feet in length. Nevertheless, Barlow declared, "No raven's wing can stretch the flight so far as the torn bandrols [flags] of Napoleon's war." Occasionally more favorable interpretations occur: Ripa depicted the bird along with an old woman and a deer, as a symbol of longevity, as it had been among the Egyptians; as I noted in connection with the crow, the habitual cry of *cras, cras* was sometimes interpreted as a sign of hope.

In our own century, however, if the raven has lost its lust for carnage, it has remained a death symbol. When the Tower of London was bombed in the Second World War, all the ravens which had lived there for centuries flew away. Traditionally, for ravens to desert their nest was ominous, foretelling the downfall of the family on whose property they lived. According to legend, if the ravens deserted the Tower, England would fall. Winston Churchill quickly averted such misfortune. He imported from north Wales and from the wilds of northwest Scotland a large supply of young ravens and clipped their wings.

Adams, p. 53; Aelian, 1.47; Ambrose, *PL*, cols. 411–12; Armstrong, *Folklore*, p. 93; Augustine, *PL*, 37, col. 1330; 38, cols. 512, 1095; D'Ayzac, p. 33; Bartholomew, xii, 11; Bechstein, p. 38; Braddy, pp. 18–19; Cahier & Martin, ii, 156; Chew, p. 239; Creuzer, iv, ii, xxvi, lvi; Evans, p. 76; Garner, *PL*, 193, col. 78; Horapollo, pp. 17–19, 140, 144–45; Hume, "The Function . . . ," pp. 60–63; Juvenal, ii, 63; Legh, f.105v; Map, p. 3; Martial, xiv, 74; Milton, *Animad-*

versions III.i.172; Panofsky, *Pandora*, pp. 28ff; Pausanias, *Des. Graec.*, IV, xxxiv, 6; Pliny, x.lx; Rabanus Maurus, *PL*, 112, cols. 902–903; Ripa, I.ii.53; Shakespeare, *Macbeth* I.v.39; Swainson, p. 89; Wenzel, p. 107.

Robin

The English still think of the robin as the symbol of a special season. Outside, with its crimson breast on the snowy windowsill, the robin pecks at the crumbs put there by little children; inside, on the mantelpiece above the coal fire and on top of the piano, the same bird appears with a blob of holly on glossy cards of various sizes, announcing: "A Merry Christmas and a Happy New Year!"

The Christmas symbolism of the robin was established before the first cards appeared in the 1860s. The Victorians, who were voluminous letter writers, were already sending Christmas notepaper decorated with a robin as the symbol of the season's greetings; from this stationery the first card developed. It was similar to the formal oblong visiting card, stiff, small, unfolded, with a robin replacing the caller's name or crest. The early Christmas card often showed the robin carrying a letter in its beak or lifting the doorknocker like the postman. Postmen

outre inde li donna deffi quen orient   Quam

The robin is an inquisitive bird.

were, in fact, called "robins" on account of their bright red coats. "Come in, Robin postman, and warm theeself awhile," says Jemima, the cook, in *Framley Parsonage*. When the uniform changed to dark blue with red trim in 1861, the nickname vanished. As David Lack observes in his magnificent study of the robin, "At the present day, red pillar-boxes still stand at street corners, and robins still strut on Christmas cards, but the link between them has been forgotten."

The association of the robin with Christmas is appropriate because the bird was the symbol of charity. According to a Breton legend, the robin stained its breast with Christ's blood while attempting to pluck a thorn from His crown. By the late fifteenth century its charity was devoted to the dead. Drayton appears to express a widely-held belief in his poem *The Owle* in 1603:

> Covering with moss the dead's unclosed eye,
> The little red-breast teacheth charity.

In John Webster's play *The White Devil* (1612), when Cornelia weeps for her murdered son, she cries:

> "Call for the robin red-breast and the wren,
> Since o'er shady graves they hover,
> And with leaves and flowers do cover
> The friendless bodies of unburied men."

Shakespeare's Arviragus makes the same association when he believes Imogen to be dead:

> "I'll sweeten thy sad grave. Thou shalt not lack
> The flower that's like thy face, pale primrose; nor
> The azured harebell . . . . The ruddock would
> With charitable bill—oh Bill, sore shaming
> Those rich-left heirs that let their fathers lie
> Without a monument!—bring thee all this,
> Yea, and furred moss besides."

Such references seem to be connected with the popular medieval Bird Mass, a parody of the church service in which birds played clerical roles. The robin's part was conspicuous. In John Skelton's poem "Philip Sparrow" (c.1509), when all the birds of East Anglia gather for the burial service of a young girl's pet sparrow savagely killed by a cat in Norwich,

> Some to sing and some to say,
> Some to weep and some to pray,
> Every birde in his lay . . . .

the robin officiates:

> And robin redbreast
> He shall be the priest
> The requiem mass to sing,
> Softly warbling . . . .

In the next century the robin was still busy in the churchyard, covering up Robert Herrick's corpse like a good sexton, or piously erecting a funereal monument for Cowley. In the story of the murdered "Babes in the Wood" the robin became a fully-fledged undertaker and ensured the tale's popularity. Some one hundred years after the first known printed version, Addison could declare in the *Spectator* that the ballad was "one of the darling songs of the common people." For a child to listen to the tale dry-eyed was a very bad sign. "It is the first trial of our humanity," observed an eighteenth-century zoologist. Since then the tale has been treated in many forms, including pantomime, and still flourishes. Everyone remembers the robin, although, in the original version, its act of charity was confined to two lines.

The robin's notorious fondness for church-going may have strengthened its fictional role. The robin regularly attended Canterbury Cathedral in the seventeenth century; in 1800 it perched on the organ and provided vocal accompaniment in Bristol Cathedral; in 1840 William Howitt met a robin which was a chorister in Winchester College Chapel. The bird has persistently sung services from lecterns, Bibles, and choir lofts in innumerable parish churches in Surrey, Suffolk, Warwickshire, and elsewhere. Its most memorable appearance was in Westminster Abbey in 1695 when it hopped about the hearse of Queen Mary II, lying in state before her funeral. According to one wit:

> "The Papists say this bird's a fiend
> Which haunts Queen Mary's ghost,
> And by its restless motion shows
> How her poor soul is tossed.
>
> But why then is this pretty bird
> So lively, brisk and merry;
> This rather proves the Queen at ease,
> And safe from Purgatory."

But the hymn-singing robin was also a martyr. Linked with the wren, it was subject to ceremonial slaughter on St. Stephen's day when the following rhyme was sung:

> We hunted the Wren for Robin the Bobbin
> We hunted the Wren for Jack of the Can
> We hunted the Wren for Robin the Bobbin
> We hunted the Wren for everyman.

This jingle and the old couplet "The Robin and the Wren / Are God Almighty's Cock and Hen" suggest that both birds were once sacred, and vestiges of their divinity survive in various taboos, portents, and ceremonies. The well-known "Who Killed Cock Robin?" has obvious medieval antecedents both in its use of formulaic question-and-answer patterns and of the Bird Mass, with the central situation reversing that of Skelton's liturgical parody. But the process whereby the dramatic tales concerning the robin evolved from earlier times and passed from chapbook thrillers to moral tales for children is unknown. For several centuries "The Marriage of Cock Robin and Jenny Wren" appeared in front of "Who Killed Cock Robin?" and both themes are common in folklore. Apparently the Wren did not make a good wife, and in some versions the Sparrow's fatal barb was intended for the Cuckoo who was making a pass at the bride, but what ancient and widespread rites lay behind these stories and that of the Babes in the Wood is a mystery. While the sparrow was primarily a symbol of lust in early times, it was also associated with Christ's passion, a notorious focus for antisemitism in the Middle Ages; in Russian folktales the sparrow betrayed Christ's hiding place in the Garden of Gethsemane, and at the crucifixion it chirped maliciously "Jif! Jif!" (He is living, He is living!) in order to urge the tormentors to further cruelties. According to M.R. James, in a fifteenth-century manuscript the robin symbolizes St. Robert of Bury, and an accompanying illustration shows St. Robert's body lying near a tree and a man shooting an arrow at the tree. St. Robert was one of those innumerable child martyrs alleged to have been murdered by the Jews. It is tempting to conjecture that "Who Killed Cock Robin?" is concerned with the ritualistic killing and is linked to the murder of the boy saint in 1181.

In the latter part of the nineteenth century instead of being a victim, the robin was the receiver of charity. Funds were raised for "Robin Dinners" for starving children; a robin was a "beggar," and "as naked as a robin" was a proverbial expression. At the same time, the bird was still the bringer of charity. In the nursery tale, it continued to cover up the babes with leaves; as the helpful archetypal guiding animal in Frances Hodgson Burnett's famous story, it showed a lonely little girl how to enter the Secret Garden. In robin poems, stories, or nature books written for children by "Auntie May," "A Clergyman's Wife" or "A Lady," when the bird became a ve-hicle for instruction in God's providence, the robin was either a pious social worker itself or the gentle, bright-eyed representative of all dumb animals to which children must show kindness. Some of these works reached the nurseries of this century, and a song which is typical of them in its basic situation, setting, and moral tone is one which I remember from my own childhood:

Said a little Robin Redbreast to a little Christmas Rose,
"Don't you think it's very, very cold today?
I've been out since early morning, and so bitterly it blows,
All my summer friends have flown away.
And I can't find any breakfast and I don't know what
    to do—"
"Don't be anxious, little Robin," said the Rose.
"There's a dear Lord up in Heaven, He cares for me
    and you,
Not a little sparrow falleth but He knows."

"Thank you, thank you," said the Robin, "I will go and
    look again,"
And he kissed the little Rose and off he flew,
And some merry little children opened wide the window-
    pane
And out upon the sill some crumbs they threw . . . .
'Twas the dear Lord up in heaven who the loving
    thought did send,
And the Robin sang once more his happy song;

And the children too were happy, for they loved their
    little friend,
And their crumbs they gave him all the winter long.

This symbolism is peculiarly English. There is no robin in classical poetry, and for centuries in Europe the robin, a very easy bird to capture because of its curiosity and friendliness, was eaten as a common dish, tormented as a child's plaything, strung up to provide a feathered colorful decoration, or caged as a songbird. England, too, had its captive robin, and a Christmas card of the 1870s even shows the bird cheerfully perched on top of a trap bearing the inscription "The Compliments of the Season." But, as Mayhew observed in *London Labour and the London Poor*, "there is a popular feeling repugnant to the imprisonment, or coercion in any way, of 'a robin.'" Wherever the English have settled, in America or in some parts of the dwindling Commonwealth, the prevailing attitude toward the robin appears to be similar to that in England. The large fat American robin is a thrush, of course, but like the English robin it is regarded as a *person*, a visitor to be warmly received. "Everyone knows the robin and ought to welcome and protect him," declares *Birds of America*. Paradoxically, that remarkable poet Emily Dickinson "dreaded the first robin so." To her the bird was a poignant symbol of unthinking beauty, a sign of the world's indifference to her pain.

Finally, we must mention another role of the robin in English life and letters. At a time when animals or birds were frequently used in topical poems to represent people, the robin served as an obvious symbol for Robert. Alas poor Essex! At twenty-one years he was the lover of Queen Elizabeth, approaching sixty, and at thirty-five he was dead. When Robert Devereux, Earl of Essex, rode high in the Queen's favor, one of his admirers wrote a poem beginning:

> Of all the birds that flieth with wing
> The Robin hath no peer,
> For he in field and house can sing
> And chant it all the year . . . .

A poem of his own invention shows Essex, who was totally committed to a life of political and amorous intrigue, longing for rural obscurity in which his tomb may become "a bush / Where harmless Robin dwells with gentle Thrush." Perhaps he chose to see Queen Elizabeth as a thrush for the purpose of rhyme. The thrush's traditional association with old age and its presence at Cock Robin's funeral—sitting on a bush, admittedly, but only to sing psalms for its dead friend—made the symbolism unfortunate. Nor were the adjectives appropriate. A few years later harmless Robin was champing through the London

*These sirens with birds' wings and fishtails
lure men to destruction.*

one alluded to in Drayton's revised edition of *The Owle*. He was Robert, Earl of Somerset, who with the "wren," Lady Frances Howard, murdered his former friend, Sir Thomas Overbury, by dosing him with sulphuric acid.

Even in this century the ghost of Cock Robin remains to be laid. The topical question "Who'll Kill Inflation?," based on the old ballad, demonstrates the firm place which this bird continues to hold in the public imagination.

Addison, *Spectator*, no. 85 (June 7, 1811); Armstrong, *Folklore*, pp. 167–79; *Birds of America*, III, 237; Brown, pp. 152, 159; Drayton, *The Owle*, ll. 87–88; Goldsmith, II, 149; Hayward, pp. 42, 98, 125; Howitt, p. 478; James, p. 19; Lack, *passim*; Mayhew, II, 60; Shakespeare, *Cymbeline* IV.ii.220–28; Webster, *The White Devil* v.iv.92–95.

streets trying to start an insurrection; and the gentle Thrush, having already sufficiently lost patience to punch him in the face, sent him to a far earlier and less peaceful death than he had anticipated. In the case of most political robins appearing in poems, broadsheets, and pamphlets of the seventeenth and eighteenth centuries, the association is in name only, even when bird fables are used. Perhaps the most reprehensible of all robins is the

Siren

"Meremaides be here" proclaim old maps of Britain, and the surrounding seas are asplash with salmon-tailed young women, combing their hair and waving tridents at the Isle of Man. Some say that their voices are still heard at Lamorna Cove in Cornwall, at Cardigan Bay in Wales, along the shores of Lough Neagh in Northern Ireland and many other places. Once a mermaid came up from the sea and sat in a church pew in the little Cornish village of Zennor. She fell in love with a choir boy and persuaded him to join her under the sea. Today, in a carving made five hundred years ago, she still decorates the bench end of the pew which she once occupied, holding a looking glass in her hand and displaying an enormous scaly tail.

Originally all mermaids were kindly creatures and probably evolved from eastern fish goddesses. They became confused with sirens, bird women whose bewitching music lured sailors to their deaths, and by the Middle Ages mermaids or sirens were synonymous and were depicted as all woman, part fish, part fowl, or even part horse. Often repeated was the story of Ulysses; how the Greek hero tied himself to the mast of his ship and stuffed the ears of his oarsmen with wax so that they could resist the fatal singing of the sirens as they passed their island. These particular sirens, as Sir Thomas Browne observed, had "no fishy composure." But however different Homer's sirens might be from the golden-haired Lorelei of the Rhine or from Milton's siren "sleeking her soft alluring hair," they had certain qualities in common. A Hellenic relief of a winged and bird-footed woman sitting astride a sleeping traveler shows the fundamental conception of the siren as *incuba*; she is the lewd demon of the nightmare. She represents the forbidden mother, the projection of repressed incestuous wishes.

The means of enticement is always the same—music. Originally only singing was used; later a trio appeared, consisting of voice, flute, and stringed instrument. This emphasis on sound is highly significant. The female voice, if it is a fascinating, forbidden voice, is phallic. It represents a fetish which in itself derives from a fear of castration. The siren's voice comes from the dreaded, incestuously desired mother, who like the incuba in the nightmare, is omniscient, all powerful, and simultaneously beautiful, malignant, and terrifying. Sir Thomas Browne was probably right in his famous remark on "what song the siren sang." He argued that if it was a puzzling question, the answer was "not beyond all conjecture." According to Bunker:

> The song of the sirens . . . symbolizes the love of the mother in all its allurement, holding forth the promise of the Land of Heart's Desire which symbolizes the possession of the beloved mother; but the end of that song is death (castration).

For many centuries symbolists had nothing good to say about either mermaids or sirens. The patristic theologians believed them to be real creatures expressly intended to serve as deterrent types of the sensual appetite. As of old, they enticed men with their singing and, having put them to sleep, tore them to pieces. "Such are they," declared the author of *De Bestiis*, "who love the delights of this world, its pomps and theatrical pleasures. Made dissolute by tragedies and comedies, as if overcome by heavy sleep, they become the prey of the devil." Isidore said that these creatures, part women and part *volucres* (birds) with wings and talons, were really prostitutes, leading men to disaster. This symbolism was repeated many times both in the Middle Ages and in the Renaissance. In addition the story of Ulysses provided a lesson which the Church was glad to appropriate. According to the usual explication, Ulysses' ship was the church. "The mast symbolizes the cross of Christ to which the faithful must cling in order to escape the seduction of the senses. As our Lord Jesus Christ was nailed to the cross and remained sinless among temptation, so let us navigate the perilous sea of life as if our ears were plugged." In one illustration of the theme an interesting variation occurs. Two of the sirens wear the philosopher's mantle and hold a scroll; they represent false teachers seeking to lead the good Christian astray with their heretical doctrines.

Similar baleful interpretations of the sirens were given in the Renaissance. Camerarius told of the sweet song of the siren with the motto *mortem dabit ipsa voluptas* (pleasure itself will give death). Whitney referred to the story of Ulysses and observed that the man who succumbed to the snare of sirens destroyed himself. Valeriano's siren had rooster's feet and held a fishtail in each hand. She represented men so obsessed with sex that they were prepared to ruin themselves financially. Aldrovandi gave a similar evaluation, while to Picinelli the siren was herself the symbol of pleasure and of the promiscuous woman.

On the other hand, as Claes Schaar observes, in Renaissance texts sirens could also represent poetic inspiration. According to the Italian scholar Gyraldus, the sirens vied with the Muses. Angels were occasionally referred to as sirens. In Crashaw's poem on Christopher Rouse, angels are heavenly sirens.

If the modern symbolism of the siren is close to Picinelli's, contemporary values may affect the application. Generally sirens

stand, it would seem, to the ancient as to the modern, for the impulses in life as yet unmoralized, imperious longings, ecstasies, whether of love or art or philosophy, magical voices calling to a man from his "Land of Heart's Desire" and to which if he hearken it may be he will return home no more—voices, to wit, whether a man sail by or stay to hearken, still sing on.

Viewed less abstractly, the siren may simply represent the woman who, depending on one's point of view, is either entrancing or terrifying. Composed of opposites, the siren is primarily a sexual fantasy: she is beautiful and she is predatory.

156

Aldrovandi, II, 269–70; Anderson, *Med. Carv.*, p. 100; Bunker, pp. 427–28; Burnell, pp. 201–207; *De Bestiis, PL,* 177, col. 78; Druce, "Some Abnormal Forms," p. 170; *EB.,* XVIII, 171; Jane Harrison, p. 206; Homer, *Od.* XII.166ff; Honorius, *PL,* 172, cols. 855, 856; Isidore, xi.3.30; Latini, pp. 131–32; Lowrie, pl. 23b; Ovid, *Met.* v.552; Picinelli, III.xxvii; Schaar, p. 414; Valeriano, f.172; Whitney, p. 10.

Sparrow

The sparrow, "Venus' son," as Chaucer called the bird, has a reputation for lechery which still survives in the Victorian music-hall refrain "Me Old Cock-sparrow!" Like the dove, the sparrow was sacred to Venus, the goddess of love, and early natural historians declared that both birds had no equals for salacity. Modern ornithologists seem to agree with such findings, although some authorities maintain that "coition is normally solicited by the female."

Today we welcome the sparrow in our noisy polluted cities because it is one of the few birds prepared to nest cheerfully behind the bright hoardings of supermarkets or gas stations. Yet in 1559 a Lutheran pastor in Dresden implored the Elector of Saxony to help him exterminate the sparrows because of "their incessant and extremely vexatious chatterings, and scandalous acts of unchastity committed during the service, to the hindrance of God's Word and of Christian Doctrine." According to a French proverb, quoted by Cotgrave (1611): "Passereaux, & moineaux sont de faux oiseaux.—*Cocke Sparrowes & (young) Monkes are (much of a disposition) Shrewd lechers.*" This proverb no doubt puns on *moineau* meaning sparrow and *moine* meaning monk. Perhaps it was current in Chaucer's day. Chaucer likened two clerical gentlemen to sparrows—the syphilitic Summoner who runs a thriving prostitution and protection racket is "as lecherous as a sparwe," and a greedy Friar "chirketh as a sparwe."

The lascivious Devil might assume the form of a sparrow. When St. Dominic was preaching from behind a grille to some sisters in a Roman convent, warning them against the different shapes taken by devils to deceive the elect, a sparrow suddenly flew through the air and hopped on to the sisters' heads. According to Blessed Cecilia, the saint told one of the nuns to catch the bird and hand it to him. Holding the bird fast in one hand he commenced plucking off the feathers with the other, saying the while: "You wretch, you rogue!" When he had plucked him clean of all his feathers amid much laughter from the Brothers and Sisters, and awful shrieks of the sparrow, he pitched him out, saying: "Fly now if you can, enemy of mankind." . . . And so it came about that he employed for God's glory what the enemy of mankind had from envy done for their hurt and hindrance.

According to Horapollo, the Egyptians symbolized a prolific man by the sparrow because of the bird's reputation for lechery. This reputation was continued in the Renaissance in allusions of such writers as Painter, Lodge, Nashe, and others. Aldrovandi pointed out that the sparrow was the hieroglyph of libidiousness, and that bird sirens were sparrows as far down as the breast. Nymphomaniac witches transformed themselves into sparrows, and physicians declared that a roasted sparrow was a splendid aphrodisiac. "This is an undeniable Aphorism," said the seventeenth-century physician Culpepper, "that whatsoever any Creature is addicted unto, they move or incite the man or woman, that eats them, to the like; and therefore Partridges, Quails, Sparrows, etc. being extremely addicted to Venery, they work the same effect in those Men and Women that eat them." But while Ripa described *Lascivia* as a woman with a mirror accompanied by sparrows, he and other emblem writers also gave the sparrow other values. In *Complessioni* the sparrow is the symbol of the melancholic man, and in another emblem the sparrow is the attribute of solitude. Here, the idea derives ultimately from the Psalm ci:8 "factus sum sicut passer solitarius in tecto," in which the psalmist likens himself to the lonely bird on the housetop, a figure difficult to associate with the gregarious sparrow but one which ensured a favorable interpretation. In general the Biblical sparrow was a very different breed from the bird which, according to Bartholomew the Englishman, was "full hot . . . and lecherous." "Are not two sparrows sold for a farthing?" said Christ. "And one of them shall not fall on the ground without your Father knoweth." Under Mosaic Law two sparrows were a purification offering, both for a leper and for a woman who had just given birth. St. Ambrose regarded the sparrows as the body and the soul, "For both are lifted up to God by spiritual wings." Rabanus Maurus used the same symbolism but said that the one was sacrificed and the other flew away. "For the sinner to be cleansed completely," he added, "it is necessary for his body to be punished through mortification and his soul to be elevated into celestial regions by contemplation." "Even the sparrow finds a home . . . where she may lay her young, at Thy altars, O Lord of Hosts!" cried the psalmist (lxxxiv.3). The same theologian took this sparrow to symbolize the righteous man who chose a heavenly dwelling for himself. Garner, on the other hand, took this sparrow to symbolize Christ. In 1559, Aldrovandi tried to sum up the complex Christian tradition of the sparrow. Like the turtledove, the sparrow signified Christ. It might also symbolize prudence, the poor, and martyrs. Edward Topsell, who translated and abridged part of Aldrovandi's work on birds, interpreted the sacrifice of a pair of sparrows and a pair of turtles as symbolizing Christ's charity and chastity. More than a century later, in the Age of Reason, a secular writer, such as Alexander Pope in his philosophical *Essay on Man* (1733–34), could still fit the Biblical sparrow into the eternal scheme of things to reach the satisfactory conclusion that "Whatever is, is right":

Who sees with equal eye, as God of all,
A hero perish, or a sparrow fall,
Atoms or systems into ruin hurled,
And now a bubble burst, and now a world.

In the last century the sparrow played a curious role as both aggressor and victim. The Victorian child in the nursery chanted the story of "Who Killed Cock Robin?" in which the sparrow shoots the fatal arrow; he also learned of the wicked boy seeking to rob a sparrow's nest who was moved to shame when he found it lined with a sheet from Isaac Watt's famous hymn "O God Our Help In Ages Past"; on reaching manhood he became a sparrow himself, solicited in Piccadilly by ladies who were popularly termed "sparrow catchers."

Stemming from the Biblical analogy, the sparrow as mankind is a figure widely known in English literature from Bede to Wordsworth and D.H. Lawrence, as Nicholes observed. In Richard Wilbur's "Still, Citizen Sparrow" (1950), the sparrow seems to stand for humanity: the humble, earth-bound sparrow which darts "in the orchard aisles," is contrasted with the vulture cruising "at the tall tip of the sky," the omniscient bird which:

Devours death, mocks mutability,
Has heart to make an end,
Keeps nature new.

The poet asks Citizen Sparrow to forgive and understand the vulture's heroic function in the eternal cycle of death and rebirth. Wilbur's choice of the sparrow seems to me to be unfortunate, traditional as the symbolism is. For centuries the signs of God's providence have been less evident than they were in ancient Judaea. God may know when a sparrow falls, but the bird has a rough time dying. In the late eighteenth century Grose described a sport called "mumbling the sparrow." With his hands tied behind his back the player had the wing of a sparrow put in his mouth.

With this hold, without any other assistance than the motion of his lips, he is to get the sparrow's head into his mouth: on attempting to do it the bird defends itself surprisingly, frequently pecking the mumbler until his lips are covered with blood.

In the next century children bought sparrows as toys. According to Henry Mayhew:

Strings are tied to their legs and so they have a certain degree of freedom, but when they offer to fly away they are checked, and kept fluttering in the air as a child will flutter a kite. One man told me that he had sometimes sold as many as two hundred sparrows in the back streets about Smithfield on a fine Sunday. These birds are not kept in cages, and so they can only be bought for a plaything.

Aldrovandi, II, 518, 519, 547–54; Ambrose, *PL*, 15, col. 1816; Chaucer, *PF*, 351; *SumT*, 1804; Cotgrave, s.v. *passereau*; Culpepper, p. 139; Fish, pp. 117–18; Garner, *PL*, 193, col. 83; Grange, *The Golden Aphroditis*, k ii verso; Horapollo, p. 156; Kittredge, p. 494; Mayhew, II, 62; Nashe (ed. McKerrow), II, 225; Nicholes, pp. 171–74; Painter (ed. Jacobs), III, 382; Pliny, x.lii; Rabanus Maurus, *PL*, 112, cols. 1022–23; Ripa, II.ii.434; I.i.195; Topsell, p. 10; B. White, p. 36; Witherby, I, 157–58; Wordsworth, *Eccl. Sonnets*, xvi.

Starling

Benvenuto da Imola stated: "Starlings are lustful as birds naturally are; starlings are light, and so are lovers; starlings cross over to the warm parts whither the heat of lechery calls them, and flee cold regions where there are no pretty women." Dante used the image of the starling to describe sinners whom he found shrieking and cursing in Hell:

> Those who sinned in the flesh, the carnal and lusty
> who betrayed reasons to their appetite.

> As the wings of wintering starlings bear them on
> in their great wheeling flights, just so the blast
> wherries these evil souls through time foregone.

Starlings, according to Pliny, could be trained to speak Latin and Greek. Laurence Sterne (1713–68), famous author of *Tristram Shandy*, added the bird as a crest to his arms because of a talking starling. Visiting Paris he saw a caged starling in his hotel and tried to free it:

> "I can't get out—I can't get out," said the starling . . . .
> The bird flew to the place where I was attempting his deliverance, and thrusting his head through the trellis, pressed his breast against it, as if impatient—I fear, poor creature! said I, I cannot set thee at liberty. . . .
> I vow I never had my affections more tenderly awakened.

The starling became the symbol of a captive to Sterne: "I beheld his body half-wasted away with long expectation and confinement, and felt what kind of sickness of the heart it was which arises from hope deferr'd." For a bottle of burgundy, he bought the bird from the hotel manager and took it to England. After passing around the nobility, the unfortunate bird went into "the hands of as many commoners." "I have nothing to add upon him," concluded Sterne rather callously, "but that from that time to this, I have borne this poor starling as the crest to my arms."

Dante (tr. Ciardi), *Inf.* v.38–42; Holbrook, p. 282; Pliny, x.lix; Sterne, *A Sentimental Journey*, pp. 121–29.

Stork

Birds have always been favorite baby-bringing symbols, as we know. But the stork illustrated in birth announcements did not always carry a baby in a pink or blue bassinet; instead the stork flew through the air with one of its parents nesting on its back. Sometimes it flourished a large fish in its beak and fed its parent at the same time. For centuries the stork was the symbol of filial piety. Aristotle, Pliny, Aelian, and others warmly praised the stork's devotion both to its parents and to its young, as well as its general virtues. The Hebrew name for stork meant "the kindly one" or "the loyal one"; in ancient Egypt the stork was praised for similar reasons. Accord-

This stork, catching a frog, is a good parent.

ing to the *Physiologus*, the bird nourished its parents with great affection in their old age. The moralist added: "So also it behoves us to observe these two divine commands, that is, to turn aside from evil and to do good . . . . Honor thy Father and thy Mother." Emblem writers gave the stork the same value. Geoffrey Whitney under the emblem *gratiam referendam* (as a thanksgiving) showed a stork with a snake in its beak flying to three young storks sitting in a nest on a chimney top:

See heare the storke provides with tender care,
And bringeth meate, unto her hatched broode:
They like againe, for her they doe prepare,
When shee is oulde, and can not get her foode:
Which teacheth bothe, the parente and the childe,
Theire duties heare, which eche to other owe:
First, fathers must be provident, and milde,
Unto theire fruicte, till they of age doe growe:
And children, muste with dutie still proceede,
To reverence them, and helpe them if they neede.

In general, the symbolism was favorable, and in emblems and printers' marks the stork was depicted feeding another stork or perched on top of a sceptre as the guardian of piety, or killing a serpent, in which case the bird represented the care for the general good. Representations of the stork with the serpent appear in tapestries and on the capital in the interior courtyard of the Palace of the Doge in Venice, and Whitney's emblem, already noted, makes use of the same device. In his work on heraldry Guillim declared "whatsoever duty a son oweth to his parents, they all are found and observed in the stork," and also made the stork as the emblem of a grateful man. Aldrovandi saw the bird as representative of gratitude, temperance, chastity, piety, and other virtues. Its very appearance was an omen of fertility and harmony. Topsell, in common with Alciatus, Valeriano, Ripa, and others, declared that the bird was *avis piissima* (a most

pious bird), and called it a bird of God.

The nest on the chimney came itself to represent piety. If the bird deserted its nest it was either a portent of death or a reproach to the householders beneath. Very widespread was the idea that the stork was "the avenger of adultery," as Chaucer once claimed. Aristotle had stated that the stork would kill its spouse if she was false, and Aelian told of a stork that struck out the eyes of a servant who seduced his employer's wife. The medieval *Gesta Romanorum* contains the curious tale of a knight who had a very beautiful castle upon which two storks built their nest. The female stork was unfaithful, and before the return of her husband she used to wash herself in a fountain. The owner of the castle, observing the female stork's behavior, closed up the fountain with the result that the male discovered his wife's defection. The male bird flew away and brought back other storks which put the adultress to death. According to the *significatio*, the two storks were Christ and the Soul; the knight was the devil and the fountain represented confession and repentance. If Christ at the Day of Judgment finds us unwashed, that is, impenitent, concluded the writer, He will come with a multitude of angels and put us to death.

The stork commonly nests on buildings rather than trees, and if its desertion of its nest meant bad luck, its presence is still considered very lucky. Its common Dutch name *ooievaar* can be traced to the old word *odebëro* (the bringer of good). That the stork should be chosen to bring the baby is probably due to the ancient belief, repeated by Gesner and others, that the stork building its nest on a house left one of its young out of gratitude to the owner. According to some versions of the tale, the infant bird was actually dropped or sacrificed, and the stork itself became the emblem of generosity. Marvell has a reference to this belief in his poem "Upon Appleton House:"

> The heron from the Ashes top,
> The eldest of its young lets drop,
> As if it Stork-like did pretend,
> That *Tribute* to its Lord to send.

The word *pretend* here suggests that the stork might have another motive such as wishing to save itself the trouble of looking after its offspring. Marvell may be looking back to another tradition which in the Middle Ages reversed the common values and associated the stork with the sin of Sloth.

Aelian, III.23; VIII.20; Alciatus, pp. 134–37, xxx; Aldrovandi, III, 296–307; Aristotle, *H.A.* IX.13; Bloomfield, 248; Camerarius, III.xl; Chaucer, *PF*, 361; *Gesta*, lxxxii; Guillim, p. 157; Horapollo, p. 122; Marvell, ll. 533–36; Neckam, pp. 112–13; *Physiologus*, pp. 106–108; Pliny, x.xxxi, xxxii; Réau, I.102; Ripa, I.i.26–27, 195; Swann, p. 251; Topsell, p. 10; Turner, p. 55; Valeriano, ff.124–27; Wenzel, p. 106; Whitney, p. 75.

Swallow

Most city dwellers would recognize the swallow by its forked tail, steel-blue upper plumage, and reddish brown parts on its breast, but they would not expect to see one in their garden. The swallow is essentially a countryman's bird, nesting in barns, boathouses, chimneys, and under the eaves of houses.

"Chelidona oikia mē dechou" (Do not receive a swallow in the house), said Pythagoras, the famous philosopher and mathematician. The advice must have surprised some of his disciples because in Greece the swallow, as in most countries, was warmly welcomed as a lodger. The famous "Swallow Song" which children sang from door to door in ancient Rhodes greeted the swallows as heralds of the spring and invited them to nest in the house:

> He has come, He has come, the Swallow!
> Happy seasons bringing,
> And happy years
> Open, open the door to the swallow!

Up to this century swallows have habitually nested in houses in Greece, Germany, Russia, England, and elsewhere, especially among peasant communities, the general belief being that the bird was an omen of good luck. Toward the end of the nineteenth century a remarkable American student of Japanese culture, Dr. Edward S. Morse (1838–1925), said that in Japan not only in the country but in large cities, such as Tokyo, the swallow nested

> in the room where the family may be most actively engaged, or in the shop fronting the street, with all its busy traffic going on. The very common occurrence of these birds' nests in houses is another of the many evidences of the gentle ways of this people and of the kindness shown by them to animals. When a bird builds its nest in the house, a little shelf is promptly secured beneath it, so that the mats below shall not be soiled.

The author added that these nests were "a household shrine to which the children paid voluntary and natural devotion." For the same reason, Peking was known as the City of Swallows.

Such respect for the bird looks back to the time when the swallow was divine, accustomed to fly unmolested in the great temples at Athens, Olympia, and Epidaurus. Even the birds of prey did not dare to touch the swallow, so Solinus claimed, because it was a sacred bird. It was also admired by the Hebrews. The Hebrew word *deror* which, according to Møller-Christensen and Jordt Jørgensen means "swallow," derives from a root meaning "to release." They add: "It is true that the swallow, unlike many other songbirds, does not thrive in captivity. The name also recognizes the fast, unrestrained, and graceful flight of this bird, a trait also hinted at in Proverbs (xxvi.2) where the swallow's style of flying is compared with that of the sparrow: 'like a sparrow in its flitting, like a swallow in its flying, a curse that is causeless does not alight.'" To some Biblical explicators, Jeremiah's swallow (Hebrew *sus*) which knew its time was John the Baptist (viii.7). With the advent of Christianity, the swallow immediately became one of the faithful: St. Francis welcomed the bird as his sister; in some countries it was known as the chicken of the Lord or the bird of the Madonna or of God Himself—"The Martin and the Swallow / Are God Almighty's birds to hallow"; it was God's assistant when He built the sky. Believed by many to hibernate in mud during the winter and become revitalized in the spring, the swallow symbolized the rebirth of the year and of hope for mankind. In some accounts of the pseudo-Matthew legend, the clay birds which the Christ Child miraculously brought to life were swallows. Rabanus Maurus regarded the bird as a symbol of *assiduitas orationis* (constant attendance to prayer). He based his symbolism on Isaiah xxxviii.14: *"Sicut pullus hirundinis, sic clamabo"* (Like the young of the swallow, I will call out). On the other hand, when he interpreted the apocryphal book of Tobit, the swallow's dung became a pejorative symbol. While Tobit was asleep the warm droppings from a swallow's nest fell into his eyes and blinded him. According to Rabanus Maurus, these excrements represented pride. Some Church Fathers saw the swallow as the symbol of maternal care and domestic contentment, even in poverty. They may have been alluding partly to the belief expressed by Pliny and others that young swallows are born blind and that their sight is restored when their parents bring to the nest the yellow flowering celandine, its name in itself deriving from the Greek chelidōn: a swallow. The swallow did in fact comprise many medicinal remedies both in ancient and medieval times: boiled in wine, for example, it promoted strength, according to the Leech-doms; its excrements aided childbirth, according to Trotula.

A sacred bird is always feared as well as respected. If the swallow's appearance was the sign of spring, its disappearance in late summer was a less happy portent. Plato in his ideal republic apparently foresaw poets clamoring to read their works in public just as they do today. Far from encouraging them with liberal government grants and governor general's awards, he recommended anointing their heads, crowning them with fillets of wool, and leading them gently away. According to Chrysostom, women

Swallows are a sign of spring.

did the same to swallows, hoping that they would not return.

Pythagoras' desire to ban the swallow was not prompted by scepticism or concern for hygiene. He probably regarded the bird as a creature of ill-omen. The famous dream expert Artemidorus said that a swallow appearing in a dream gave a warning of untimely death. In some countries a swallow flying down a chimney or through

165

a window was believed to bring a similar message. While a diet of swallows cured drunkenness according to King Orus of Assyria, the Chewsurs of the Caucasus believed that a generous swig of wine or brandy was the best way to fortify oneself against the evil consequences of seeing the first swallow. In parts of Scotland and Ireland the swallow was the devil's bird; in Caighness it was called "witch hag"; every Irishman possessed a certain hair on his head which, if seized by the swallow, brought disaster. In *Antony and Cleopatra* Shakespeare used the swallow as an omen of impending catastrophe:

> Swallows have built
> In Cleopatra's sails their nest: the augurers
> Say they know not, they cannot tell; look grimly,
> And dare not speak their knowledge.

The typical attitude toward a swallow was ambivalent. According to Horapollo, when the Egyptians "would signify that the whole of a parent's substance has been left to the son, they depict a swallow. For she rolls herself in the mud, and builds a nest for her young, when she is herself about to die." Valeriano took the bird as a symbol of impartiality because, according to Aristotle, the swallow fed all its offspring equally. Ripa and others regarded the swallow as an attribute of military architecture because of the bird's remarkable way of building its nest. Here the opinion of the swallow's nest-building appears to be different from that once held in China where, according to Williams, "the fragile nest of the bird is metaphorically applied to positions of insecurity and danger."

The swallow is often represented in opposition to the sparrow. The sparrow was eternally cursed for its behavior at Christ's passion; the swallow, according to the Scandinavians, was known as the *svalow*, or the Bird of Consolation because at the crucifixion it cried *"Svale! Svale!"* (Console Him! Console Him!). It was the swallow which tried to carry away the nails from Calvary; the sparrow which brought them back. In Russian folktales, it was the swallow which fluttered around the cross crying *"Umer! Umer!"* (He is dead! He is dead!), trying to persuade the torturers to desist; it was the sparrow which chirped *"Jif! Jif!"* (He is living! He is living!) to encourage the soldiers to further cruelty. According to the Spaniards, the swallow acquired the patch on its throat when it tried to peck out the thorns from Christ's crown.

This opposition of the two birds may have a sexual basis. Both birds were associated with love and in ancient Rome were used as terms of endearment. In the *Book of Secrets* Albertus Magnus, a firm believer in sympathetic magic, recommended both birds as aphrodisiacs:

And because the Swallow loveth greatly, as Philosophers saith, therefore they choose her greatly to stir up love. Likewise the Dove and the Sparrow are holden to be of this kind especially when they are delighted in love, or carnal appetite, for then they provoke and bring love without resistance.

Like the dove, the sparrow was Venus' bird, insatiably lecherous and an obvious phallic symbol. The swallow, according to Suidas' lexicon, represented the female pudendum, and its associations with women persisted for many centuries. Among the wild theories concerning the bird's migratory habits was the view that, far from sleeping under water in a river bed as even Dr. Samuel Johnson had believed, swallows flew to the moon, the most obvious of feminine symbols. Medieval misogynists were quick to note that some natural historians linked the swallow with the salacious mouse as the most intractable of all creatures and they added further accusations of greed and loquacity. According to the writer of "The Pain and Sorrow of Evil Marriage,"

> Wyves been bestes [beasts] very unstable
> In ther desires, which may not chaunged be,
> Like a swallowe which is insaciable . . . .

Chaucer likened the loud eager voice of the flighty young wife of old John, the carpenter, to a swallow chittering on a barn, presumably alluding to the swallow's shrill cry made in excitement or alarm. In the Renaissance, Gesner, the natural historian, referred to the swallow as *garrulitas* (garrulous); Ripa represented loquacity as an open-

The swallow is often a feminine symbol.

mouthed woman with a swallow on her head and a raven in her right hand. Here, the swallow "signifies the tiresome and importunate nature of loquacity, which offends the studious mind." Alciatus and Valeriano gave a similar symbolism. Guillim, in common with Valeriano and Camerarius, saw the swallow as resembling "fained and

167

temporizing friends" who will fraternize gladly "in the Spring of Honours, and Summer of Abundance" but will desert those who experience "the Winter of Adversity." Whitney, showing a swallow carrying a grasshopper to its nest, repeated an idea that was a favorite among the emblem writers. Here the swallow turns on a friend and becomes a tyrant. Dissension among equals, said the writer, was the worst. The bird's migratory habits also made it the symbol of the wanderer.

The swallow's twittering, pleasant as it was to seem to the Romantic poets, reminds us that the bird is the unhappy Progne of one of the oldest legends in the world. Progne's husband Tereus kidnapped, raped, and imprisoned her sister Philomela, and tore out her tongue to ensure secrecy. Philomela wove her story into a tapestry, sent the dumb but revealing work of art to Progne, and then joined her sister in exacting so horrible a revenge that all three ceased to be human and were changed into birds. In the Ovidian version Progne became a swallow with blood-stained breast, Philomela a nightingale singing at night of eternal passion and eternal pain, and Tereus a hoopoe. Robert Graves provides a characteristically ingenious explanation for the origin of the tale. The Phocian Greeks devised it to explain a set of Thraco-Pelasgian religious pictures which they found in a temple at Daulis and could not understand. The pictures all showed different methods of divination. Philomela was a priestess inducing a trance by chewing laurel leaves; what interpreters had taken for her tongue was really another laurel leaf which an attendant was handing her to chew. The scene in which Tereus eats his son shows a priest taking omens from the entrails of a sacrificed child. The scene of Progne transformed into a swallow shows a priestess in swallow disguise taking auguries from the flight of the swallow. The other bird transformations should be similarly interpreted. Unfortunately, Graves provides no evidence that such representations ever existed. In another version of the legend Philomela becomes the swallow and Progne the nightingale. Algernon Swinburne (1837–1909) used Ovid's version in "Itylus," one of the most haunting of a collection of poems which earned him the extraordinary title of "the libidinous laureate of a pack of satyrs." Implicit in this lyrical treatment is the traditional idea of the swallow's instability:

> Swallow, my sister, O sister swallow,
>   How can thine heart be full of the spring?
>   A thousand summers are over and dead.
> What hast thou found in the spring to follow?
>   What hast thou found in thine heart to sing?
>   What wilt thou do when the summer is shed?
>
> O swallow, sister, O fair swift swallow,
>   Why wilt thou fly after spring to the south,
>   The soft south whither thine heart is set?

Shall not the grief of the old time follow?
  Shall not the song thereof cleave to thy mouth?
    Hast thou forgotten ere I forget? . . . .

O sweet stray sister, O shifting swallow,
  The heart's division divideth us.
    Thy heart is light as a leaf of a tree;
But mine goes forth among sea-gulfs hollow
  To the place of the slaying of Itylus,
    The feast of Daulis, the Thracian sea.

O swallow, sister, O rapid swallow,
  I pray thee sing not a little space.
    Are not the roofs and the lintels wet?
The woven web that was plain to follow,
  The small slain body, the flowerlike face,
    Can I remember if thou forget?

O sister, sister, thy first-begotten!
  The hands that cling and the feet that follow,
    The voice of the child's blood crying yet.
Who hath remembered me? who hath forgotten?
  Thou hast forgotten, O summer swallow,
    But the world shall end when I forget.

Aelian, I.52; III.24–25; Albertus Magnus, *Secrets*, p. 81; Alciatus, pp. 247–49, lxx; Aldrovandi, II, 681; Altick, p. 198; Ambrose, *PL*, 14, col. 244; Aristotle, *H.A.* IX.7; Artemidorus, II, 66; Bannerman, III, 376; Brand, p. 92; Camerarius, III.lxxxv, lxxxvi; Evans, pp. 7, 55; Friedman, p. 8; Gesner, III.iii.549; Graves, p. 436; Gubernatis, II, 240; Guillim, p. 163; Horapollo, p. 107; Ingersoll, pp. 96, 152; Leechdoms, II, 154; Mayer (ed.), p. 401; Møller-Christensen & Jordt Jørgensen, pp. 184–85; Morse, p. 227; Plato, *Republic*, III, 9, p. 398a; Pliny, VIII.xli; x.xlix; Pythagoras, Jamblicus, *Adhort. ad. philos.* (ed. Kiessling), p. 314; Rabanus Maurus, *PL*, 112, col. 954; Ripa (ed. Richardson), pp. 77, 90–91; Rowland, *Blind Beasts*, p. 24; Shakespeare, *Antony and Cleopatra* IV.xii.3; Trotula, XVI; Valeriano, ff.161v–63v; Whitney, p. 4; Williams, p. 350; Witherby, II, 227.

Swan

Although the word *swan-song*, meaning "last work or the last appearance of a writer or performer," is in all dictionaries, swans are anything but musical. As Oliver Goldsmith observed:

The tame swan is one of the most silent of all birds; and the wild one has a note extremely loud and disagreeable. It is probable, the convulsions of the wind-pipe may have contributed to increase the clangour of it; for such is the harshness of its voice, that the bird from thence has been called the hooper. In neither is there the smallest degree of melody.

Swans like singing to the harp.

Nevertheless, from earliest times the swan has been associated with music. Among the Egyptians the swan was the hieroglyphic of music, and Horapollo said that a swan signified a musical old man because "when old it sings the sweetest melody." In Greece it was Apollo's bird and was often represented as singing to the lyre. Aristotle gave the

swan's fabled ability as a fact of natural history, and while it was challenged by Pliny in the first century it still needed to be refuted in the seventeenth and eighteenth centuries by Sir Thomas Browne and Oliver Goldsmith. These last two writers were particularly indignant that the famous Italian naturalist Aldrovandi in 1559 declared that the English bred swans in large numbers on the sea near London and these birds greeted every returning fleet with "loud and cheerful singing." In his fourteenth-century *Bestiary of Love*, Richard de Fournival expressly likened the singing swan to the love sick poet: "The better the swan harmonizes with the harp, the more certain he is to die soon; for this reason the poet has left off singing and sends to his love in writing." Early in the nineteenth century, Coleridge's amusing couplet shows that the ancient association which gave the name of swan to Anacreon, Pindar, Virgil, Shakespeare, and many other poets still prevailed:

> Swans sing before they die; 'twere no bad thing
> Did certain persons die before they sing.

Because the swan was believed to foresee its own fate Socrates alluded to himself as a swan before his death. He declared that his swan-song derived not from grief but from joy at his prophetic vision of the blessings in the other world. By the sixteenth and seventeenth centuries the swan's prophetic vision had become a further proof of its virtue either as a poet or as an aged holy man. While some emblem writers such as Alciatus and Whitney used the swan on a shield expressly for *Insignia Poetarum* (the insignia of poets) who "must be cleane, and pure, and must of crime beware," others made the swan symbolize virtuous and eloquent old age or purity itself. In his work *De Volatilibus*, 1595, Camerarius put a swan on a tombstone with the motto *Sibi canit et orbi* (It sings for itself and for the world). The implication is that the swan's celebration of death is triumphal.

In Christian terms the dying swan was a type of martyrdom, of Christian resignation, of serenity in death, and of Christ himself speaking from the cross. In a passage not found in other bestiaries, a French prose bestiary praises the swan's wonderful singing and its ability to harmonize with the harp. It adds, *Cest chine que si bien cante encontre sa mort, senefie l'ame qui a joie en tribulation* (This swan which sings so well against its death signifies the soul which has joy in tribulation). The same symbolism occurs in religious tracts such as *A Tretyse of Love*. Neckam, on the other hand, finds the swan a symbol of the repentant sinner. "What shall we say of the swan," he asks, "who seems to be clad in its tender age in a dusky hue but before long changes to a dazzling whiteness? Even thus some men seem first to be darkened by a cloud of sin, and afterwards are clad in the spiritual raiment of the dazzling whiteness of innocence."

Other medieval writers discovered less admirable qualities in the swan. To Rabanus Maurus the swan represented Pride, *Cygnus est superbia, ut in lege prohibetur, ne quis manducet cygnum* [Leviticus xi.18], *id est ne exhibeat se elatum* (For the eating of swan is forbidden under the law, that is to say, one must not display oneself proudly). Medieval moralists also regarded swans as symbols of hypocrisy "because they have fine wings, and yet can scarce raise themselves from the earth, so that the wings are of no use to them; besides, the feathers of a swan are white perfection, but their flesh is very black, as are the hypocrites, appearing outwardly virtuous, and being inwardly very wicked." The concept of the swan as a hypocrite was one which was to pass over to secular literature. Chaucer's friars that are

> Fat as a whale and walkynge as a swan,
> Al vinolent as botel in the spence
>
> (Fat as a whale and walking like a swan,
> As full of wine as a bottle in the wine-cellar)

are probably to be associated with hypocrisy. Instead of being abstemious, the friars walk awkwardly like swans, swaying from side to side as though drunk. The image is also appropriate because various proverbial expressions imply that the bird is always thirsty and exemplifies the sin of Sloth.

Alas Sloth, that devoute woman
Which hath the proprete of a swan
Evyr to be in plenty of licour . . .

exclaims the anonymous writer of "Colin Blowbol's
Testament."

A more unusual association in medieval times is with the
Immaculate Conception. The swan was the form which
Zeus had taken in order to seduce the beautiful mortal
Leda. The story acquired Christian significance as a result
of scholars' keenness to give pagan myths a contemporary
meaning, and they interpreted Zeus's action as a foreshadowing of the union of the Virgin with the Holy
Ghost. The myth itself points to the ancient idea of the
swan as a divine being. Very widespread are the ideas of
the transformation of humans into swans, of the bird as
the human soul which brought death to anyone who tried
to kill it. The legend of the Knight of the Swan who
mysteriously appears and disappears in a boat drawn by
a white swan occurs in various versions down to Wagner's
Lohengrin in 1850. Other folktales were grafted on to it
at a very early date, usually concerning royal children who
take the forms of swans with gold necklaces. Rituals in
Siberian tribes still contain allusions to the story motif
of the enchanted swan maiden who becomes mortal when
her lover steals her feathers but resumes her bird form
when she retrieves them. The fact that in some European
versions the visitation of swan maidens occurs on the
night of St. John's Eve, the summer solstice, suggests that
we have the remnants of a forgotten ceremonial worship
of the swan.

As a heraldic bird the swan made its appearance as
early as 370 B.C. It was the blazon of the Ionian city of
Clazomenae and it strutted on a most impressive four-
drachma piece, wings up, wild and aggressive, a perfect
foil to the handsome, virile-looking, square-jawed Apollo
on the other side. In medieval Europe the widespread use
of the swan in chivalry reflects the rich myth and ritual
associated with the bird in earlier times. The Counts of
Boulogne claimed descent from the Knight of the Swan.
John Rous, a chantry priest, writing in the late fifteenth
century, stated that the first Saxon Earl of Warwick, and
the Earls of Hereford and Stafford, who bore the swan as
their crest, were descended from Eneas, called the Knight
of the Swan. Eneas, a king's son, was the eldest of six
brothers and sisters born at one birth, of whom the rest
were changed by enchantment into swans with collars
and chains of gold. It was customary for knights to make
their vows of arms "before the swan." Edward I is said
to have sworn an oath on two swans decorated with gold
necklaces when he was being invested as a knight. Two
swans with trappings of gold were brought into the royal
palace when his son was knighted at Westminster. As
the knights sat feasting, a gaily dressed minstrel entered
and demanded that the knights should make their vows

before the swan. The swan was the heraldic badge of the Bohuns, a powerful family in thirteenth- and fourteenth-century England, and from them it passed to the Duke of Gloucester, the uncle of Richard II. As such, the swan appears in several political poems of the 1390s by John Gower and others deploring the King's misrule and lamenting the death of Gloucester, the Swan, after he had been declared guilty of treason. Later, in 1440, Frederick II of Brandenburg instituted an Order of the Swan, and in 1453 Phillip the Good, Duke of Burgundy, held a tournament at which the Knight of the Swan awarded his bravest opponent with a gold swan decorated with a golden chain. The joust for the occasion was proclaimed at a banquet given by Duke Adolf of Cleves, whose family also claimed descent from the Swan Knight.

On a more mundane level, the swan served as a very popular inn sign. It was an eye-catching figure, and in addition, as Colin Blowbol's Testament shows, the bird was proverbially associated with drinking. The swan on the hoop was the sign on a metal hoop, the ale-stake whereby the brewer advertised his house. The *Liber Albus* in 1419 complained that these signs were often very heavy and projected too far into the road, creating a hazard to passers-by. The inn, "The Swan With Two Necks," looks back to the time when the swan was a royal bird and the privilege of keeping swans was granted from the crown. Swan marks or notches were carved on the bills of the

The Swan Poet dances with the maidens.

173

bird to denote ownership. A swan with two nicks belonged to the Vintners' Company.

From Homer to Yeats the bird has been a fine subject for the poet. Spenser's great prewedding poem "Prothalamion," with its haunting refrain "Sweet Thames, run softly till I end my song," reverses the customary phallicism of Apollo's bird and gives the swan the quality assigned to it by the emblem writers, *animi candor* (purity of the soul). The whole poem is built around the two white swans which sail in triumphal procession along the Thames to their wedding in London, and they are a magnificent symbol for the two brides, Lady Elizabeth and Lady Katherine Somerset, to whom the poem is dedicated. Apart from forming a splendid pictorial image, in their whiteness and "beauties bright," the swans reflect the qualities and virtues of the brides:

> With that, I saw two Swannes of goodly hewe,
> Come softly swimming downe along the Lee;
> Two fairer Birds I yet did never see:
> The snow which doth the top of Pindus strew,
> Did never whiter shew,
> Nor Jove himselfe when he a Swan would be
> For love of Leda, whiter did appeare:
> Yet Leda was they say as white as he,
> Yet not so white as these, nor nothing neare;
> So purely white they were . . . .

Aelian, x.36; Alciatus, p. 587, clxxxiii; *Allit. Poem.* (ed. Wright), pp. 15, 56n; Aristotle, *H.A.* ix.12; Armstrong, "The Symbolism," p. 58; *Folklore*, pp. 48–61; Bannerman, vi, 180–86; Browne, iii.xxvii.1; Burn, p. 235; Cahier & Martin, iii, 233; Camerarius, iii.xxiii; Chaucer, *SumT*, 1929–31; Chew, pp. 99, 122n.50, 124, 196; "Colin Blowbol," p. 6; Creuzer, iv, ii, ccx; Douglas, pp. 108–109; Evans, p. 239; De Fournival, pp. 13–14; Goldsmith, ii, 226–27; Guillim, iii.156; Heckscher, p. 218; Horapollo, p. 111; *Liber Albus*, iii, pt. iii, 389; Neckam, p. 101; *Political Poems* (ed. Wright), 1.363–66; Rabanus Maurus, *PL*, 112, col. 894; Réau, 1.103; Ripa, 1.i.71–72; Rows Roll, no. 18; Rowland, *Blind Beasts*, pp. 60–61, 89–90; Seltman, 105 a & b; Seznec, p. 89; Sneyd, p. 62; Swainson, p. 151; Swan, pp. 413–14; Swann, p. 253; Thompson, pp. 179–86; Todd, *passim*; *Tretyse of Love*, p. 112; Valeriano, ff.164–65v; Wagner, pp. 127–38; Whitney, p. 126.

Thrush

The thrush eyes you sadly from the closely packed cages of singing birds that daily line the left bank of the Seine in Paris: it huddles in a cage suspended from a nail in the century-old Sunday bird market off Kalitnikovskaya

Street, Moscow—an enterprise currently praised in the West as one of the few free commercial activities permitted in the Soviet Union. In the last century when Mayhew observed that "among the working-men of England no bird is a greater favourite than the thrush," he meant the caged bird and it was bred for the street market. "These men," Mayhew added, "exert themselves to bring up thrushes to sing well, and then they command good prices."

Among the Romans, Agrippina, the mother of Nero, noted for her cruelty, had a thrush which mimicked what people said. Pliny said that its ability was unprecedented. Thrushes were also bred for the table like battery chickens:

> The doors [of the Aviaries] were very low, there were but few windows, and always so turned, that the prisoners could see neither the woods nor country, nor even the birds which hovered outside, so that nothing might hinder them from growing fat.

The nineteenth-century editors of Oliver Goldsmith's work on animals and birds, who describe these practices with extraordinary gusto, find the flesh of the song thrush or mavis "the most delicate of any," while that of the mistletoe or missel thrush is inferior because its diet of hips, flax-seed, and berries in general "impart to it a disagree-able taste, and cannot produce the delicate fat which renders the other thrushes so highly esteemed in some places as an article of game." Similarly, the mavis is more highly valued for its song. It is "susceptible of education, learns even to speak, and whistles very agreeably many airs of the bird-organ and the flageolet." There is some confusion over the names. Newton distinguishes the song thrush, also known as the mavis, from the less musical missel thrush which in the mating season takes its stand on a tall tree "like an enchanter calling up the gale," and "with a loud voice proclaims in wild and discontinuous notes the fervor of his love for his mate." Whether John Skelton was making the distinction when he referred to the "threstill, with her warblynge" and the mavis with her "whistell" in *Phillip Sparrow* is not clear. Certainly Spenser appears to differentiate when he describes the birds singing on his wedding day:

> The merry larke hir mattins sings aloft
> The thrush replyes, the mavis descant playes.

Whatever the distinction, the thrush's role here looks back to the medieval Bird Mass, a traditional poetic form in which birds blithely sang various parts of the church service in honor of sacred or profane love. Essentially the thrush was a member of the bird choir warbling in the garden of love in *The Romaunt of the Rose*, "The Parlia-

175

ment of Fowls," "The Armonye of Byrdes," "La Messe des Oisiaus," and other poems.

In some early works the bird was quarrelsome. Carleton Brown, noting that a love lyric described the thrush as "doughty in argument," remarks that the bird had "a reputation for contentiousness." Presumably this trait belonged to the missel thrush. Not only was the bird known as the "storm-cock" from its habit of singing in bad weather, but its harsh cries uttered in anger or alarm gave rise to local names such as "schreech," "shrite," and "skrike," all traceable to the Old English *scric*, glossed as *turdus*, thrush, in early vocabulary books. But the roles of the missel thrush and the mavis are not always consistent. The threstlecok angrily denounces women in the early part of "The Thrush and the Nightingale," while in "The Court of Love," it sings with a harmony surpassing that of the first legendary musician, Tubal Cain. It is the mavis in "The Court of Love" which introduces a jarring note by scorning the gentle song of the turtledove.

The thrush had other values. It had no place in the bestiaries, but, as Wenzel notes, in a religious treatise by the Franciscan, Malachy of Limerick, the bird was likened to the deadly sin of Sloth. *Turdus*, Latin for thrush, was erroneously associated with *tardus*: late or slow. In the next century Vincent de Beauvais made a similar etymological distinction: *Turdi autem a tarditate vocati sunt*. In the Renaissance the bird was associated with *taciturni-tas* and was said to have been sacred to Harpocrates, the god of silence. Some praised it for a lack of garrulity; others quoted as a proverb *surdior turdo* (deafer [or dumber] than a thrush). Aldrovandi referred to it as a bird of prophecy: when thrushes gathered in large flocks they were an omen of imminent plague.

With the industrial revolution in Britain, to the city dweller such as Wordsworth's poor Susan, the thrush at the corner of Wood Street symbolizes lost happiness as it brings a fleeting vision of the countryside:

> Green pastures she views in the midst of the dale,
> Down which she so often has tripped with her pail;
> And a single small cottage, a nest like a dove's,
> The one only dwelling on earth that she loves.

Similarly nostalgic are the emotions felt by Robert Browning as he thinks of the thrush in a blossoming pear tree, singing each song twice over:

> Lest you should think he never could recapture
> The first fine careless rapture!

Chaucer wrote of the "throstil old" and Hardy of the "aged thrush," probably not because of the folk belief that the thrush lived to an extreme old age but because the thrush often looks old. Chaucer's thrush is one of a catalog of birds; Hardy's is a symbol of hope. In the "Darkling Thrush," Hardy at the beginning of a new year sees a world of grayness and death. But with the joyous voice of "an aged thrush, frail, gaunt, and small," scarcely one of Darwin's fittest who will survive, the death lament turns into ecstatic carolings, and the bird's song symbolizes, says Hardy, "some blessed Hope, whereof he knew / And I was unaware." The meaning of Frost's thrush music in "Come In!" is less clear. In the darkness of the woods the music is "almost like a call to come in / To the dark and lament." Frost refuses. Instead he is "out for the stars" which, as opposed to the thrush music, seem to epitomize gaiety and aspiration.

Aldrovandi, II, 575ff.; "Armonye of Byrdes," p. 6, ll. 86–90; Carleton Brown, p. 225; Browning, "Home-Thoughts From Abroad," ll. 14–16; Camerarius, III.lxxii; Chaucer, *PF*, 364; "Court of Love," ll. 1388–93, 1401–1407; Gesner, II.ii.762–63; Goldsmith, pp. 138–40; Harrison, *They Tell of Birds*, p. 81n; Hudson, pp. 59–67; Lampe, "Parlement," p. 177; "Tradition," p. 54; Mayhew, II, 61; "La Messe des Oisiaus," p. 6; Newton, *EB.*, XXVI, 892; Pliny, x.lix; *Romaunt*, ll. 619, 665; Spenser, *Epith.* l. 81; Valeriano, f.184; Vincent de Beauvais, *Spec. Nat.* XVI.cxlii; Wenzel, p. 107.

Vulture

"The sloth, the filth, and the voraciousness of these birds, almost exceeds credibility," wrote Oliver Goldsmith in the late eighteenth century.

> In the Brazils, where they are found in great abundance, when they light upon a carcass, which they have liberty to tear at their ease, they so gorge themselves that they are unable to fly; but keep hopping along when they are pursued . . . . But they soon get rid of their burden; for they have a method of vomiting up what they have eaten.

Although the bird to this day remains the symbol of voracity, in warm countries where decomposition occurs very rapidly it was regarded as an emblem of the highest good. According to Horapollo, the vulture symbolized many things. It was a symbol of vision in ancient Egypt because it saw more keenly than other birds; of a boundary because it marked out the spot where a battle was to be fought by going there seven days beforehand; of foreknowledge and of the year itself. Above all, it was the symbol of purification, compassion, and maternity.

Great mother goddesses had vulture heads or vulture attributes, and from Egypt where the bird was associated with Maut, the goddess of eternity, came the widely disseminated belief that the vulture was impregnated by the wind.

> To denote a mother . . . they delineate a vulture. They signify by it a *mother*, because in this race of creatures

there is no male. They are produced, however, in this way. The vulture is kindled with a desire to conceive, opening her womb to the North Wind, she is, as it were, embraced by him for five days, during which time she partakes neither of food nor drink, being intent upon procreation. There are also other kinds of birds which conceive by the Wind, but their eggs are of use only for food and not for procreation, but the eggs of the vultures that are impregnated by the Wind possess a vital principle.

This story got into patristic literature to support the dogma of the virgin birth of Christ. In the fourth century both St. Basil and St. Ambrose made use of the vulture's parthenogenesis. "What say those who are accustomed to smile at our mysteries," observed St. Ambrose,

when they hear that a virgin may generate . . . . Is that thing thought impossible in the Mother of God which is not denied to be possible in vultures? A bird bears without a mate and none confutes it, and because Mary bore when betrothed, they question Her chastity. Do we not perceive that the Lord sent beforehand many examples from nature itself to which incarnations He proved the virtues of the suspected ones and added truth [to the story]?

Among other Christian commentators the vulture had a dual symbolism. In Job xxviii.7, *Nec intuitus est eam oculus vulturis* (Nor has the eye of the vulture perceived it), the vulture is the Savior, according to Rabanus Maurus; the vulture in Leviticus xi.15, that must not be eaten, is any rapacious man. In the bestiaries, the vulture is described as a bird which follows armies to feed on corpses; whenever two lines of battle are drawn up against each other, the birds pursue in a long column and show by the length of the column how many men will die in the struggle. The vulture readily eats the eyes and then extracts the whole of the brain (*la chervele*) through the eyes. It can smell carrion from a distance of a three-day journey. This bird, according to medieval moralists, was the Devil, and the same meaning persisted for many centuries in Germany in the popular expression *hol dich der Geier* (may the vulture [the devil] seize you). For obvious reasons, in representations of the Five Senses, the vulture signified the sense of Smell.

Some writers attribute to the vulture rather than to the eagle the habit of seizing tortoises and then throwing them down from a height to break their shells. This cruel sport was said to have caused the death of the Greek playwright Aeschylus. After meticulously avoiding houses and trees because soothsayers warned that he would be killed by something falling on his head, he had his brains dashed out on an open plain by a tortoise falling from the sky.

The famous artist Leonardo da Vinci made a strange reference to the vulture:

It comes to my mind as a very early memory when I was still in the cradle, a vulture came down to me, opened my mouth with his tail and struck me many times with his tail against my lips.

This was not memory but fantasy, said Freud:

This phantasy conceals nothing more or less than a reminiscence of nursing—or being nursed—at the mother's breast, a scene both human and beautiful, which he, as well as other artists, undertook to depict with the brush in the form of the Mother of God and Her Child. . . . In continuing the work of interpretation we now encounter the strange problem: why this memory content was elaborated into a homosexual situation. The mother who nursed the child, or rather from whom the child suckled, was transformed into a vulture which stuck its tail into the child's mouth. We maintain that the "coda" (tail) of the vulture following the common substituting usages of language, cannot signify anything else but a male genital or penis.

Leonardo appears to have realized that the vulture not only represented the mother, but, according to a well-known tradition, was supposed to give birth without copulation. His fantasy reveals that because of his illegitimate birth he wished he were a vulture-child produced as a result of parthenogenesis. His statement also reveals the homosexual's intensive erotic attachment to a feminine

The vulture feeds on corpses.

person, manifest in very early childhood and later forgotten.

In contrast, the vulture which Michelangelo depicts in his portrayal of Tityus is wholly sinister. Tityus was a giant whose body covered nine acres of land. He tried to rape the virgin Artemis and as a punishment was flung into Hades where a vulture perpetually gnawed his liver.

179

In the early Renaissance he became the symbol of the unhappy lover. "The misery of the lover," stated one writer, "grows because he feeds his tortures with his own self. This is Tityus who with his liver feeds the vulture." The liver perpetually renewed in the case of both Prometheus and Tityus was supposed to be the seat of the physical passions. As Panofsky observes, in one of the two drawings given by Michelangelo to Cavalieri in 1532, Tityus, tormented in Hades by the vulture, "symbolizes the agonies of sensual passion, enslaving the soul and debasing it even beneath its normal terrestrial state." Later, Ripa presented an allegory called the "tortures of love," which consisted of "a sad man ... with his breast open and lacerated by a vulture," and Valeriano made the vulture the symbol of sensuality.

Nevertheless the vulture continued to be an ambivalent figure. Topsell observed that vultures who lived on carrion symbolized those living in idleness upon the labors of others. He added: "they also are to be abhorred which wish the death of their freindes, that they might possesse their goodes." Milton, who, as T.P. Harrison points out, invariably used bird metaphors to vilify his enemies, regarded bishops as "vultures gorging themselves on the bait of church livings." On the other hand, Ripa's emblem of *Natura* or Nature perpetuated the idea of the vulture as a benevolent maternal figure. The vulture is perched on the wrist of a nude woman who has milk pouring from her breast. Valeriano included the vulture in a similar figure, and referred to its impregnation by the wind. He also made the vulture the symbol of Justice.

Aelian, II.46; Ambrose, *PL*, 14, col. 248; Cahier & Martin, II, 146; IV, 80; Ham (ed.), p. 236; Freud, pp. 52, 57, 58; Goldsmith, II, 42; Harrison, *They Tell of Birds*, pp. 101–103; Harting, pp. 40–41; Horapollo, pp. 23–27; McCulloch, pp. 184–86; Milton, *Animadversions*, III, pt. 1; Neumann, p. 164; Pliny, x.lxxxviii; Panofsky, *Studies*, p. 218; Rabanus Maurus, *PL*, 112, col. 1083; Ripa, I.i.119; II.ii.507–508; Topsell, p. 9; Valeriano, ff.131v–133; Zircle, pp. 104–11.

Woodpecker

The loud-voiced, hard-working Woody Woodpecker of the cartoons has a long ancestry. The widespread belief that this bird could call down rain points to its earlier roles as the god-sent bird in the ancient sacred grove; as the bird who, according to legend, cared for Romulus and Remus, and as the oracular bird of Mars, god of war. Such roles in turn suggest the existence of an ancient cult in Greece and Rome in which the woodpecker was itself a god. Even in late Rome, Plautus seems to have been aware that the woodpecker was a prophetic bird. In one

180

of his comedies, when a delinquent servant sees a woodpecker tapping an elm, a tree used to make canes for corporal punishment, he regards it as a bad omen. But it is the folklore of the woodpecker rather than the myth which contributed most toward the bird's symbolism, and this was concerned with the belief that if its nest became blocked in any way, the bird could remove the obstacle.

According to Pliny and others, if a spike was inserted in the entrance to the bird's nest, the woodpecker would bring a certain herb and the spike would drop out. In the Middle Ages the details of the plant were sometimes omitted, as in *De Bestiis*:

Picus a Pico Saturni Filio nomen sumpsit, eo quod ipse in auspiciis ea ave uteretur. Nam ferunt hanc avem quiddam habere divinum, indicio illo quod in quacunque arbore nidificaverit, clavum vel quidquid aliud ei infixum diu haerere non posset quin statim excidat, ubi illa insederit.

(The woodpecker received its name from Picus, the son of Saturn, because it practiced divination with that bird. For men said that this bird had something divine about it because of the following evidence: in any tree in which it built its nest, a nail or anything else inserted in it could not stay there for long without falling out forthwith when the bird settled there.)

In the second half of the seventeenth century this belief was still being solemnly tested. According to John Aubrey (1626–97):

Sir Bennet Hoskins, Baronet, told me that his keeper at his parke at Morehampton in Herefordshire, did for experiment sake, drive an iron nail thwert the hole of a woodpecker's nest, there being a tradition that the damme will bring some leafe to open it. He layed at the bottome of the tree a cleane sheet, and before many houres passed the naile came out and he found a naile lying on the sheete . . . They say [the herb] moonewort will doe such things. This experiment may easily be tryed again.

As Armstrong observes, educated country gentlemen of some two hundred years ago were "curious, interested in experimentation, but casual as to method and credulous as to result." John Ray replied forthrightly: "the story . . . is without doubt a fable," yet this eminent naturalist blamed the death of his daughter from jaundice on the use of new-fangled scientific remedies instead of an old-fashioned cure—beer flavoured with horse manure.

While the belief lasted, the woodpecker's curious knack of unplugging its nest lent itself to symbolic exegesis. According to some bestiaries the woodpecker building its nest was the good Christian; those who plugged his nest were devils. The herb was confession and repentance which enabled the man to free his soul:

*The woodpecker carries an herb which will unplug
its nest.*

C'est example de nos meismes. Li hom qui est en bones
oevres, il fait son ni por manoir en la parfaite joie de
nostre Segnor. Cil qui sa vertu voelent esprover, et
estopher l'entree de son ni, ce sont diables . . . .

(This is an example for us. The man engaging in good
works is preparing a nest where he may dwell in the
perfect joy of our Lord. Those who wish to test his virtue
and stop the entrance of his nest are devils . . . .)

In *secular* terms, in Richard de Fournival's *Bestiary of
Love*, the woodpecker's herb is the means of securing a
lady's affection. The lover longs to know what the herb is.
The nest is the object of his devotion, and he wants to
unlock it and take out the heart.

In many tales from antiquity the woodpecker acts
against the commands of the Almighty. In connection
with the woodpecker's widespread function as a rainbird,
for example, a common story was that because of the
woodpecker's disobedience God commanded that the bird
should drink nothing but rainwater; hence the unhappy
bird always called to the clouds for rain—"To this day the
country people doe divine of raine by their [woodpeckers']
cry," said Aubrey. The persistence of such stories may
account for a symbolism which is very different from that
associated with the bird's miraculous powers. According
to the *Physiologus* attributed to Epiphanius, the woodpecker has many colors and symbolizes the crafty (*ver-
sipellus*) Devil. Just as the woodpecker seeks out the rotten
tree in which to make its home, so the Devil seeks out
the sinner. The same work likens the woodpecker to
chattering women, and the bird is still a symbol of idle
chatter in Sebastian Brant's *Narrenschiff* (*Ship of Fools*),
in 1494. The engraving shows a man in traditional fool's
costume; in a tree nearby, where some birds are nesting
in the leaves, a woodpecker is tapping. The heading is
"of idle talk" (*von vil schwetzen*), and the translation
runs:

182

Who guards his speech and holds his tongue
by anguish ne'er his soul is stung;
woodpeckers' screech betrays their young.

In the Renaissance, Aldrovandi quotes Epiphanius on the woodpecker, and Jacob Cats (1577–1660), affectionately known to his fellow Dutchmen as "Father Cats," carries on the pejorative tradition in his emblems. Cats, the lawyer-poet who was knighted by Charles I, farmed in Zeeland for twenty years, but country life apparently did not endear him to the bird. In his emblems the woodpecker tapping away at the bark of a tree is a symbol of ineffectuality, arrogance, presumption, and mindless self-admiration. The bird's action teaches us that further effort is required for success. "Don't pretend that you are wise," states one caption.

The woodpecker flutters everywhere, sweeps through thickets and hedges,
It seems as though he wants to declare war on the trees.
He pecks into every kind of wood and he looks for an open space.
But the bark hardly smells his breath.

Similarly, says Cats, people delude themselves about their capabilities. Another emblem, showing a woodpecker

Boys shoot at a popinjay.

183

about to peck at an oak tree, tells of the mortification of an impetuous young man who fell in love with a girl called Rosemund. The rubric runs: Sive Amator, Sive Gladiator, Repete! (Whether you are a lover or a fighter, strike again!). After the aphorism "no tree grows in one day / No tree can be felled at one blow," the discomforted lover himself speaks:

> As soon as I found myself caught within the net of
>   Venus
> I said to Rosemund, "Please yield to my desire."
> At the time it appeared to me that she was ready to do
>   that.
> However, I received this answer to my foolish request:
> The woodpecker, the stupid creature, pecks at all trees.
> Yet everything that he does consists of nothing but vain
>   dreams.
> He believes that he digs a hole, but the wood is too
>   thick!
> My friend, an oak tree really requires someone who is
>   able to peck harder.

Emblem writers Camerarius and Picinelli, on the other hand, thought that the bird was industrious and provided an admirable lesson for humanity. Picinelli under the rubric *latentia tentat* (he seeks hidden things) likens him to the studious man with an enquiring mind. Camerarius has the motto *Merces haec certa laborum* (this crown, the reward of labors). And the lines:

Spernit humum picus, petit ardua sic quoque virtus
Appetit excelsis sacra reposta locis.

(The woodpecker despises the earth, he seeks the heights. So also virtue seeks sacred things stored in lofty places.)

Aldrovandi, 1, 841; Aristotle, *H.A.* ix.9; Aubrey, see Armstrong, *Folklore*, p. 106; Brant, ch. 19; Cahier & Martin, ii, 160; Camerarius, iii.lxvii; Cats, 7, 1–3; *De Bestiis, PL*, 177, cols. 95–96; De Fournival, pp. 59–60; Halliday, pp. 110–12; Ham (ed.), p. 235; Mayer (ed.), p. 401; *Physiologus*, pp. 102–105; Picinelli (ed. 1678), iv.lvi; Plautus, *Asin.*, ii.i.262–63; Pliny, x.xx; Pollard, pp. 355–56; Swainson, p. 101; Stith Thompson, vi, 883.

Wren

The vast grassy fields of Curragh in county Kildare were for centuries the regular meeting place for people of southern Ireland. The word *cuirrech*, cognate with the Latin *cursus*, means a race course, and chariot races took place there as early as the first century A.D. In the Crimean War (1853–56), it became famous not only for its racetrack, but also for its military camp which remained there

184

for many years. The camp followers were called wrens. "These creatures," said one writer in 1867, "are known in and about the great military camp and its neighborhood as wrens. They do not live in houses or even huts, but build for themselves 'nests' in the bush." Fortunately the significance had long been forgotten when, in the Second World War, British women joined the navy and were given the same name as an abbreviation of the Women's Royal Naval Volunteer Service.

Today the stocky, bustling wren, distinctive for its small size, russet brown coloring, short cocked tail, and rattling warble of clear shrill notes in quick time, fails to excite the imagination as it once did. Yet it is the subject of some of the oldest folklore. The story of how the wren became king of the birds is of ancient origin and so widely disseminated that in most European languages the wren's name implies royalty. The wren, of course, managed to fly higher than all the other birds by concealing itself on the eagle's back and then taking off from its carrier like a rocket in the final stage of the contest. Although the fable is not in the surviving collection of Aesop's fables, it has been attributed to him. Plutarch made oblique reference to the story when, after describing some famous people, he remarked: "Such then, are the men to whom young statesmen should attach themselves and cling closely, not snatching glory away from them, like Aesop's wren who was carried up on the eagle's shoulders, then suddenly flew out and got ahead of him." The eagle was eminent in Asia; the wren in Europe. Armstrong suggests that the conflict between the two birds points to their fundamental significance:

The eagle is the king of heaven, the representative and symbol of the sun and powers of the sky, the wren belongs to the earth, creeping into holes and crevices in or near the ground. According to Argive tradition Trochilos, the wren, was the son of Triptolemos, the inventor of the plough and therefore, presumably connected with the earth. . . . The wren was believed to have oracular, and probably supernatural, powers. It may well have been regarded as possessing qualities rather similar to those of the snake which also creeps into holes and is closely in touch with chthonic forces. In folklore the eagle and the owl are alike enemies of the wren and the snake. Thus in the rivalry between the eagle and the wren we seem to have evidence of the supersession by solar beliefs from Asia of chthonic magico-religious ideas lingering in Europe.

The wren was undoubtedly a sacred bird for many centuries and as such was the subject of the most elaborate bird ritual surviving in Western Europe. The event often did and still does occur on a special day each year, such as St. Stephen's Day, Twelfth Night, New Year's Day, or in connection with an annual fete. At other times it was unlucky to kill the wren, but on the special day men or

The little wren is at the top of the tree.

heavy burden. In some instances jingles were chanted such as:

> We hunted the Wren for Robin the Bobbin,
> We hunted the Wren for Jack of the Can,
> We hunted the Wren for Robin the Bobbin,
> We hunted the Wren for everyone.

Later the bird might be given a very elaborate funeral or be presented to the priest in a solemn mass. That the wren should also be popularly known as "God's bird" and "St. Mary's hen" does not obscure the meaning of these ceremonies. As is often the case with birds and animals, the wren had ambivalent values, and by its sacrifice, the powers of darkness were defeated, and light and life triumphed.

In the Renaissance, Aldrovandi, who called the wren *regulus*, gave no symbolism for the bird. Allusions by Shakespeare are mainly concerned with the bird's courage, smallness, and cheerful sound. Lady Macduff's contention that "the poor wren, / The most diminutive of birds, will fight, / Her young ones in her nest, against the owl" is apparently very unlikely. An unfledged four-week-old owl, kept as a pet, has been recorded as swallowing a whole wren, but the bird is not in the habit of robbing nests, and the parent wren would probably not be there if he did. The emblem writer Ripa brought the two rival birds, the eagle and the wren, together in the personification of Pre-

boys might hunt it mercilessly with sticks, stones, and even guns. The corpse was placed in a rough nest of fresh evergreen leaves and tied to the top of a gaily decorated pole and carried through the village as though it were a

186

eminence as a woman dressed in royal robes. She holds a wren in her right hand and her left hand rests on the head of an eagle standing beside her. The accompanying explanation suggests an unrealistic concept of society, an anticipation of the reassuring idea that any man can be President:

Among the prodigies that happened the day preceding the death of Caesar, this little bird, called Trochilus by Aristotle . . . was seen flying towards the senate house, with a branch of laurel in its mouth, and many other birds following it. For this reason the wren was assigned as a symbol to empire, and called the king of birds in preference to all others. It is reported that the eagle frequently contends with the wren for superiority; and tho' it is well-known that the former is much greater in power and might than the latter, yet the wren is here placed in the most distinguished situation; which denotes, that ingenious and brave men, of whatever station, who, by their merit in arts or in arms, raise their reputation by some memorable exploit, have an equal claim to honour and preferment with those of the most distinguished rank.

Aldrovandi, II, 649; Armstrong, p. 139; Harting, pp. 143–44; Ingersoll, pp. 117–18; Ripa (tr. Richardson), I, 107; Shakespeare, *Cymbeline* IV.ii.305; *Henry VI*, pt. 2, III.ii.42; *Macbeth* IV.ii.9; *Merchant of Venice* V.i.106; *Twelfth Night* III.ii.59; Witherby, II, 213–14.

Selected Bibliography

This bibliography refers to works cited in the text. It is not intended to be comprehensive. Well-known authors for which standard editions have been used are omitted. See bibliographic note, pages xv–xvii.

Adams, John F. "Classical Raven Lore and Poe's Raven." *Poe Studies*, 5 (1972), 53.

Albertus Magnus. *The Book of Secrets*, ed. Michael R. Best & Frank H. Brightman. Oxford, 1973.

———. *De Animalibus Libri XXVI*, ed. H. Stadler. 2 vols. Munster, 1916, 1920.

Alciatus, Andreas. *Omnia Andreae Alciati V.C. emblemata cum commentariis . . . per Claudium Minoem*. Paris, 1583.

Aldhelm. *Opera*, ed. Rudolph Ewald. *Mon. Germ. Hist.*, vol. 15. Berlin, 1919.

Aldrovandi, Ulisse. *Ornithologia, hoc est de Avibus Historiae libri XII*. 3 vols. Bonn, 1646 (colophons 1645, 1640, 1640).

———. *On Chickens*, tr. L.R. Lind. Norman, Okla., 1963.

Allen, Hope E. "The Fifteenth-century 'Association of Beasts, Birds, and of Men': The Earliest Text with 'Language for Carvers.'" *Publications of the Modern Language Association*, 51 (1936), 602–606.

Alliterative Poem on the Deposition of King Richard II, ed. Thomas Wright. London, 1838.

Altick, Richard D. *Victorian People and Ideas*. New York, 1973.

American Slang, Dictionary of, ed. Harold Wentworth and S.B. Flexner. New York, 1960.

American Underworld Lingo, Dictionary of, ed. Hyman E. Goldin et al. London, 1950.

Ancren Riwle, ed. James Morton. London, 1853.

Anderson, M.D. *The Mediaeval Carver*. Cambridge, 1935.

Aptowitzer, V. "Die Seele als Vogel," in *Monatsschrift für Geschichte . . . des Judentums*, 69. Breslau, 1925.

"Armonye of Byrdes." *Early English Poetry*, ed. J.P. Collier. London, 1842.

Armstrong, Edward A. "The crane dance in east and west." *Antiquity*, 17 (1943), 71–76.

——. *The Folklore of Birds* (1958). New York, 1970.

——. "The Symbolism of the Swan and the Goose." *Folk-Lore*, 55 (1944), 54–58.

Artemidorus Daldianus. *Onirocriticon Libri V*, ed. Rudolph Hercher. Leipzig, 1864.

"Der äthiopische Physiologus," ed. Fritz Hommel. *Romanische Forschungen*, 5 (1890), 13–36.

D'Ayzac, Félicie. "De la zoologie composite . . . ." *Revue de l'art chrétien*, ser. 4, 4 (1886), 13–36.

Bain, Carl E. "The Nightingale and the Dove in *The Kingis Quair*." *Tennessee Studies in Literature*, 9 (1964), 19–29.

Baldwin, Anne W. "Henry II and the Owl and the Nightingale." *Journal of English and Germanic Philology*, 66 (1967), 207–29.

Bannerman, David. *The Birds of the British Isles*. 9 vols. Edinburgh, 1953–61.

Barclay, Alexander (tr.). *The Ship of Fools* (1509). New York, 1966.

Barke, James. *The Merry Muses of Caledonia*, ed. James Barke & Sydney Goodsir Smith. New York, 1964.

Bartholomaeus Anglicus. *De Proprietatibus Rerum*. Frankfurt, 1601; rpt. 1964. [cited as Bartholomaeus]

——. *On the Properties of Things: John Trevisa's Translation of Bartholomaeus Anglicus De Proprietatibus Rerum*. 2 vols. Oxford, 1972. [cited as Bartholomew]

——. *Bartholome, Batman Uppon. His Booke De Proprietatibus Rerum*. London, 1582. [cited as Batman]

Bartsch, Karl. *Chrestomathie de l'Ançien Français*. 12th ed. New York, 1968.

Baudelaire, Charles. *Les Fleurs du Mal* (1857). Paris, 1936.

Bawcutt, Priscilla. "Aspects of Dunbar's Imagery." *Chaucer and Middle English Studies in Honor of Rossell Hope Robbins*, ed. Beryl Rowland. London, 1974.

——. "The Lark in Chaucer and Some Later Poets." *Yearbook of English Studies*, 2 (1972), 5–12.

Bechstein, J.M *The Natural History of Cage Birds*. London, 1888.

Bennett, J.A.W. *Chaucer's Book of Fame*. Oxford, 1968.

Berchorius, Petrus. *Reductorium Morale*. Venice, 1583.

Beres, David. "A Dream, a Vision and a Poem." *International Journal of Psychoanalysis*, 32 (1951), 97–115.

Berry, Reginald. "Chaucer's Eagle and the Element Air." *University of Toronto Quarterly*, 43 (1974), 285–97.

Le Bestiaire Divin de Guillaume le Clerc de Normandie (1852), see Hippeau.

"Bestiary." *An Old English Miscellany*, ed. R. Morris. EETS, OS, 49. London, 1872.

Birds of America, ed. G. Pearson et al. (1917). 3 pts. New York, 1936.

Bloomfield, Morton W. *The Seven Deadly Sins* (1952). East Lansing, Mich., 1967.

Boutell, Charles. *English Heraldry* (1867). 7th ed. London, 1902.

Braddy, Haldeen. *Three Dimensional Poe*. El Paso, Tex., 1973.

Brand, John. *Observations on Popular Antiquities*. Newcastle, 1777.

Brehm, Alfred. *Brehm's Tierleben.* 4 vols. Leipzig, 1926.

Breton, Nicholas. "Amoris Lachrimae." *Brittons Bowre of Delights* (1591), ed. Hyder Edward Rollins. Cambridge, Mass., 1933.

Brown, Carleton (ed.). *English Lyrics of the XIIIth Century* (1932). Oxford, 1962. [cited as Carleton Brown]

Brown, W.J. *The Gods Had Wings.* London, 1936. [cited as Brown]

Bugge, John. "The Virgin Phoenix." *Mediaeval Studies,* 38 (1976), 332–50.

Bunker, Henry Alden, Jr. "The Voice as (Female) Phallus." *The Psychoanalytic Quarterly,* 3 (1934), 391–429.

Bunyan, John. *Divine Emblems.* 9th. ed. London, 1724.

Burn, J.H. *A Descriptive Catalogue of the London Traders' Tavern, and Coffee House Tokens.* London, 1855.

Burnell, F.S. "Ino and her Veil." *Folk-Lore,* 60 (1949), 201–207.

Cahier, Charles, & Arthur Martin. *Mélanges d'Archéologie.* 4 vols. Paris, 1847–56.

Calder, R.F. "A note on Magic Squares in the Philosophy of Agrippa of Nettesheim." *Journal of the Warburg and Courtauld Institute,* 12 (1949), 196–99.

Camerarius, Joachim. *Symbolorum et emblematum,* ed. L. Camerarius, the younger. 3 vols. in 1. Leipzig, 1605.

Capgrave, John. *The Life of St. Katherine of Alexandria,* ed. C. Horstmann. EETS, OS, 100. London, 1893.

Cassell, Anthony K. "The Crow of the Fable and the *Corbaccio*: A Suggestion for the Title." *Modern Language Notes,* 85 (1970), 83–91.

————, tr. and ed. *The Corbaccio.* Urbana, Ill., 1975.

Cawdray, Robert. *A Treasurie or Store House of Similes.* London, 1600.

Chandler, A.R. *Larks, Nightingales and Poets.* Columbus, Ohio, 1937.

————. "The Nightingale in Greek and Latin Poetry." *Classical Journal,* 30 (1934), 78–84.

Le Chant du Roussigneul, ed. E. Walberg. Lund, 1942.

Chester, Robert. *Love's Martyr,* ed. Alexander B. Grosart. London, 1878.

Chew, S.C. *The Pilgrimage of Life* (1962). New York, 1973.

Clanvowe, John. "The Cuckoo and the Nightingale." *Chaucerian and Other Pieces,* supplement to *The Complete Works of Geoffrey Chaucer,* ed. W.W. Skeat. Oxford, 1897; rpt. 1935, 1959, pp. 347–58.

Child, Francis J. *The English and Scottish Popular Ballads.* 5 vols. Boston, 1882–98.

Colgrave, Bertram. "*The Owl and the Nightingale* and the Good Man from Rome.'" *English Language Notes,* 4 (1966), 1–4.

"Colin Blowbol's Testament." *Nugae Poeticae,* ed. J.O. Halliwell-Phillipps. London, 1844.

Collins, Arthur H. *Symbolism of Animals and Birds.* London, 1913.

Cotgrave, Randle. *A Dictionarie of the French and English Tongues* (1611). Columbia, S.C., 1950.

Cottrell, R.D. "Le lai du laustic." *Philological Quarterly,* 47 (1968), 449–505.

"Court of Love." *Chaucerian and Other Pieces*, supplement to *The Complete Works of Geoffrey Chaucer*, ed. W.W. Skeat. Oxford, 1897; rpt. 1935, 1959, pp. 409–47.

Creuzer, Georg Friedrich. *Réligions de l'Antiquité . . . de Dr. Frédéric Creuzer*, ed. J.D. Guigniaut. 4 vols. Paris, 1825–41.

Crooke, W. *An Introduction to the Popular Religion and Folklore of Northern India*. Allahabad, 1894.

Culpepper's Compleat and Experienc'd Midwife in Two Parts, Made English by W— S—. London, 1718.

Dahlberg, Charles R. "Chaucer's Cock and the Fox." *Journal of English and German Philology*, 53 (1954), 277–90.

"Devotions of the Fowles," in *Lydgate's Minor Poems*, ed. J.O. Halliwell-Phillipps. London, 1840.

Douglas, Norman. *Birds and Beasts of the Greek Anthology*. New York, 1929.

Dronke, Peter. *The Medieval Lyric*. London, 1968.

Droulers, E. *Dictionnaire des Attributs, Allégories, Emblèmes et Symboles*. Turnhout, Belg., 1948.

Druce, George C. "The Caladrius and its Legends, Sculptured upon the Twelfth-century Doorway of Alne Church, Yorkshire." *Archaeological Journal*, 69 (1912), 381–416.

———. "Some Abnormal and Composite Human Forms in English Church Architecture." *Archaeological Journal*, 72 (1915), 135–86.

Duchaussoy, Jacques. *Le Bestiaire Divin*. Paris, 1958.

Dunbar, William. *Poems of William Dunbar*, ed. W.M. Mackenzie. London, 1932.

Durandus, William. *The Symbolism of Churches and Church Ornaments*, ed. J.M. Neale & B. Webb. London, 1906.

Edwards, C.H. "Dickey's Deliverance: the owl and the eye." *Critique*, 15 (1973), 95–101.

Eliade, Mircea. *Myths, Dreams and Mysteries* (1957), tr. Philip Mairet. London, 1960.

Epulario or the Italian Banquet, tr. from Epulario of Giovanni de' Rossellini. London, 1598.

Erec et Enide, Les Romans de Chrétien de Troyes, I, ed. Mario Rogues. Paris, 1963.

Etienne de Bourbon. *Anecdotes Historiques*, ed. A. Lecoy de la Marche. Paris, 1877.

Evans, E.P. *Animal Symbolism in Ecclesiastical Architecture*. New York, 1896.

Field, John Edward. *The Myth of the Pent Cuckoo*. London, 1913.

The Floure and the Leafe, ed. D.A. Pearsall. London, 1962.

Ford, Newell. "The Symbolism of Shelley's Nightingale." *Modern Language Review*, 55 (1960), 569–74.

De Fournival, Richard. *Li Bestiarires d'Amours di Maistre Richart de Fornival e li Response du Bestiaire*, ed. Cesare Segre. Milan, 1957.

Freeman, Rosemary. *English Emblem Books*. New York, 1966.

Freud, Sigmund. *Leonardo da Vinci*, tr. A.A. Brill. New York, 1947.

Friedmann, Herbert. *The Symbolic Goldfinch*. Bollingen Series 7. New York, 1946.

Fulgentius, Fabius Planciades. *Mythologiae, Auctores Mythographi Latini*, ed. Van Staveren. Leyden, 1742.

Garrod, H.W. "The Nightingale in Poetry." *The Profession*

of Poetry and Other Lectures. Oxford, 1929.

Garver, Milton Stahl. "Sources of the Beast Similes in the Italian Lyric of the Thirteenth Century." *Romanische Forschungen*, 21 (1905–1908), 276–320.

Gérard, Albert. "The Eagle and the Star." *English Studies*, 35 (1955), 145–53.

Gerald of Wales. Giraldus Cambrensis. *Topographia Hibernica, Opera*, ed. J.F. Dimock. Vol. 5. London, 1867.

Gesner, Conrad. *Historiae animalium liber III qui est de avium natura.* Frankfort, 1585.

Gesta Romanorum, ed. Hermann Oesterley. Berlin, 1872; rpt. Hildesheim, 1963.

Giffin, Mary. *Studies on Chaucer and his Audience.* Hull, Quebec. 1956.

Giovio, Paolo, & Gabriel Symeoni. *Le Sententiose Imprese.* Lyons, 1561.

Goldsmith, Oliver. *Animated Nature* (1774). 2 vols. Glasgow & Edinburgh, 1876.

Gower, John. *The Complete Works*, ed. G.C. Macaulay. 4 vols. Oxford, 1899–1902.

Graham, Victor. "The Pelican as Image and Symbol." *Revue de Litérature comparée*, 36 (1962), 233–43.

Graves, Robert. *The White Goddess* (1948). London, 1962.

Greenway, John. "The Flight of the Grey Goose: Literary Symbolism in the Traditional Ballad." *Southern Folklore Quarterly*, 18 (1954), 165–74.

Grose, Francis. *A Classical Dictionary of the Vulgar Tongue* (1785). Enlarged ed. Chicago, 1971.

Gubernatis, Angelo de. *Zoological Mythology* (1872). 2 vols. Detroit, 1968.

Guillim, John. *A Display of Heraldry.* London, 1610.

Gunston, David. "The Magpie." *Contemporary Review*, 194 (1958), 338–41.

Hadfield, J.A. *Dreams and Nightmares.* Harmondsworth, Middlesex, 1954.

Halliday, W.R. "Picus-Who-Is-Also-Zeus." *Classical Review*, 36 (1922), 110–12.

Halliwell [Phillipps], J.O. *A Dictionary of Archaic and Provincial Words.* 2 vols. London, 1847.

Ham, Edward B. (ed.). "The Cambrai Bestiary." *Modern Philology*, 36 (1939), 225–37.

Harbaugh, H. *The Birds of the Bible.* Philadelphia, 1854.

Hardy, James. "Popular History of the Cuckoo." *Folk-Lore Record*, 2 (1879), 47–91.

Harrison, Jane Ellen. *Prolegomena to the Study of Greek Religion.* 3rd ed. Cambridge, 1922.

Harrison, Thomas P. "The Birds of Gerard Manley Hopkins." *Studies in Philology*, 54 (1957), 448–63.

———. "Keats and a Nightingale." *English Studies*, 41 (1960) 353–59.

———. *They Tell of Birds.* Austin, Tex., 1956.

Harting, James Edmund. *The Birds of Shakespeare* (1871). Chicago, 1965.

Haslewood, Joseph (ed.). *The Dialogue of Creatures Moralised.* London, 1816.

Hawkins, Henry [H.A.]. *Partheneia Sacra* (1633), introd. Iain Fletcher. Aldington, Kent, 1950.

Haydon, Benjamin Robert. *The Autobiography and Memoirs*

of, ed. Alexander P.D. Penrose. New York, 1929.

Hayward, Jane Mary. *Bird Notes*. London, 1895.

Heckscher, W.S. "Relics of Pagan Antiquity in Mediaeval Settings." *Journal of the Warburg and Courtauld Institute*, 1 (1938), 204–20.

Henderson, Joseph L. "Ancient Myths and Modern Man." *Man and his Symbols*, ed. Carl G. Jung. New York, 1964.

Henkel, Arthur, & Albrecht Schöne. *Emblemata*. Stuttgart, 1967.

Hippeau, C. (ed.). *Le Bestiaire Divin de Guillaume Clerc de Normandie* (1852). Geneva, 1970.

———. *La Chanson du Chevalier au Cygne et de Godefroid de Bouillon* (1874–77). Geneva, 1963.

Holbrook, R.T. *Dante and the Animal Kingdom*. New York, 1902.

Hopkins, Gerard Manley. *The Poems of*, ed. W.H. Gardner. London, 1952.

Horapollo. *The Hieroglyphics of Horapollo Nilous*, ed. Alex-Turner Cory. London, 1840.

Howe, William Norton. *Animal Life in Italian Painting*. London, 1912.

Howitt, William. *Visits to Remarkable Places*. 2nd ed. London, 1840.

Hubaux, Jean, & Maxime Leroy. *Le Mythe du Phénix dans les littératures grecque et latine*. Liège, 1939.

Hudson, William Henry. *British Birds* (1906). London, 1923.

Hulme, F.E. *The History, Principles and Practice of Symbolism in Christian Art*. London, 1892.

Hume, Kathryn. "The Function of the *Hrefn Blaca*: *Beowulf*, 1801." *Modern Philology*, 67 (1969), 60–63.

———. *The Owl and the Nightingale: The Poem and Its Critics*. Toronto, 1975.

Ingersoll, Ernest. *Birds in Legend, Fable and Folklore*. New York, 1923.

Isidore of Seville. *Etymologiarum sive originum libri XX*, ed. Wm. Lindsay. 2 vols. Oxford, 1911.

Jackman, Brian. "Europe's birds run the gauntlet of death." *Sunday Times* (Oct. 26, 1975), pp. 20–21.

Jackson, Robert L. "The Symbol of the Wild Duck in Dr. Zhivago." *Comparative Literature*, 15 (1963), 39–45.

Jacques de Vitry. *The Exempla of*, ed. Thomas Frederick Crane. London, 1890.

James, M.R. *Suffolk and Norfolk*. London, 1930.

Jameson, William. *The Wandering Albatross*. London, 1958.

Jean de Condé. Francesco Novati, " 'Li Dis du Koc' di Jean di Conde e il gallo del campanile nella poesia medievale." *Studi Medievali*, 1 (1904–1905), 465–90; append. 1, 491–510; 11, 510–12.

Jennison, George. *Animals for Show and Pleasure in Ancient Rome*. Manchester, 1937.

Jones, Ernest. "The Madonna's Conception by the Ear." *Essays in Applied Psychoanalysis* (1912). Vol. 2. New ed. London, 1964.

Jubinal, Achille (ed.). *Nouveau Recueil de Contes, Dits, Fabliaux, et autres pièces inédites des XIIIe, XIVe et XVe siècles*. 2 vols. Paris, 1842.

Jung, C.G. *Symbols of Transformation* (1916), tr. R.F.C. Hull. 2 vols. New York, 1946.

Junius. *Hadriani Junii Medici Emblemata*. Antwerp, 1565.

Kantorowicz, Ernst. H. *The King's Two Bodies: A Study in Mediaeval Political Theology*. Princeton, N.J., 1957.

Kantrowitz, Joanne Spencer. "The Anglo-Saxon Phoenix and Tradition." *Philological Quarterly*, 43 (1964), 1–13.

Katzenellenbogen, Adolf. *Allegories of the Virtues and Vices in Mediaeval Art* (1939). New York, 1964.

Kelchner, G.D. *Dreams in Old Norse Literature and Their Affinities in Folklore*. Cambridge, 1935.

Kiernan, K.S. "The Mysteries of the Sea-eagle in Exeter Riddle 74." *Philological Quarterly*, 54 (1975), 518–22.

Kittredge, G.L. *Witchcraft in Old and New England* (1929). New York, 1956.

Klingender, Francis. *Animals in Art and Thought to the End of the Middle Ages*. Cambridge, Mass., 1971.

Knight, Richard Payne. *The Symbolical Language of Ancient Art and Mythology* (1818). New York, 1876.

Kunstmann, J.G. *The Hoopoe: A Study in European Folklore*. Chicago, 1938.

Lack, David. *Robin Redbreast*. Oxford, 1950.

Lactantius. "De Ave Phoenix." *Minor Latin Poets* (1934), ed. J.W. Duff & A.M. Duff. Cambridge, Mass., 1961.

Lampe, David E. "The Poetic Strategy of the *Parlement of the Thre Ages*." *The Chaucer Review*, 7 (1973), 173–83.

———. "Tradition and Meaning in *The Cuckoo and the Nightingale*." *Papers in Language and Literature*, 3 (1967), 49–62.

Lanoe-Villène, Georges. *Le Livre des Symboles*. 6 vols. Paris, 1926–37.

Latham, C. "West Sussex Superstitions." *Folklore Record*, 1 (1878), 9.

Latini, Brunetto. *Li Livres dou Trésor*, ed. Francis J. Carmody. Berkeley, Calif., 1948.

Lazar, Moshé. *Amour Courtois et 'Fin' Amors' dans la Littérature du XIIe siècle*. Paris, 1964.

Legh, Gerard. *The Accedence of Armory*. London, 1562.

Lévy-Brühl, Lucien. *L'expérience mystique et les symboles chez les primitifs*. Paris, 1938.

Leyerle, John. "Chaucer's Windy Eagle." *University of Toronto Quarterly*, 40 (1971), 247–65.

Libellus de Natura Animalium. A Fifteenth-Century Bestiary, introd. J.I. Davis. London, 1958.

Liber Albus. Munimenta Gildhallae Londoniensis, ed. T.H. Riley. London, 1859.

Lowrie, W. *Art in the Early Church*. New York, 1947.

Lydgate, John. *Pilgrimage of the Life of Man*, ed. F.J. Furnivall. EETS, ES, 77. London, 1891.

———. *Poems*, ed. John Norton-Smith. Oxford, 1966.

———. *Lydgate's Minor Poems. The Two Nightingale Poems*, ed. Otto Glaunig. EETS, ES, 80. London, 1900.

McCulloch, Florence. *Mediaeval Latin and French Bestiaries*. Rev. ed. Chapel Hill, N.C., 1962.

McKenzie, Kenneth. "Unpublished Manuscripts of Italian Bestiaries." *Publications of the Modern Language Association*, 20 (1905), 380–433.

Mandeville, John. *Mandeville's Travels*, ed. P. Hamelius. 2 vols. EETS, OS, 153, 154. Rpt. London, 1960, 1961.

Mannyng, Robert, of Brunne. *Handlyng Synne*, ed. F.J. Furnivall. EETS, OS, 119, 123. London, 1901–1903.

Map, Walter. *De Nugis Curialium*, ed. E.S. Hartland. London, 1923.

Marie de France. *Die Lais der Marie de France*, ed. Karl Warnke. Halle, 1900.

Martigny. *Dictionnaire des Antiquités Chrétiennes par M. l'Abbé Martigny*. 2 vols. Paris, 1865.

Matheolus. *Les Lamentations de*, ed. A.G. Van Hamel. 2 vols. Paris, 1892–1905.

Matthews, W.H. *Mazes and Labyrinths* (1922). New York, 1970.

Mayer, Alfons (ed.). "Der waldensische Physiologus." *Romanische Forchungen*, 5 (1890), 392–417.

Mayhew, Henry. *London Labour and the London Poor* (1851). 2 vols. London, 1967.

Medallic Illustrations of the History of Great Britain and Ireland to the Death of George II (1885). Edward Hawkins, comp.; ed. A.W. Franks & H.A. Grueber. London, 1969.

Du Méril, Édélestand. *Poésies inédites du Moyen Âge*. Paris, 1854.

———. *Poésies populaires latines antérieures au douzième siecle*. Paris, 1843; rpt. Bologna, 1969.

Meyer, P. (ed.). "Le Bestiaire de Gervaise." *Romania*, 1 (1872), 420–43.

"La Messe des Oisiaus." *Dits et Contes de Baudouin de Condé et de son fils Jean de Condé*, ed. Aug. Scheler, Vol. 3. Brussels, 1867.

Middle English Sermons, ed. Woodburn O. Ross. EETS, OS, 209. London, 1940.

Mills, Jerry Leath. "Satan as Cormorant, 'Paradise Lost,' IV, 196." *Notes & Queries*, 17 (1970), 414–15.

Møller-Christensen, V, and K.E. Jordt Jørgensen, *Encyclopedia of Bible Creatures*. Philadelphia, 1965.

Morgan, H.T. *Chinese Symbols and Superstitions*. S. Pasadena, Calif., 1942.

Morse, Edward S. *Japanese Homes and Their Surroundings* (1886), ed. Terence Barrow. Tokyo, 1972.

Neale, J.M. *The Unseen World*. London, 1847.

Neckam, Alexander. *De Naturis Rerum et de Laudibus Divinae Sapientiae*, ed. Thomas Wright. Rolls Series 34. London, 1863.

Neilson, W.A. *The Origins and Sources of the Court of Love*. Cambridge, Mass., 1899.

Neumann, Erich. *The Great Mother* (1955). 2nd ed. Princeton, N.J., 1963.

Newton, Alfred. *A Dictionary of Birds*. London, 1896.

Nicholes, E.L. "The Simile of the Sparrow in The Rainbow by D.H. Lawrence." *Modern Language Notes*, 64 (1949), 171–74.

Nichols, J.G. "Observations on the Heraldic Devices discovered on the Effigies of Richard II and his Queen." *Archaeologia*, 29 (1842), 32–59.

Nott, John. *The Cook's and Confectioner's Dictionary or the Accomplish'd Housewife's Companion*. London, 1723.

Odo of Cheriton. *Les Fabulistes Latins* (1896), ed. Léopold Hervieux. Vol. 4. Hildesheim, N.Y., 1970.

Olson, Paul A. "Chaucer's Merchant and January's 'Hevene in erthe heere.'" *English Literary History*, 28 (1961),

203–14.

Opie, Iona & Peter (eds.). *The Oxford Dictionary of Nursery Rhymes*. Oxford, 1951.

Orvell, Miles D. " 'The Raven' and the Chair." *Poe Studies*, 5 (1972), 54.

Ovide Moralisé, ed. C. de Boer. Amsterdam, 1915.

The Owl and the Nightingale, ed. E.G. Stanley. London, 1960.

Owst, G.R. *Literature and Pulpit in Medieval England* (1933). Oxford, 1961.

Panofsky, Dora & Erwin. *Pandora's Box* (1956). New York, 1965.

Panofsky, Erwin, *Studies in Iconology* (1939). New York, 1962.

Paradin, Claude. *Les Devises héroiques*. Anvers, 1567.

Partridge, Eric. *The Routledge Dictionary of Historical Slang*, abridg. J. Simpson. London, 1973.

Peacham, Henry. *Minerva Britanna*. London, 1612.

Perella, Nicholas James. *The Kiss Sacred and Profane*. Berkeley, 1969.

Peterson, Roger, et al. *A Field Guide to the Birds of Britain and Europe*. London, 1954.

Petti, Anthony G. "Beasts and Politics in Elizabethan Literature." *Essays and Studies*, 16 (1963), 68–90.

Pettie, George. *A Petite Palace of Pettie His Pleasure*, ed. H. Hartman. New York, 1938.

Philippe de Thaon. *Le Bestiaire de Philippe de Thaün*, ed. Emmanuel Walberg. Paris and Lund, 1900.

Physiologus, attrib. to Epiphanius, ed. D. Gonsali Ponce de Leon. Antwerp, 1588.

Picinelli, Filippe. *Mondo Simbolico*. Milan, 1669.

Political Poems and Songs Relating to English History, ed. Thomas Wright. Rolls Series 14. 2 vols. London, 1859–61.

Pollard, J.R.T. "The *Birds* of Aristophanes—a Source Book for Old Beliefs." *American Journal of Philology*, 49 (1948), 353–76.

Prosalegenden, ed. C. Horstmann. *Anglia*, 8 (1885), 102–96.

Prudentius. *Carmina*, ed. A. Dressel. Leipzig, 1860.

Pugin, A. Welby. *The Present State of Ecclesiastical Architecture in England* (1843). Oxford, 1969.

Pyles, Thomas. "Innocuous linguistic decorum: a semantic byway." *Modern Language Notes*, 64 (1949), 1–8.

Raby, F.J.E. "Philomena praevia temporis amoeni." *Mélanges Joseph de Ghellinck*. II. Gembloux, Belg., 1951.

Randall, Lilian M.C. "Exempla as a source of Gothic Marginal Illumination." *The Art Bulletin*, 39 (1957), 97–107.

Réau, Louis. *Iconographie de l'art chrétien*. 6 vols. Paris, 1955–59.

Reusner, Nicolaus. *Emblemata . . . in quatuor libros*. Frankfort, 1581.

Riddell, W.H. "The Domestic Goose." *Antiquity*, 17 (1943), 148–55.

Rigg, A.G. (ed.). *A Glastonbury Miscellany of the Fifteen Century*. London, 1968.

Ripa, Cesare. *Iconographia*. 2 vols. Padua, 1630.

———. *Iconology . . . from compositions of C. Ripa, etc.* tr. George Richardson. 2 vols. London, 1778–79.

Robbins, Rossell Hope (ed.). *Secular Lyrics of the Four-*

teenth and Fifteenth Centuries (1952). Rev. ed. Oxford, 1955.

Robertson, D.W., Jr. "*Buzones*, an alternative etymology." *Studies in Philology*, 42 (1–45), 741–44.

———. *A Preface to Chaucer*. Princeton, N.J., 1962.

Rogers, Thorold, J.E. *Six Centuries of Work and Wages* (1884). 12th ed. London, 1917.

Rolland, Eugène. *Faune Populaire de la France*. 3 vols. Paris, 1877–81.

Rolle, Richard. *Yorkshire Writers*, ed. C. Horstmann. 2 vols. London, 1895–96.

Rowland, Beryl. *Blind Beasts: Chaucer's Animal World*. Kent, Ohio, 1971.

———. "The Mill in Popular Metaphor from Chaucer to the Present Day." *Southern Folklore Quarterly*, 33 (1969), 69–79.

———. "Owles and Apes in Chaucer's *Nun's Priest's Tale*, 3092." *Mediaeval Studies*, 27 (1965), 322–25.

———. "Sitting up with a Corpse: Malthus according to Melville in 'Poor Man's Pudding and Rich Man's Crumbs.'" *Journal of American Studies*, 6 (1972), 69–83.

Rows Roll. *This rol was laburd & finishid by Master John Rows Warrewyck*, trans. L. Larking, ed. W. Courthope. London, 1845–59.

Rutebeuf, Oeuvres Complètes de. ed. A. Jubinal. Paris, 1839.

Sandys, George. *Ovid's Metamorphosis Englished and Represented in Figures*. London, 1640.

Schaar, Claes. *Studia Neophilologica*, 47 (1975), 414.

Schnier, Jacques. "The Symbolic Bird in Medieval and Renaissance Art." *American Imago*, 9 (1952), 89–117.

Seltman, Charles. *A Book of Greek Coins*. Harmondsworth, Middlesex, 1952.

The Seven Sages of Rome, ed. Karl Brunner. EETS, OS, 191. London, 1933.

Seznec, Jean. *The Survival of the Pagan Gods* (1953). New York, 1961.

Shelvocke, George. *A Voyage Round the World*. London, 1726.

Sherman, C. "Some Fabulous Birds." *New York Folklore Quarterly*, 14 (1960), 36–47.

Shippey, Thomas Alan. "Listening to the Nightingale." *Comparative Literature*, 22 (1970), 46–60.

Sisam, Kenneth (ed.). *Fourteenth Century Verse and Prose*. Oxford, 1933.

Skelton, John. *John Skelton's Poetry*. ed. S.E. Fish. New Haven, 1965.

Sneyd, C.A. (tr.). *A Relation or Rather a True Account of the Island of England*. London, 1847.

Spence, Lewis. *Myth and Ritual in Dance, Game, and Rhyme*. London, 1947.

Steadman, J.M. "Chaucer's Eagle: A Contemplative Symbol." *Publications of Modern Language Association*, 75 (1960), 153–59.

———. "Chaunticleer and Medieval Natural History." *Isis*, 50 (1959), 236–44.

Sterne, Laurence. *A Sentimental Journey Through France and Italy* (1768). New York, 1900.

Stuart, Dorothy Margaret. *A Book of Birds and Beasts*. London, 1957.

Sühling, Friedrich. *Die Taube als religiöses Symbol im christlichen Altertum*. Freiburg im Breislau, 1930.

Suidas, *Lexicon Graece et Latine*. Halle, 1843.

Svendsen, Kester. "The Prudent Crane." *Notes & Queries*, 183 (1942), 66–67.

Swaen, A.E.H. (ed.) "The Booke of Hawkyng." *Studia Neophilologica*, 16 (1943), 5–32.

Swainson, C. *Provincial Names and Folk Lore of British Birds*. London, 1885.

Swan, John. *Speculum Mundi*. Cambridge, 1635.

Swann, H. Kirke. *A Dictionary of English and Folk-names of British Birds*. London, 1913.

Swart, J. "John Skelton's Philip Sparrow." *English Studies*, supplement 45 (1964), 161.

————. "On Re-reading William Dunbar." *Chaucer and Middle English Studies in Honor of Rossell Hope Robbins*, ed. Beryl Rowland. London, 1974.

Taylor, A. "Three Birds of Ill Omen in British Folklore." *Washington University Studies*, 4 (1917), 151–73.

Telfer, J.M. "The Evolution of a Mediaeval Theme." *Durham University Journal*, 45 (1952), 25–34.

Tervarent, Guy de. *Attributs et symboles dans l'art profane, 1450–1600*. Geneva, 1958.

Thompson, D'Arcy Wentworth. *A Glossary of Greek Birds*. Oxford, 1936.

Thompson, Stith. *Motif Index of Folk Literature* (1932). 6 vols. Bloomington, Ind., 1955–58.

Thynne, Francis. *Emblemes and Epigrames*, ed. F.J. Fur-

nivall. EETS, OS, 64. London, 1876.

Tilley, M.P. *A Dictionary of Proverbs in England in the Sixteenth and Seventeenth Centuries*. Ann Arbor, Mich., 1950.

Tillyard, E.M. *Studies in Milton*. New York, 1951.

Tindall, William York. *The Literary Symbol*. Bloomington, Ind., 1955.

Todd, H.A. "La naissance du Chevalier au Cygne ou les enfants changés en cygnes." *Publications of the Modern Language Association*, 4 (1889), i–xv.

Topsell, Edward. *The Fowles of Heauen or History of Birdes*, ed. Thomas P. Harrison and F. David Hoeniger. Austin, Tex., 1972.

La Tour-Landry, The Book of the Knight of, ed. Thomas Wright. EETS, ES, 33. London, 1868.

The Tretyse of Love, ed. John H. Fisher. EETS, OS, 223. London, 1951; rpt. 1970.

Trotula. *De Passionibus Mulierum* . . . . Venice, 1547.

Turner, William. *Avium Praecipuarum*. Cologne, 1544.

————. *Turner on Birds*, tr. A.H. Evans. Cambridge, 1903.

Twining, Louisa. *Symbols and Emblems of Early and Medieval Christian Art*. London, 1885.

Typotius, Jacobus. *Symbola Divina et Humana*. Prague, 1601–1603.

Valeriano, Giovanni Pierio. *Hieroglyphica*. Basel, 1575.

Varty, Kenneth. *Reynard the Fox*. Leicester, 1967.

De Vitry. *The Exempla of Jacques de Vitry*. ed. T.F. Crane. London, 1890.

Wagner, Anthony R. "The Swan Badge and the Swan Knight." *Archaeologia*, 97 (1959), 127–38.

Wailes, Stephen L. "The Crane, the Peacock, and the Reading of Walther von der Vogelweide." *Modern Language Notes*, 88 (1973), 947–55.

Walberg, E. (ed.). *Le Chant du Roussigneul*. Lund, 1942.

Wenzel, Siegfried. *The Sin of Sloth: Acedia in Medieval Thought and Literature*. Chapel Hill, N.C., 1960; rpt. 1967.

Whitaker, Virgil K. (ed.). *The History of Troilus and Cressida, William Shakespeare, The Complete Works*, ed. Alfred Harbage. Rev. ed. Baltimore, 1969.

White, Beatrice. "Medieval Beasts." *Essays & Studies*, 18 (1965), 34–44.

White, T.H. *The Bestiary. A Book of Beasts* (1954). New York, 1960.

Whitney, Geoffrey. *Whitney's "Choice of Emblemes,"* ed. Henry Green. London, 1866.

Wilbur, Richard. *The Narrative Poems, William Shakespeare, The Complete Works*, ed. Alfred Harbage. Rev. ed. Baltimore, 1969.

Williams, C.A.S. *Outlines of Chinese Symbolism*. Peiping, 1931.

Wilson, William S. "The Eagle's Speech in Chaucer's House of Fame." *Quarterly Journal of Speech*, 50 (1964), 153–58.

Wimberly, Lowry C. *Folklore in English and Scottish Ballads*. New York, 1959.

Wither, George. *Collection of Emblems, Ancient and Modern*. London, 1635.

Witherby, H.F., et al. *The Handbook of British Birds*. 5 vols. London, 1943.

Wittkower, Rudolf. "The Eagle and Serpent: A Study in the Migration of Symbols." *Journal of the Warburg and Courtauld Institute*, 11 (1939), 293–325.

Wood, Chauncey. "Chaucer and Sir Thopas: Irony and Concupiscence." *Texas Studies in Language and Literature*, 14 (1972), 389–403.

Wood, J.G. *Animate Creation*. 5 vols. New York, 1898.

———. *Bible Animals*. Guelph, Ontario, 1877.

Woodruff, Helen. "The Physiologus of Bern." *Art Bulletin*, 12 (1930), 226–53.

Wormhoudt, Arthur. "The Unconscious Bird Symbol in Literature." *American Imago*, 7 (1950), 173–81.

Wulff, August. *Die Frauenfeindlichen Dichtungen in den Romanischen Literatüren Des Mittelalters*. Halle, 1914.

Zimmer, Heinrich. *Myths and Symbols in Indian Art and Civilization* (1946), ed. Joseph Campbell. New York, 1962.

Zircle, Conway. "Animals Impregnated by the Wind." *Isis*, 25 (1936), 95–130.

Index

Adams, John F., 148, 189
Addison, Joseph, 150, 154
Aelian, xvi, 18, 19, 34, 51, 57, 63, 64, 66, 70, 73, 82, 83, 84, 85, 86, 124, 127, 132, 135, 139, 145, 148, 161, 163, 174, 178, 180
Aeschylus and the eagle, 57, 178
Aesculapius, 20, 21
Alan of the Isles, 94, 96
Albatross: bad omen, 5; cruelty to, 3; good omen, 3; in "The Ancient Mariner," 3-5; used to make pipes and tobacco pouches, 4
  symbol of mother or breast, 4; poet, 5; unsurmountable burden, 5
Albertus Magnus, 11, 13, 48, 63, 64, 86, 92, 94, 96, 104, 105, 116, 136, 139, 166-67, 169
Alciatus, Andreas, 24, 27, 33, 34, 37, 38, 41, 57, 85, 86, 91, 92, 119, 120, 132, 162, 163, 167, 169, 171, 174, 189
Aldegrever, Henri, 54
Aldhelm, 109, 111, 189
Aldrovandi, Ulisse, xvi, 13, 19, 23, 24, 26, 27, 29, 30, 36, 38, 46, 47, 48, 51, 68, 70, 71, 73, 74, 76, 77-78, 79, 80, 81, 85, 86, 87, 91,

Aldrovandi, Ulisse (*cont.*)
  92, 96, 97, 98, 101, 129, 130, 143, 156, 157, 158, 160, 162, 163, 170, 174, 176, 177, 183, 184, 186, 187, 189
Alerion: described in *Physiologus*, 6; device of the Dukes of Lorraine, 5
  symbol of dishonest rich man, 6
Alexander the Great, 18, 72
Alliterative Poem on the Deposition of Richard II, 173, 174, 189
Altick, Richard D., 169, 189
St. Ambrose, xvi, 21, 28, 57, 92, 124, 127, 148, 158, 160, 178, 180
Ancren Riwle, 131, 133, 189
Anderson, M. D., 57, 189
Ape with owl, 118
Aptowitzer, V., xv, 189
Aquinas, St. Thomas, 47
Aristophanes, 35, 93, 96
Aristotle, xvi, 18, 19, 26, 33, 34, 41, 52, 53, 57, 82, 83, 127, 129, 130, 161, 163, 166, 170, 174, 184
"Armonye of Byrdes," xv, 176, 177, 189
Armstrong, Edward, xv, 32, 34, 70, 74, 105, 134, 144, 148, 154, 174, 181, 184, 190

200

Cock (*cont.*)

uxoriousness, 25; vigilance, 24; warrior, 25; wrath, 26

white, symbol of purity, 23; black, sacrified to demons, 23, 24; cure for epilepsy, 24; for restoring speech, 24; red, sacrificed to Osiris, 24; emblem of protection against fire in China, 24 *See also* Sugar cocks

Coleridge, S. T., 3–5, 97, 101, 170

"Colin Blowbol's Testament," 172, 173, 174

Collins, Arthur H., 139, 191

Color symbolism of Doves, 45–46, 48

"Columbine kiss," 43, 44

Conception by the ear, xv, 43

Coot: associated with baldness, 29; inferiority, 29; madness, 29; stupidity, 29

symbol of the good Christian, 29; hermit, 29

synonym for "buffle-head," 29

Cormorant: symbol of Christ rising from hell, 31; exploiters, 31; greed, 30; insatiability, 31; monopolists, 31

Cotgrave, Randle, 78, 157, 160, 191

Crane: associated with alphabet, 34; disdain, 34; gluttony, 34; happiness, 32

crane dance, epitomizing fertility and death rituals, 31; consisted of nine steps and a leap, 32; performed in China, 32

emblem of longevity in China and Japan, 32

symbol of cautious man, 33, 34; Christian's foresight and wisdom, 33; discretion, 34; inquisitive man investigating sublime things, 34; prudence, 33; vigilance, 33; watchful prelate, 33

Crawshaw, Richard, 131, 133, 156

Cretan labyrinth, 31

Creuzer, Georg Friedrich, 54–55, 57, 72, 73, 130, 148, 174, 192

Crooke, W., 70, 192

Crow: divine, 36; ominous, 35; tell-tale bird, 36, 37

symbol of bad nun, 35; black widow, 36; conjugal harmony, 36; God's providence, 37; happiness, 36; hope, 37; longevity, 36; "loose woman," 36; pretentiousness, 36; procrastination, 36; spendthrift, 37; talkative woman, 36

Ctesias, 121

Cuckoo: symbol for avarice, 39; boasting, 40; cowardice, 39; cuckold, 38–39; fool, 38, 39, 40; fruitfulness, 40; good luck, 40; ill-luck in love, 38; ingratitude, 38; jealousy, 39; longevity, 40; "ravisher of the heart" (to Hindu poets), 40; spring, 41; Virgin Mary *parturiente*, 41

Cuckoo pens, 40–41

"Cuckoo's nest," the pudendum, 40

Culpepper's Compleat and Experienc'd Midwife, 158, 160, 192

Dahlberg, Charles, 28, 192

Dante Alighieri, 52, 55, 64, 72, 93, 96, 131, 133, 160, 161

Davis, J. E., captain of the *Challenger*, 3

D'Ayzac, Félicie, 115, 148, 190

Dekker, Thomas, 74

"Devotions of the Fowles," xv, 98, 101, 192

Dickinson, Emily, vii, 153

Diver: symbol of those preoccupied with sexual matters, 50

Doctor Faustus, xiii, xv

St. Dominic, 157

Donne, John, 56

Douglas, Norman, 174, 192

Dove: symbol of the active life, 45; the Ascension, 42; charity, 42; Christ, 42, 45, 47; Church, 42, 45, 47; creator of the world, 43, 44; cry of the penitent, 45; defenselessness, 42; deliverance, 44; divine breath, 44; faithfulness, 41; fertility, 41, 42; filial piety, 41; fire, 44; gift of the Holy Spirit, 45; God's grace, 45;

Dove (*cont.*)

Holy Ghost, 42, 45, 47; inspiration, 47; longevity, 41; love, 44; martyrdom, 42; peace, 44; persecuted Israel, 41; phallus, 43; preacher, 45; purity, 41; sacred teaching, 47; sacrifice, 47; scripture, 47; seven gifts of the Holy Spirit, 47; simple and upright men, 47; sorrow, 42, 47; soul, 41; spiritual love, 42; the twelve apostles, 47; Virgin Mary, 47; virgins, 42

See also Color symbolism; Turtledove

Drayton, Michael, 9, 10, 31, 97, 101, 119, 154

Dronke, Peter, 99, 101, 192

Droulers, E., 101, 192

Druce, George C., 19, 157, 192

Duchaussoy, Jacques, 57, 192

Duck: emblem in China of faithful married life, 49; common people, 50; happiness, 50; illusions, 50; treachery, 50

Dunbar, William, 11, 13, 109, 192

Durandus, W., 21, 28, 113, 115, 192

Dying swan: symbol of Christ speaking from cross, 171; Christian resignation, 171; martyrdom, 171; serenity in death, 171; soul, 171

Eagle: attribute of acute sight, generosity, hope, longevity, pride, sublimity, success, 54

symbol of air, 54; apotheosis, 52, 55; Christ, 52, 53; deity, 51; demon, 57; desire for knowledge, 51; the divine, 51; good augury, 54; military power, 52; old man, 53; pious and compassionate king, 57; poet and poetry, 55; regeneration, 52; resurrection, 52; rhetoric, 55; Roman persecution, 52; St. John, 54; soul of dead king, 52; souls of the just, 51; success, 54; wise Christian, 53

eagle and dove, eagle's feathers, eagle and snake, eagle and tortoise, two-headed eagle, their symbolism, 56

Eliade, Mircea, xv, 192

Eliot, T. S., 108

Elizabeth I: with crane, 33; with phoenix, 137–39; with Robert Devereux, Earl of Essex, 139, 153

Epulario or *The Italian Banquet*: recipe for baking blackbirds in a pie, 12, 13, 192; for peacocks, 130

Étienne de Bourbon, 7, 9, 192

St. Eucherius, 21, 28, 127

Evans, E. P., 19, 28, 48, 57, 114, 115, 124, 127, 148, 169, 174, 192

Farmer, J. S., & W. E. Henley, *Slang and its Analogues*, 8, 16, 29, 37, 48, 106, 110

Four-and-twenty blackbirds: as allegory, 12–13; as nursery rhyme, 12; in cooking, 12; as parody, 13

Field, J. E., 41, 192

Finch: associated with prophetic power, 63; sweet song, 63; women, 64

The Floure and The Leafe, 66, 192

De Fournival, Richard, 11, 13, 19, 28, 34, 170, 174, 182, 184, 192

St. Francis, 164

Frazer, Sir James George, 42

Freeman, Rosemary, 137, 139–40, 192

Freud, Sigmund, 179, 180, 192

Friedmann, Herbert, 13, 19, 65, 66, 169, 192

Frost, Robert, 177

Ganymede: prefiguration of St. John, 55

Garner of St. Victor, Paris, 28, 45, 48, 63, 77, 79, 94, 96, 115, 147, 148, 158, 160

Garrod, H. W., 109, 111, 192–93

Garuda, 52

Garver, Milton Stahl, 38, 130, 140, 193

Owl (*cont.*)

    symbol of Athenians, 116; Christ, 119; despotism, 119; evil, 118, 119; humility of Christ, 119; hypocrisy, 119; ill-omen, 117, 119; Jew, 117; melancholy, 119; seeker of "vain knowledge," 118; sloth, 118; wisdom, 116

"The Owl and the Nightingale," 107, 119

Owling, 120

Owst, G. R., 10, 130, 197

Painter, William, 158, 160

Pandora's jar, 37

Panofsky, Dora & Erwin, 38, 63, 148–49, 197

Panofsky, Erwin, 55, 57, 180

Paradin, Claude, 6, 24, 28, 57, 62, 63, 137, 140, 197

Partridge: symbol of deceit, 124; Devil, 124; envy, 124; fearfulness, 124, 125, 126; prostitute, 126; treachery, 124

Pâte de foie gras: how obtained, vii

Pausanias, 144, 149

Peacham, Henry, 10, 28, 76, 101, 119, 120, 197

Peacock: ashamed of its feet, 129; flesh believed to be incorruptible, 127

    symbol of apotheosis of Roman emperors, 127; ascent of the soul, 127; Devil, 129; falsity, 129; immortality, 127; lust, 129; predatory woman, 130; pride, 129, 130

Pearl, 136–37, 142

Peckham, John, 109, 111

Pelican: symbol of bad-tempered nun, 132; Christ, 131; filial ingratitude, 132; fool, 132; garrulity, 132; gluttony, 132; good king, 132; self-sacrifice, 132

Perella, Nicholas James, 48, 197

St. Peter: and the cock, 22–23

Petrarch, Francis, 137

Petronius, 44, 48

Pettie, George, 94

Pheasant: symbol of authority, 133; pleasure, 134; woman, 134

Philippe de Thaon, 29, 30, 53, 57, 120, 197

Phoenix: symbol of Christ, 134, 137; eternity, 134, 137; fire, 134, 137; good woman, 139; hope, 134, 137; immortality, 136; Jane Seymour, 139; just man, 136; kingship, 137; love, 19; man returning home, 137; monastic recluse, 136; mystery of the Trinity, 136; overflowing of the Nile, 137; penitent sinner, 136; perpetuity of sovereignty, 137–38; Queen Elizabeth I, 138–39; rarity, 137; rebirth, 137; Resurrection, 136; solitariness, 137; soul, 137; Virgin Mary, 134, 136, 137

Physiologus, xvi, 6, 19, 47, 57, 80, 81, 129, 130, 161, 163, 182, 184, 197

Pica, 104

Picinelli, Filippe, 35, 41, 64, 73, 92, 143, 156, 157, 184, 197

Pilgrimage of the soul, 97, 101

Plato, xiii, 28, 165, 169

Plautus, Titus Maccius, 38, 41, 93, 96, 143, 180, 184

Pliny the elder, xvi, 21, 24, 26, 28, 33, 35, 38, 41, 48, 57, 66, 70, 73, 81, 86, 87, 89, 92, 95, 96, 105, 111, 117, 120, 121, 123, 124, 125, 127, 129, 130, 133, 134, 135, 140, 142, 143, 144, 145, 149, 160, 161, 163, 165, 169, 170, 175, 177, 180, 181, 184

Plover, 16, 17

Plutarch, xvi, 31, 35, 185

Poe, Edgar Allan, 143–44, 145

Political Poems, ed. Wright, 81, 174, 197

Pollard, J. R. T., 184, 197

Pope, Alexander, 159

Prester, John, 6

Prudentius, *Carmina*, 28, 197

Pugin, A. Welby, 42, 48, 197

Vulture (*cont.*)

thenogenesis, 177–78; Prometheus, 180; Tityus, 179–80

symbol of bishops, 180; boundary, 177; Christ, 178; compassion, 177; Devil, 178; envy, 94; foreknowledge, 177; idlers, 180; Justice, 180; maternity, 177, 179, 180; rapacious man, 178; purification, 177; sense of smell, 178; sensuality, 180; vision, 177; voracity, 177; year, 177

Wagner, Anthony R., 174, 199

Wailes, Stephen L., 130, 200

Waldensian Bestiary. See Mayer, Alfons (ed.)

Watt, Isaac, 159

Webster, John: *Duchess of Malfi*, 100, 101; *The White Devil*, 150, 154

Wenzel, Siegfried, 48, 149, 163, 176, 177, 200

Whitaker, Virgil K. (ed.), 141, 143, 200

White, Beatrice, 160, 200

White, T. H., 17, 19, 30, 50, 51, 133, 200

Whitney, Geoffrey, 37, 38, 50, 51, 63, 95, 96, 137, 140, 156, 157, 161–62, 163, 171, 174

"Who Killed Cock Robin?," 151, 152, 159

Wilbur, Richard, 19, 159, 200

The Wild Duck, 50

Wild geese: symbol of fighting Irishmen, 70

Williams, C. A. S., 9, 28, 35, 51, 63, 70, 105, 134, 140, 166, 169, 200

Willughby, Francis: *Ornithology* (1676), 9

Wilson, William S., 57, 200

Wimberly, Lowry C., 28, 200

"Winchester goose," 68

Wither, George, 34, 200

Witherby, H. F., et al., 5, 10, 14, 51, 63, 74, 87, 97, 105, 127, 134, 160, 169, 187, 200

Wittkower, Rudolf, 56, 57, 200

Wood, Chauncey, 61, 63, 200

Wood, J. G., 83, 87, 88, 103, 104, 105, 200

Woodpecker: associated with divinity, 180–81; miraculous herb, 181–82; prophecy, 182

symbol of arrogance, 183; Devil, 182; good Christian, 181; idle chatter, 182; industry, 184; ineffectuality, 183; mindless self-admiration, 183; presumption, 183; studious man, 184; virtue, 184

Woodruff, Helen, 19, 200

Wordsworth, William, 97, 176

Wordsworth, William and Mrs., 48, 159, 160

Wormhoudt, Arthur, xv, 95, 96, 200

Wren: associated with chthonic forces, 185; divinity, 185; eagle, as rival, 185–87; ritual killing, 186; royalty, 185

Wulff, August, 105, 200

Yeats, W. B., 32, 70, 174

Dr. Zhivago, 50–51

Zimmer, Heinrich, 67, 70, 200

Zircle, Conway, 180, 200

About the Book and Author

Drawing upon references to birds in all periods and documenting her sources, Beryl Rowland provides symbolic meanings for nearly sixty birds and illustrates their wide application in literature and art. She shows that the concept of the bird as the possessor of a human soul is universal; the bird's supernatural associations have strikingly influenced its symbolism, and if animals usually represent earthly passions such as greed, lust or envy, birds often stand for man's spiritual aspirations or for his gods. This unusual work is accompanied by an equal number of illustrations, taken mainly from rare medieval manuscripts and reproduced, in many instances, for the first time.

Beryl Rowland is Professor of English at York University, Toronto. She is the author of *Blind Beasts: Chaucer's Animal World*, *Animals with Human Faces*, and the editor of the *Companion to Chaucer Studies* and of *Chaucer and Middle English Studies in Honour of Rossell Hope Robbins*. Known mainly for her work on Chaucer, she has published many articles in professional journals and has lectured extensively at universities in Canada, the United States, Europe, and Australia.

Birds with Human Souls was cast on the Linotype in eleven-point Granjon with one-point spacing between the lines. Handset Garamond was selected for display.

The Granjon type design came into being in 1924 through the hands of George W. Jones, one of England's great printers. Granjon continues to meet the most exacting requirements for fine books, which is a tribute to the honest design and legibility distinguishing this type.

This book was designed by Lynn Ezell and Jim Billingsley and manually composed in hot metal at Heritage Printers, Inc., Charlotte, North Carolina. It was printed by offset lithography at Thomson-Shore, Inc., Ann Arbor, Michigan and bound by John H. Dekker & Sons, Grand Rapids, Michigan.

THE UNIVERSITY OF TENNESSEE PRESS / KNOXVILLE